GROWTH. TRADE

al

ENVIRONMENTAL
VALUES

edited by

Ted Schrecker

and

Jean Dalgleish

Westminster Institute for Ethics and Human Values
London, Ontario
1994

CANADIAN CATALOGUING IN PUBLICATION DATA

Main entry under title:

Growth, trade and environmental values

Includes bibliographical references
ISBN 1-895175-04-6

    1.   International trade–Environmental aspects–
Congresses. 2. Commerical policy–Environmental
aspects--Congresses. 3. Environmental policy–
Congresses. I. Schrecker, Ted II. Dalgleish,
Jean, 1952- . III. Westminster Institute for
Ethics amd Human Values.

HF1412.G76 1994363.7 C94-900288-7

ACKNOWLEDGEMENTS

The Board of Governors of the Westminster Institute for Ethics and Human Values provided the special funding which made the Growth, Trade and Environmental Values symposium possible. Jean Dalgleish of the Westminster Institute staff provided the planning and logistics expertise that made the symposium a success.

Subsequent to the conference, Jean Dalgleish spent countless hours on the transformation of conference papers into book chapters, to the point where her role evolved into that of co-editor. Janet Baldock, Judy Noordermeer and Edith Richardson spent many hours on the tedious but essential tasks that accompany book production. Busy contributors responded with alacrity to requests for manuscripts, clarifications and proofreading of galleys.

Finally, the financial support of the Ontario Ministry of Environment and Energy under the Environmental Education and Awareness Program (EEAP) is gratefully acknowledged; without it this publication would not have been possible.

Ted Schrecker
Westminster Institute for Ethics and Human Values
January 1994

THE EDITORS

Ted Schrecker is Associate Director (Environmental Ethics) of the Westminster Institute for Ethics and Human Values, and holds a teaching appointment in the Department of Political Science at The University of Western Ontario. He has more than 15 years' experience in the environmental policy field as a legislative researcher, academic and consultant; he is the author of the Law Reform Commission of Canada's studies of *Workplace Pollution* and *Political Economy of Environmental Hazards*, as well as numerous articles and book chapters.

Jean Dalgleish is Assistant Director & Projects Manager at the Westminster Institute. She has held part-time teaching appointments in the Department of History at The University of Western Ontario and has worked as a private researcher and consultant.

TABLE OF CONTENTS

INTRODUCTION

Environmental policy today is no longer settled simply between national or sub-national governments and their citizens. The environmental stresses associated with economic activity often extend far beyond the borders of the nation-state involved; acid precipitation, global warming and ozone depletion are among the most familiar examples. The *Montreal Protocol* for phasing out production of ozone-destructive CFCs suggests that international agreement on these issues is possible. Other environmental issues with an international dimension may prove considerably more intractable, both ethically and politically. Politically, the costs and benefits of international efforts to protect the environment will often be distributed unequally and inequitably. Ethically, the question arises of whether rich countries and their citizens are insisting on a form of extraterritoriality when they advocate protection of resources outside their own borders. If, for example, a poor country should choose rapid liquidation of its tropical timber resources as the least destructive route to obtaining the investment capital necessary to improve the living standards of its people, can this decision be gainsaid by outsiders?

The Canada-US Free Trade Agreement, the North American Free Trade Agreement (NAFTA) and the recent renegotiation of the General Agreement on Tariffs and Trade (GATT) have all raised the issue of how trade policy is, and should be, connected to environmental policy. There are no simple answers. Environmentalists like Steven Shrybman of the Canadian Environmental Law Association have argued that trade liberalization will lead to the lowering of environmental standards as nations are pressured or obliged to harmonize environmental standards toward a lowest common denominator, and investors seek "pollution havens": countries with lax environmental standards, or demanding standards but lax enforcement.[1] (Parenthetically, this point illustrates that it is important to keep in mind the growing substitutability of direct investment for trade flows.) Indeed, some commentators view current trade liberalization initiatives, like the GATT and the NAFTA as being "about more than sending First World factories into the Third World; they are about importing Third World economic pressures and social conditions into the West."[2]

Economist Arvind Subramanian, on the other hand, has criticized the use of trade policy measures for environmental protection, because: "They are aimed at negating the very source of comparative advantage which could legitimately be conferred by differences in environmental endowments, pollution assimilation capacities or social preferences regarding environmental outcomes."[3] The critic of trade liberalization might reply that eliminating such sources of comparative advantage is precisely the point. Countries ought not to be permitted to seek comparative advantage by (for instance) being less careful to avoid killing dolphins while catching fish on the high seas, or less careful in the disposal of toxic industrial wastes. Also important here might be the question of whether trade liberalization simply encourages countries which are heavily reliant on their resource endowments as a source of economic growth to exhaust or liquidate those endowments even more rapidly than might otherwise be the case–an economic development strategy which to many observers, although not all, is the antithesis of sustainability.

In response, it can be argued that the trade-offs of economic rewards against environmental risks accepted by the governments of poor countries ought to be respected, even though they may reflect a willingness to tolerate environmental damage that would be unacceptable in, say, Canada or the United States. Pursuing this line of reasoning, environmental criteria for trade policy could be characterized as ways for the rich countries to protect their industries and achieve their desired levels of environmental protection in the poor countries, without having to pay for doing either. In addition, it is sometimes pointed out that the rich countries themselves enjoyed the benefits of comparably destructive practices at an earlier stage in their own development; the area of old-growth forest cleared in southern Ontario is of the same order of magnitude as that currently endangered in the Amazon Basin. In many respects, "the Third World is being asked to forgo the very development path that enriched the North (and polluted the global ecosystem) in favour of a more financially costly path."[4]

In the background of this discussion are more fundamental questions of growth and economic development. The World Commission on Environment and Development (the Brundtland Commission) stressed the need for sustained economic growth in the poorer countries of the world if the needs of their poor are ever to be met, and emphasized that in an increasingly interdependent international economy achieving such growth depends on continued liberalization of trade. It also called for an expansion of the mandate of GATT to include sustainable development, and for measures to speed the diffusion of environmentally sound technology and to ensure responsibility in transnational investment. Some critics of the Brundtland report argue for a much more radical approach to economic development, pointing to the fundamentally exploitative nature of the relations between rich and poor countries, and question the presumption that continued economic growth is desirable or even possible. Questioning this presumption, of course, means that the connections among growth, trade and environmental values must be looked at in an entirely different way. It also raises the critical question of how basic needs are to be met, in poor countries and for that matter in rich ones, in the absence of continued economic growth.

In September 1992, the Westminster Institute organized two workshops as part of the planning process for a three-year programme of facilitating research on sustainable development, growth, and distributive justice. (This programme has now been funded by the Social Sciences and Humanities Research Council of Canada, and involves an expanding network of more than 50 Canadian researchers.) The single area mentioned most frequently by participants in those workshops as requiring further research was the connection among trade policy, environmental policy and economic distribution. In order to contribute to Canadians' understanding of the issues, the Institute sponsored a two-day symposium on Growth, Trade and Environmental Values at The University of Western Ontario in February, 1992. The papers presented at that symposium, revised for publication and with one addition and two substitutions,[5] comprise this book.

Part I of the book provides an overview of the connections between trade policy and the environment. With admirable clarity, John Whalley and Peter Uimonen describe the basic institutions of international trade policy. Sarah Richardson argues that a policy approach she refers to as "developmental trade" provides important opportunities for achieving more sustainable economic development. William Rees, on the other hand, provides a far more sceptical view of the impact of trade liberalization on ecological integrity. Finally, David Runnalls' contribution outlines a series of principles for linking trade and sustainable development. These principles, which formed the basis of Mr. Runnalls' presentation at the February symposium, were elaborated and agreed to by a diverse group of individuals working under the auspices of the Institute for International Sustainable Development.

Part II moves on to specifics. Michelle Swenarchuk provides an overall critique of the environmental implications of NAFTA, arguing that on balance these are substantially negative. David Bennett analyzes the way in which NAFTA will affect the policy treatment of certain kinds of environmental risks. With reference to recent developments in trade policy, Brenda Leith explains the divergences between economic theory and the real world of agricultural commerce. David Conklin and Ross Archibald point out that aggressive approaches to environmental protection in the accounting field may have unexpected and unanticipated costs in terms of the location of investment, and point out the ethical importance of asking who will bear those costs. Finally, David Conklin and Jeffrey Gandz offer a provocative argument about national obligations to take on unpleasant environmental duties whose benefits may be transnational or even global in nature.

Part III explores the connections among trade policy, environmental issues and global economic integration. O.P. Dwivedi outlines a distinctive Third World perspective on these questions. Deborah Poff argues that environmental protection objectives are ultimately incompatible with global economic integration, certainly to the extent that such integration is taken to imply a declining role for the nation-state. Finally, John Cartwright and Susan Holtz offer two contrasting views of an alternative vision known as bioregionalism, which actively challenges the desirability of a world in which economic interdependence increases irrespective of "natural" boundaries.

As we near the end of the twentieth century, global economic integration is perhaps the single most dominant characteristic of the political landscape. For some people, this trend toward a "borderless world" (the phrase used by management consultant Kenichi Ohmae) is entirely desirable. For others, it suggests the possibility of a savagely Darwinian socioeconomic system in which the gap between the powerful and the powerless becomes unbridgeable. (Italian sociologist Laura Balbo has referred to this as the *Blade Runner* model" of the future.) It is imperative that Canadians understand what is behind these conflicting interpretations of a trend on whose basic factual contours there is widespread agreement. Trade liberalization is only one element of global economic integration, and the environmental and resource management questions raised by trade policy are only one dimension of its social impacts. This book is one effort among many on the part of Canada's academic and professional communities to assist a wider audience in reaching that understanding.

Endnotes

[1] Steven Shrybman, "International Trade and the Environment: An Environmental Assessment of the General Agreement on Tariffs and Trade," *The Ecologist* 20 (January/February 1990), 30-34; Steven Shrybman, *Selling the Environment Short: An Environmental Assessment of the First Two Years of Free Trade Between Canada and the United States* (Toronto: Canadian Environmental Law Association, November 1990).

[2] Walter Russell Mead, "Bushism, Found: A Second-Term Agenda Hidden in Trade Agreements," *Harper's*, September 1992, 41.

[3] A. Subramanian, "Trade Measures for Environment: A Nearly Empty Box?" *The World Economy* 15 (1992), 151.

[4] David Runnalls, *Trade and Sustainable Development: A New Research Agenda* (Winnipeg: International Institute for Sustainable Development, 1993), 35.

[5] The chapter by David Conklin and Jeffrey Gandz was not originally presented at the conference. Instead of revising the paper presented at the conference, Michelle Swenarchuk chose to substitute a slightly revised version of a previously prepared analysis of the environmental implications of NAFTA. John Whalley's conference presentation was based on an article previously published in *Ecodecision*, which we have reprinted here with permission. Full acknowledgements appear in the relevant chapters of the book.

PART I

TRADE, ENVIRONMENT

AND

THE GLOBAL ECONOMY

OVERVIEW

CHAPTER 1

TRADE AND ENVIRONMENT: SETTING THE RULES

John Whalley
Peter Uimonen

John Whalley is a Professor of Economics and academic research economist in the Department of Economics at The University of Western Ontario, where he is also the Director of the Centre for the Study of International Economic Relations. He is a Research Associate with the National Bureau of Economic Research, Cambridge, Massachusetts; Senior Fellow with the Institute for Policy Reform; and was a Visiting Fellow of the Institute for International Economics in Washington, D.C. His career has spanned several different areas of economics and his coverage of policy interests has subsequently grown to issues in development and, most recently, environmental issues. In the process of this work, he has also been involved with several major policy efforts. He was the coordinator for international trade research with the Macdonald Commission in Canada which was to lead to Canada's participation in bilateral trade negotiations with the United States in the mid-1980s. More recently, he has been a member of a dispute settlement panel under the Canada-US Free Trade Agreement.

Peter Uimonen has been a research assistant with the Policy Development and Review Department of the International Monetary Fund since August 1991. He was previously a research assistant with the Institute for International Economics. The views expressed are those of the authors and do not necessarily reflect those of the International Monetary Fund.

This article was originally published in *Ecodecision*, the Environment and Policy Magazine, Edition no. 8, March 1993; 276 St. James Street, Montreal, Quebec H2Y 7N3. Permission to reprint is gratefully acknowledged.

Over the last few years, a number of clashes between international trade arrangements and environmental concerns have emerged (see Table). Tuna bans, trade in ivory, tropical lumber exports, the environmental consequences of North American free trade, and other topics have all received substantial media attention. But what, if anything, should or even can be done about all this? How deep is the conflict? How might one (and indeed should one) begin to lessen the sense of clash between trade and environment by developing a linked-rule regime and hence better integrating these two policy subsystems?

It is widely believed that trade and the environment are in inevitable conflict and that more trade means more production, pollution, environmental degradation and endangerment of species. The implication appears to be that action should be taken, and quickly, through new trade rules that control trade that has negative environmental effects. But trade economists and trade policy-makers have taken a different stance on these matters.

They have argued that freer trade and higher environmental quality go hand in hand because the higher incomes that accompany freer trade allow for stronger environmental protection. Furthermore, trade policies are typically only a second-best way to deal with environmental concerns and in some circumstances can be counter-productive, worsening the environmental problems they were supposed to solve. Finally, environmentally motivated trade actions run the risk of being sought by special interests, thus generating new protectionism in the global economy.

The press release sent out with the 1992 Annual Report of the General Agreement on Tariffs and Trade (GATT) supported the latter positions. It suggested that "expanding trade can help solve environmental problems," and went on to argue that

> increased world trade leads to higher *per capita* incomes, and with that the freedom and incentive to devote a growing proportion of national expenditure to the environment. GATT rules do not prevent governments adopting efficient policies to safeguard their own domestic environment, at the same time, trade measures are seldom likely to be the best way to secure environmental objectives and, indeed, could be counter-productive.[1]

In some of the recent papers in the World Bank collection on Trade and Environment edited by Patrick Low (several written by Bank staff), similar positions can be found.[2]

Economists thus view trade policy as an economically costly and ineffective means of achieving environmental goals compared to policies attacking the problem closer to the source, such as direct taxation on pollution. Primo Braga[3] goes so far as to argue that such policies may even be perverse, citing export bans on logs in Indonesia which have resulted in more plywood being produced at home with older technology which has higher log input per unit output.

RECENT CLASHES BETWEEN TRADE AND ENVIRONMENT POLICIES

1. The Use of Trade Restrictions for Environmental Reasons

   1. Import bans going beyond those justified by the 1975 CITES convention covering endangered species. Grounds for actual or proposed bans include cruel methods of capture (leghold traps dolphins killed in tuna catch); slowing deforestation (tropical lumber imports); and others. Consistency of such actions with established trade rules (e.g. GATT) is a central issue.

      Global environmental treaties (Montreal CFC protocol, and possibly an eventual global carbon-limitation treaty) may increasingly resort to trade actions against non-signatories as an enforcement mechanism against free riding.

      Future bilateral pressures on developing countries may specify compliance with environmental objectives, coupled with trade threats (China on coal burning Brazil on deforestation). Trade actions which result could well be incompatible with GATT.

2. Trade Negotiations and International Environmental Standards

   2. Can trade negotiations mean eroding environmental standards; driving the higher standard countries down to the lower standards of others (Canada-US asbestos case)?

3. Environmental Regulation and Competitiveness

   3. (i) Lax standards in exporting countries. How far do lax standards serve to attract production from high-standards to low-standard countries? Does trade from low-standard to high standard countries "evade" high production standards? Are such low-standards equivalent to a production subsidy? Should such subsidies fall under the GATT subsidies code and be countervailable?

      (ii) Special rules for environmental products. Should subsidies for installation of pollution control equipment be non-countervailable in importing countries? Should exports of pollution control equipment be exempt for GATT limits on use of export subsidies?

4. Trade Consequences of Major Global Environmental Interventions

   4. Potentially large impacts on world trade patterns and volumes would follow from a global carbon limitation treaty designed to significantly lower the growth rate of global carbon emissions.

5. Constraints on New Environmental Laws Implied by Existing Trade Treaties

   5. Do (and should) existing trade arrangements constrain the adoption of seemingly sensible environmental polities? (Danish bottle recycling laws and the Treaty of Rome)

6. Environmental Transparency Treaties be More Mandatory?

   6. Should environmental impact analysis of new trade legislation and How to make environmental impacts of policies more transparent?

Source: Uimonen and Whalley (Institute for International Economics.)

In this chapter, we suggest that despite the validity of many of the arguments from the trade policy community, the pressures for trade rules to be modified on environmental grounds are likely to intensify over the next few years. There is debate in the wake of the GATT and World Bank reports as to whether their arguments should be widely accepted. The contention that incomes are higher with free trade does not guarantee that such income gains are spent on higher environmental quality in an optimal fashion. And while trade policy is generally second-best environmental policy, if exporting countries are unwilling to implement first-best policies, this type of policy may be an improvement on no action at all.

The North-South Aspect

There is now a significant North-South component to the trade and environment debate as well. Developing countries see environmentally-motivated trade restrictions as potentially truncating their growth and development, as responding more to Northern than Southern concerns, and as late attempts to use trade to deal with environmental issues after decades of developed (rather than developing) country neglect. In their view, the issues should be dealt with by compensation; that is cash transfers to countries adopting environmental policies, not trade restrictions implemented because of the lack of such policies.[4] Their claim is that environmentally-motivated trade restrictions constitute "eco-imperialism," reflective of the way the developing world has been treated on trade issues by the developed world in the past. Somewhat paradoxically, discord over this set of issues is rising at a time when North-South tensions on other trade issues have been sharply reduced.[5]

Balancing the Effects

What kinds of approaches to rule writing and institutional responses in this area make sense? To what extent do all the uncertainties created by the current ambiguities in arrangements impede both trade performance from the global economy and environmental management of the global ecology? What can one say about compensation versus trade sanctions as far as developing countries are concerned?

Despite recent scientific investigation, the true dimensions of the extent to which trade and environment are linked remain uncertain. Scientific opinion on such matters as how rapidly, if at all, global warming is occurring; how rapidly rain forests are disappearing; and the precise health and other risks from ozone depletion, various gaseous emissions and other environmental contaminants varies greatly.[6]

Imputing the trade component of such uncertain effects is equally, if not even more, difficult. Economists' estimates of the gains to the global economy from freer trade also have a surprisingly wide variance,[7] and hence trading off foregone trade gains and environmental costs (or benefits) is at best an extremely imprecise art.

While environmental concerns over the directions trade policies seem to be taking may be legitimate in some cases, the nature of the linkages as well as the quantitative dimensions involved are far from clear. Moreover, any adverse environmental effects from trade have to be balanced against the harm to the global economy that could accompany overzealous attempts to curb trade. For example, cross-border Mexico-US trade involving *maquiladora* production with high levels of sulphur emissions, hepatitis from infected aquifers, and large untreated discharges of toxic wastes into major rivers may seem to demonstrate the link between trade and environment. However, a North American Free Trade Agreement (NAFTA) that liberalizes the trade and investment regime in Mexico may serve to reduce the special incentives for firms to locate along the border and result in less pollution in that region. Yet another example: allowing increased imports of small fuel-efficient cars can reduce gasoline consumption and actually benefit the environment.

Developing a New Rule Regime

In discussing possible approaches toward achieving a joint trade-and-environment rule regime, changes have been proposed within the present framework of multilateral trade rules in the GATT as well as in other areas, such as regional arrangements like NAFTA. One GATT approach, sometimes suggested, builds on waivers that allow more consistent use of trade measures on environmental grounds. This might involve a framework of understanding indicating where GATT waivers (individual country or even bloc-wide) could be granted on environmental grounds. GATT waivers decided on a case-by-case basis by the contracting parties would, if approved, permit the use of trade measures that are otherwise inconsistent with existing trade rules for particular environmental reasons. Another approach might be a new broad-based exception to existing GATT rules on environmental grounds (a GATT environmental accord). Yet another might be a possible new GATT code on environment, clarifying and elaborating on various GATT articles so far as their environmental implications are concerned, and a piecemeal rewriting of individual GATT articles or chapters of other existing trade agreements to reflect environmental concerns.

These approaches are not mutually exclusive and could be used together. Each has both good and bad points. Waivers are flexible, but they are ad hoc and may not be applied consistently. An open-ended GATT accord might generate too much new protection. A GATT code or a major rewriting of GATT articles could prove unworkable. We see rule writing as clearly being most effective if done piecemeal, rather than as part of a *de novo* redesign of existing trade arrangements.

Whatever approach is chosen to link trade and environmental policies, a clear test of the necessity of the trade measure as a response to the environmental problem will be needed, in either regional or multilateral negotiations. Where environmental effects occur largely within national borders, there is clearly no rationale for using trade measures to deal with them. Where cross-border effects occur, if small numbers of countries are involved, compensation for environmental restraint may suffice. For remaining situations, non-border measures (domestic excise taxes) may be sufficient. Trade measures for environmental reasons, therefore, under such an approach would be treated as something of a final recourse. Determinations of the level at which barriers would be set also need to be codified. One approach might use calculations designed to equate marginal benefits of improved environmental quality with the measure and marginal social costs of foregone trade.

To some degree, the GATT is already quite flexible regarding the environmental measures it permits. As long as they are not arbitrarily discriminatory, measures "necessary" to protect domestic health and safety of humans, animals and plants are permitted. Other trade measures that relate to resource conservation in a country are also permitted. Pollution abatement subsidies that are generally available are permitted, as well as are border charges on imported products when like domestic products are subject to environmental excise taxes.

However, questions arise with respect to determining exactly when a trade measure taken for protection of the domestic environment may be considered "necessary." Further, the way GATT trade rules treat trade restrictions against non-signatories to an international environmental agreement is unclear. As far as regional trade arrangements are concerned, the substantive content of the environmental provisions of one such arrangement, NAFTA, while vague in certain respects, represent a first small step toward trade arrangements that include an environment component. This outcome may reflect Mexican willingness to move speedily toward compliance with demands made of the country on environmental issues. In future regional negotiations, we see environmental concerns as playing an ever larger role, with a high premium on transparency of process, environmental impact statements for the trade policy changes involved, and provisions that safeguard environmental concerns. This seems likely to bring domestic environmental law and its enforcement into trade bargaining, further strengthening future linkage between trade and environmental policies.

Issues for the Future

But despite all this, at present we have two sets of institutional arrangements: trade arrangements that have been negotiated largely as if environmental issues did not exist, and environmental arrangements that increasingly seek to utilize trade arrangements for their enforcement, regardless of the potential for impaired performance from the trading system. Fundamental issues of property rights, reflected in the compensation/environment-based trade measures issue, divide developed and developing countries. Thus, it is likely that trade rules will have to be modified because of environmental pressures, and trade policy constraints on environmental policies will have to be accepted. Further, some new institutional structure will need to emerge to help arbitrate disagreements. The pressures for some accommodation of international trade rules to environmental concerns are, in our view, likely to be so strong over the next few years that even reluctant trade policy practitioners will need to consider the options.

Environment/trade linkage will, we feel, also increasingly play a major role in new international environmental and in conventional trade negotiations. In the Montreal Protocol on CFCs, possible trade sanctions against third-party non-signatories could eventually be used as part of the enforcement mechanism in the agreement. And while we are still at an early stage in terms of a possible global carbon treaty, a similar structure could also evolve there. The direct trade implications of enacting such a treaty (for energy-intensive and energy-non-intensive exports, for instance) could also prove to be quantitatively large. And the North-South dimensions of such environmental treaties add distributional conflicts. We would suggest the same test of necessity of the use of trade measures be applied to these agreements as to requests for exceptions under existing trade treaties. We would also suggest that if bringing added environmental transparency to the trade policy process is desirable, trade policy implication statements for new environmental laws should also be added so as to alleviate trade policy concerns over new environmental laws being enacted independently of existing trade laws.

In closing, we would also note that the principles underlying today's global trading system (embodying such principles as most favoured nations (MFN) and national treatment in the GATT) make trade-offs between trade and environmental concerns much more difficult to achieve than in a trading system whose principles are more explicitly access-based. Trading off environmental damage against, say, a compromise of the principle of non-discrimination in the GATT is something that comes less naturally than trading off repair of environmental damage against foregone gains from trade. Thus, in the longer term, it may also be that in addition to clarifying and endorsing the central trade and environment principle of necessity of the trade measure, some degree of refocusing in the present trade and environment policy subsystems may be helpful in facilitating the evolution of a linked policy regime.

Endnotes

[1] GATT Press Release, February 3, 1992, 1.
[2] Widely respected research economists are also increasingly espousing or supporting these positions. A recent paper by Grossman and Krueger argues that after country *per capita* income levels of $5,000 are reached, key *per capita* emission levels decrease with income and on this basis freer trade arrangements such as the North American Free Trade Agreement (NAFTA) could well reduce US and Mexico emissions. See G. Grossman and A. Krueger, "Environmental Policy in the United States," Discussion Paper #158*Discussion Papers in Economics* (Princeton, New Jersey: Woodrow Wilson School, Princeton University, 1991); K. Anderson, "The Standard Welfare Economics of Policies Affecting Trade and the Environment and Welfare," 25-48; "Effects on the Environment and Welfare of Liberal-

izing World Trade: The Cases of Coal and Food," 145-172; in K. Anderson and R. Blackhurst, eds., *The Greening of World Trade Issues* (London: Harvester-Wheatsheaf, 1992); "Agricultural Trade Liberalization and the Environment: A Global Perspective," *World Economy*, 15 (1) 153-172; P.J. Lloyd, "The Problem of Optimal Environmental Policy Choice," 49-72; R. Snape, "The Environment, International Trade, and Competitiveness," 73-92 in K. Anderson and R. Blackhurst, eds., *The Greening of World Trade Issues*, 25-48. All argue the relative inefficiency of trade policies for environmental ends. Birdsall and Wheeler argue a similar linkage of income *per capita* and emissions (and hence to trade) as Grossman and Krueger. See N. Birdsall and D. Wheeler, "Trade Policy and Industrial Pollution in Latin America: Where are the Pollution Wastes?" in P. Low, ed., *International Trade and the Environment*, World Bank Discussion Paper #159 (Washington, D.C.: World Bank, 1992), 159-168.

3 Carlos Alberto Primo Braga, "Tropical Forests and Trade Policy: The Case of Indonesia and Brazil" in Low, ed., *International Trade and the Environment*, 173-193.

4 See "Malaysia Calls for Cash to Protect Environment," *Financial Times*, April 28, 1992, which reports on a speech by Dr. Mahatir Mohammed, the Malaysian prime minister, to a conference in Kuala Lumpur, held in advance of the Rio Earth Summit, which produced the Kuala Lumpur declaration on environment and trade. The speech argued that developed countries would have to provide substantial financial assistance and transfers of technology to developing countries to induce them to adopt new environment preserving domestic policies.

5 See, for instance, the Symposium on Trade and Environment in *World Economy*, (January 1992); and C. Arden-Clark, "The General Agreement on Tariffs and Trade, Environmental Protection and Sustainable Development," World Wildlife Fund Discussion Paper, 1991.

6 See, for instance, "Skeptics are Challenging Dire 'Greenhouse' Views," *New York Times*, December 13, 1989, which reports on how a number of leading scientists have become increasingly skeptical of the predictions of significant global warming, all of which rest on computer-based general circulation models. Further skepticism is set out by A. Solow in "Is There a Global Warming Problem?" in Rudiger Dornbusch and James M. Poterba, eds., *Global Warming: Economic Policy Responses* (Cambridge, Massachusetts: The MIT Press, 1991), 1-31. Solow was a member of the International Panel on Climate Change (IPCC). See also Margulis and Reis, who list the wide range of estimates now available as to the rate at which deforestation is occurring in the Amazon. See S. Margulis and E. Reis, "Options for Slowing Amazon Jungle Clearing," in Dornbusch and Poterba, eds., *Global Warming: Economic Policy Responses*, 335-380.

7 See T.N. Srinavasan, John Whalley and Ian Wooton who, in reviewing studies of the effects of regional trade agreements, point out the differences between older studies from the 1950s and 1960s based on traditional competitive assumptions valuing the annual gains of trade liberalization at around 1/10-1/20th of 1 per cent

of GDP, and new studies incorporating market structure and scale-economy effects valuing the annual benefits at around 10 per cent of Gross Domestic Product (GDP). It should also be noted that older studies used data for periods when trade barriers were considerably higher. T.N. Srinivasan, John Whalley and Ian Wooton, "Measuring the Effects of Regionalism," in R. Blackhurst and K. Anderson, eds., *Regional Intergration and the Global Trading System.* (London: Harvester-Wheatsheaf, 1993), 52-79.

CHAPTER 2

THE TRADE-ENVIRONMENT LINKAGE: FUTURE CHALLENGES OF LIBERALIZED TRADE AND ENVIRONMENTAL COMPLIANCE

Sarah Richardson[1]

Sarah Richardson is a lawyer, and in her position as the Foreign Policy Advisor at the National Round Table on the Environment and the Economy, she specializes in the relationship between trade and the environment. She has a B.A. (Hons) in International Relations from the University of Toronto, an LL.B. from Dalhousie University and an LL.M. (Masters in Law) from Columbia University. Among her publications, Richardson edited and contributed to *Trade, Environment and Competitiveness*, published by the NRTEE in 1992.

Since the 1940s, improved transportation, communication, and the increased liberalization of global trade through successive rounds of multilateral and regional negotiation, have led to the increased integration of national economies around the world. Through this economic integration, international trade policy has increasingly begun to penetrate the domestic policy prerogatives of government and the daily lives of the citizens in countries engaged in global commerce. In fact, managing domestic policies and practices whose differences might otherwise inhibit trade is at the very core of the agendas of the Uruguay Round of the General Agreement on Tariffs and Trade (GATT), the European Community's 1992 Program (EC 1992), the Canada-US Free Trade Agreement, the recently completed North American Free Trade Agreement (NAFTA), and prospectively, the burgeoning Asia-Pacific Economic Cooperation Forum (APEC).

In the European Community (EC), the goal of creating a European customs union, and possibly one day a political union, has led to a strong push towards domestic policy harmonization well beyond narrowly defined economic areas. Harmonization has come to include areas such as environmental and social policies traditionally thought of as unrelated to trade. The potential competitiveness and trade-distorting effects of domestic policy differences are most apparent, and thus of concern to publics and policy-makers, in those cases where economic integration occurs between countries at widely varying levels of development.

The addition of the developing country of Mexico to the Canada-US free trade area through the creation of NAFTA has brought this issue to North America. Moreover, NAFTA goes substantially further along the road to integration than the Canada-US Free Trade Agreement, notably in such areas as investment and financial services. In addition, the "side deal" on the environment negotiated along with a labour agreement during the spring and summer of 1993 and signed in August 1993, contains elements of supranational authority which are unprecedented in US external relations.[2]

In order to meet the imperatives of sustainable development, there is a clear need to ensure that integration is positive and the harmonization of standards of any kind is upward to encourage efficient growth, environmental protection and an improved quality of life for current and future generations. While these values are governed largely by domestic policies, mechanisms to facilitate their realization can be put in place within trade regimes now.

What mechanisms could and should such regimes include? This chapter argues that movement towards more liberalized trade results in pressures among competing countries to harmonize and level the so-called "playing field." An upwards harmonization of standards, however, is only as good for the environment, sustainable development and a productive and cooperative trading relationship as a country's ability to devote real material resources to give substance to rhetorical declarations of principles. Failing this, the benefits of the trade agreement could well be negated through successive rounds of disputes which will do nothing either to promote sustainable development or to protect the environment, and the offending country will be less able to direct or redirect scarce resources in ways that will effectively raise its standards.

This chapter attempts, in a preliminary fashion, to assess some existing and emerging trade regimes against two competing approaches to the integration of trade and sustainable development. As outlined in Section I, these models are "developmental trade" which directly promotes sustainable development, and "adversarial trade" which will not necessarily enhance the environment or promote sustainable development. In order to ensure that trade does in fact enhance environmental protection, regimes must be put in place that will address the underlying causes of low standards or poor enforcement. A "developmental" trade regime is more likely to do this than an adversarial one.

In practice, existing multilateral and regional regimes incorporate a developmental approach to widely varying degrees. Section II looks briefly at the most sophisticated attempt at the multilateral level to promote developmental trade, the Montreal Protocol. Section III details the most venerable and developed regional economic community, the European Community, which has evolved to the point where it is relatively successful in promoting the values of sustainable development through a Social and Economic Cohesion Fund to promote integration by even the poorest countries in the Community.

Section IV demonstrates that the new NAFTA, despite its impressive attention to environmental considerations (particularly compared to the Canada-US Free Trade Agreement five years before), lacks mechanisms to encourage movement, through trade, to sustainable development outside the working of the free market. On the other hand, as Section V indicates, the new parallel accord accompanying NAFTA is a promising beginning to seriously addressing the need for social safeguards. Nevertheless, the "side deal" remains flawed to the extent that it does not adequately tackle the root of environmental problems and infrastructure deficiencies within Mexico or the challenges of harmonization across North America. Recently, however, there has been some promising bilateral movement between the US and Mexico to create a North American Development Bank to tackle the environmental cleanup of one of the most polluted areas in North America–the Mexico-US border.

The chapter concludes by suggesting that for the future, when issues of economic and trade liberalization are pursued, especially among countries of widely varying degrees of development, increased attention be given to the advisability of addressing the key obstacles and roadblocks to sustainable development within prospective trading partners. There is little doubt that bringing economies at different levels of development together as equals is an expensive proposition.

I   Competing Approaches to Trade and Sustainable Development

There are two competing models to consider if one is concerned that free trade alone will not promote sustainable development. These might be termed "adversarial trade" and "developmental trade."

"Adversarial" trade exists when trade sanctions are used to alter an individual country's behaviour, in this instance to compensate for, or encourage through punition, what are perceived as inadequate environmental or social standards or practices. Often what one country perceives as an unfair trade practice or a competitive advantage reflects differences in the societal values, domestic priorities, and available material resources of another country.

In the long run, adversarial trade is an inefficient and unproductive method of influencing and changing the behaviour of countries. The adjustment costs to the offending country of changing its regime will in some cases exceed the trade benefits to be gained from avoiding the occasional trade sanction. There will be cases when an offending country simply cannot afford to enforce even domestically legislated and articulated environmental and social values. Adversarial trade in those cases might drive offending parties to find trading partners willing to buy their goods, whatever the environmental and social costs, permitting the so-called "playing field" to remain at a lower common denominator. Moreover, adversarial trade is an expensive route to take with no guarantees of success at a time of shrinking resources in both government and the private sector. Finally, its effects are felt unfairly in countries, component regions, and sectors whose economies are relatively heavily dependent upon trade.

"Developmental" trade exists when parties achieve an international agreement which reflects shared social and environmental values at a higher level. Where standards are not being met, whether because of a lack of will or a lack of resources, under the developmental model compliance should be encouraged and where possible, facilitated by positive incentives. Efforts to ensure consistent and stringent standards and compliance across national boundaries must be a natural extension of this trade agenda. Trade sanctions in themselves will do little to create the resources necessary to hire inspectors, retrofit existing plants and improve public infrastructures.

Arguably, more effective and/or better means of "enforcement" are brought about by the positive effectiveness of public participation, widespread education and extensive reporting, all based on and backed up by genuinely sound science. As well, new institutions and funding mechanisms created to assist countries in implementing and enforcing agreed upon standards within trade areas will go a long way to ensure that trade is not just an end in itself, but a means to rapidly and directly achieving environmentally sustainable, equitably distributed economic development.

Sustainable development is not simply the integration of environmental and economic values. Central to the concept of sustainable development is the notion of inter-generational equity. The developmental trade model promotes inter-generational equity by ensuring that standards are not harmonized downwards as a result of liberalized trade for any short-term economic gain. Equally important to developmental trade is the idea that the costs of meeting common standards of environmental protection are borne up-front by the generation that produced, and enjoyed the benefits of, those environmental costs. Developmental trade involves a clear application of the Polluter Pays Principle (PPP) on a global stage. The PPP is a concept which originated at the Organization for Economic Cooperation and Development (OECD) in the 1970s. It found favour at the United Nations Conference on Environment and Development (UNCED) and is now being incorporated into international law. The application of the PPP will help ensure that while trade continues to be a major tool for economic growth, it also becomes a tool for sustainable development. Developmental trade will encourage largely voluntary compliance and provide the tools to ensure it, rather than insisting on sometimes unrealistic demands through command and control approaches backed by strong-arm tactics and threats of trade sanctions.[3]

II   International Mechanisms to Promote Sustainable Development

Mechanisms to promote compliance and facilitate movement towards a developmental trade model were endorsed at UNCED and have already been adopted in some international environmental treaties. One of the most important of these treaties is the Montreal Protocol on Substances that Deplete the Ozone Layer. The Montreal Protocol addresses the critical global environmental issue of ozone destruction. It demands from its signatories the adoption of new technologies in order to meet agreed upon targets. The Protocol attempts to use trade measures to ensure that signatories phase out CFCs in a timely manner. In this way, the Protocol has the potential to effect the competitiveness of countries unable to meet the demands of the agreement by cutting them off from their trading partners.[4]

The Montreal Protocol uses trade up-front as one means of achieving an environmental end. Article 4 of the Protocol controls trade with countries not party to it. It requires the ban of both the import and export from non-party countries of CFCs and other substances covered by the Protocol. Article 4 also threatens future trade restrictions on products containing, or products made using the controlled chemicals.[5] Despite these elements of adversarial trade, however, the accompanying mechanisms set up to implement the Protocol strongly embody the approach of developmental trade.

In conjunction with the Montreal Protocol, an Interim Multilateral Fund was set up. It is designed, through financial and technology transfer, to support the early adoption of ozone-protecting technologies in order to facilitate the early elimination of the production and consumption of ozone depleting substances in developing countries.[6] The Fund exists to foster compliance with the Protocol; it is administered by the World Bank, United Nations Environment Program (UNEP) and the United Nations Development Program (UNDP) and is well-funded with an initial three year budget of US$160 million made up of contributions from its signatories. The accession of India to the Montreal Protocol in 1992, and of China in 1993, has meant an increase in the fund to US$500 million. The purpose of the fund is to finance the incremental costs of complying with the Protocol, technical assistance, and feasibility studies.[7]

A similar approach to promoting compliance is taken by the Global Environment Facility (GEF). The GEF is a pilot funding mechanism which was created in 1991 in anticipation of the global environmental agreements arising out of UNCED. At UNCED, the GEF was designated as the interim funding mechanism for the Climate Change and Biodiversity Conventions. The GEF is governed by representatives of the 28 countries which have paid a minimum of US$5.7 million to become "participants."

III   The EC Experience:
Liberalized Trade and Environmental Compliance

In the European Community, member States are encouraged to set environmental standards based on a high level of protection. In order to ensure that these standards do not unduly distort trade and prevent the free movement of goods in the Community, the EC has put a fund in place to encourage compliance with higher standards.

The experience of the European Community clearly illustrates the dynamics of the pressure when creating a free trade area to harmonize standards in policy areas which are not traditionally thought of as being "economic." The EC has based its attempt to create a single market on the four fundamental freedoms: free movement of capital, goods, persons and services. Over time, in an effort to achieve a single market, the EC has had to include among its areas of competence those of environment and social policy. This movement is apparent in the *Single European Act (SEA)* of 1985 and was reinforced in December 1991 at the European Council in Maastricht. This additional integration is undertaken at the price of transferring a certain amount of national sovereignty from the member States to the Community's institutions.

In the lead-up to the *SEA*, the EC identified priorities for the years 1985 to 1992. Among them were the internal market, economic and social cohesion (which is aimed at narrowing the development gap between regions), environmental policy and the social dimension, with a view to European integration. The Maastricht Treaty (Maastricht), signed in February 1992 and put into effect in November 1993, confirms economic and social cohesion as one of the pillars of the Community. In time, Maastricht might become the cornerstone of political union.

In the area of environmental policy, Maastricht builds on the significant changes introduced by the *SEA*. The *SEA* had provided, for the first time, an explicitly legal basis for the Community's common environmental policy. In the text agreed to in Maastricht, the environment has acquired full status as a policy area falling within the Community's priority objectives. Environmental measures are now also dealt with in the Council of Ministers by qualified majority voting (QMV). One important characteristic of directives issued in areas where the Community has absolute jurisdiction is that they are enforceable in the domestic courts of the member States. This extra enforcement mechanism of the domestic courts is granted by virtue of the principle of "direct affect."

There is some debate as to the effect of the principle of subsidiarity, which is left somewhat vague by Maastricht. Subsidiarity dictates that action can be taken at the Community level in areas where the Community does not have exclusive competence, when it would be more effective than national action, but only to the minimum extent necessary. It is anticipated that this principle will give the institutions of the Community considerable leeway, with the blessing of the European Court of Justice (ECJ).[8]

The increased use of qualified majority voting across broad policy areas will facilitate the integration of both environmental and social policy. Because unanimity is no longer required in the Council of Ministers, so-called "dirty" countries can no longer block initiatives unilaterally. However, the increased use of QMV might also create some problems of implementation and enforcement. Because of differing national standards, the use of qualified majority voting implies that member States will be obliged at times to implement environmental measures on which they are unable to follow through because of the prohibitive capital expenditures required. It also means that member States will inevitably be asked to implement directives to which they are fundamentally opposed. This conflict can either be dealt with based on an adversarial model with no guarantee of either freer trade or environmental protection, or through the facilitation of development. The EC has chosen the latter route.

On the one hand, in order to provide an incentive for reluctant member States to enforce Community policy, the Treaty of Rome has been amended to allow the ECJ to impose fines for non-compliance with directives.[9] In extreme cases, formal provision is made for temporary derogation from complying with directives.[10] However, in order to facilitate compliance, and thereby encourage developmental trade, the European Community Fund for Social and Economic Cohesion (the "Cohesion Fund") is gradually being realized. The Cohesion Fund supports major transport infrastructures and environmental projects in respect of the four poorest EC member States. It was agreed at the Edinburgh Summit in December 1992 that 15 billion ECUs would be made available to Ireland, Greece, Portugal and Spain (i.e., those member States with a per capita gross national product of less than 90 per cent of the Community average) over a six year period ending in 1999. The permanent fund can now be established, because the Maastricht Agreement has been ratified. In the meantime, the Council had adopted a Regulation for an Interim Fund which was implemented on April 1, 1993.

While the possibility of derogating from particular items of EC legislation holds out the prospect of a "slow lane" in the movement towards higher environmental standards in the Community, the availability of funds for the poorer member States increases the chances that higher standards will indeed be realized. As well, the Maastricht Treaty reaffirms an existing right set out in the *SEA* for member States to maintain or introduce more stringent protective measures, providing that they are compatible with the Treaty and are notified to the Commission.[11]

IV North American Free Trade

By the time NAFTA was being negotiated, environmental issues were on the agenda of trade discussions, even if they were of peripheral importance to the negotiators. The fact that the environment is included in the NAFTA at all is due in large part to the strong Environmental Non-Governmental Organization (ENGO) lobby in the US, and fuelled by the preliminary ruling of the GATT tuna-dolphin panel between the US and Mexico in September 1991.[12] This ruling went a long way to discredit the GATT in the eyes of some American policy-makers and came to embody what many perceived as the lack of sensitivity of the international trading regime towards the environment. The completed NAFTA is the first trade agreement to address environmental issues head-on and it will probably set the minimum standards for trade agreements in the future.

Sustainable development is included in the preamble of NAFTA as a primary objective of the Agreement and there are further provisions which address specific environmental issues. For example, there is a broad exception for specific trade obligations set out in certain international and bilateral environmental and conservation agreements such as the Montreal Protocol. The standards section protects the rights of governments to determine the level of environmental protection that they consider appropriate. The chapter on investment contains an important provision that would formally discourage a government from lowering its own environmental standards for the purpose of encouraging an investment.

In a more general way, the dispute settlement procedure provides for the creation, over and above the regular dispute settlement panel, of expert panels to consider scientific and technical issues. The NAFTA also gives the responding party the right to require that any disagreement be considered exclusively under the NAFTA procedure. The NAFTA procedure is an improvement over the GATT, which does not provide recourse to outside panels of experts. Also, NAFTA has extended GATT Article XX(b) to exempt from its provisions environmental measures which are necessary to protect human, animal or plant life or health, including the conservation of living and non-living exhaustible natural resources.

Even with this environmental content, NAFTA, as it was negotiated, would not necessarily address issues of equity, promote sustainable development or ensure the free movement of goods. Pressure for harmonization would exist, but with no guarantees that harmonization would necessarily be upwards. Some observers are concerned that the lure of lower pollution control regulations will create a pollution haven south of the US border without the existence of monitoring mechanisms.[13]

In order to address these concerns and thereby achieve fast-track authority to negotiate the NAFTA from Congress, in 1991 President Bush committed the US administration to negotiating "side deals" on the environment and labour. This mandate was carried out by the Clinton administration.

V   The North American Agreement on Environmental Cooperation: The NAFTA Side Agreement

During the spring and summer of 1993, the governments of Canada, the United States and Mexico negotiated the details of a promised North American Agreement on Environmental Cooperation (NAAEC). Among other things, the Agreement establishes a North American Commission for Environmental Cooperation, a new institution to oversee and strengthen environmental cooperation on the development and continuing improvement of environmental laws and regulations in the three countries. The Commission will also contribute to the prevention or resolution of environment-related trade disputes. A preliminary examination of the side deal, and the enforcement mechanisms which it contains, indicates that although it promotes cooperation among the Parties on issues of the environment, at the end of the day, if the Parties choose not to cooperate, it might become either virtually impotent or adversarial, resulting in little enhanced environmental protection in North America.

During the negotiations, there were proposals on the table that would have provided this Commission with some of the powers that would ensure the further integration of the environmental policies of the three countries, and move towards a system of common rule-making and harmonization. These were rejected at an early stage. In fact, all three Parties have articulated quite similar values for workplace safety and environmental protection through their national laws. Mexico's 1988 environmental law, based largely on American legislation, is strict but has not been adequately enforced.[14] The issue therefore became one of enforcement or compliance.

Economic theory might allow for competitive advantage to be had by virtue of low wages, but neither economic theory nor the values of sustainable development will justify the cost advantages and movement of jobs driven by lax enforcement of environmental regulations. American and Canadian acceptance of lax enforcement of environmental regulations at home or in the *maquiladora* undermines living standards in all three North American countries and free trade without an improvement in environmental compliance will only exacerbate these effects. The *maquiladora* is the most obvious example of environmental degradation and has been the most highly publicized, but disparities between the developed and the developing world are even broader and more profound, encompassing massive social inequities in education, health and housing among others.

The suggestion that a North American Commission on Environmental Cooperation be empowered to enforce domestic environmental laws, to ensure a "level playing field," was rejected during the negotiations. Enforcement powers vested in a supranational body clearly raise issues of sovereignty and early in the negotiations, the Mexican government announced that it would not accept a Commission with enforcement powers.[15]

The compromise reached under the Agreement chose what appears to be an adversarial regime. The Agreement provides for penalties in the form of government-to-government fines in cases where a dispute settlement Panel finds a persistent pattern of failure by a Party to enforce its environmental laws effectively. Prior to the imposition of fines, the Commission will produce a final report and give the offending party a chance to address the concerns in an "action plan." Only "where warranted" will the Panel impose the fine.[16] One of the criteria that the Panel must take into account when assessing the fine is the level of enforcement that could reasonably be expected of a Party, given its resource constraints. Although this has not yet been interpreted by a panel, in theory it suggests that if a legitimate argument can be made contending a lack of infrastructure, personnel and/ or resources to rectify the violation, a Panel's finding will have little effect and will not facilitate a change in the situation.

If fines are imposed, and either the US or Mexico fails to pay fines levied against it, trade sanctions can be applied. Under the Agreement, trade sanctions are limited to an amount no greater than that sufficient to collect the monetary assessment. The ultimate mechanism for enforcement of fines against Canada requires the Canadian government to adopt a procedure in its domestic courts whereby the panel determination can be filed with the Court and become an Order of the Court. The Commission may then take proceedings for the enforcement of the panel determination in court against the person against whom the determination is addressed. A panel determination that has been made an Order of the Court is not subject to review or appeal in domestic courts, and neither is the final order made by the Canadian court in the proceedings.

Mexico and the US both rejected the Panel decision being substituted into their domestic court system and becoming an Order of the Court. Instead, those two countries have agreed that in the case of non-payment, they would be subjected to trade sanctions which would put them back into the position they were in before NAFTA was signed.

The resistance by Canada to trade sanctions goes beyond the question of sovereignty. There is nothing new about countries abandoning claims of national sovereignty as a result of a negotiated provision in an international treaty. All international agreements have binding commitments that penetrate national sovereignty to the extent that national governments honour them. Countries come to accept these intrusions into their national sovereignty in order to obtain the benefits of increased foreign market access. Of more concern to the government of Canada in the trade sanctions debate was the increased use of adversarial trade and punitive trade measures, not to coerce behaviour, but to harass domestic industries with no positive implications for the environment. With the Canadian economy based as it is largely on the trade of natural resources, Canada is particularly vulnerable to ill-conceived trade measures.

By accepting the ruling of the Panel as legitimate to the point of making the ruling enforceable without appeal in domestic courts, Canada was giving up more claims on sovereignty than either the US or Mexico were willing to consider. From a Canadian perspective, the government has, through its actions, made a decision of the tri-national Panel under the Commission effectively an Order of the Canadian court for purposes of collection, giving it "direct effect." This is a degree of supranationalism heretofore seen only in the EC as part of a larger scheme to encourage the creation of a single market.[17]

However, unlike the EC model, nowhere in the NAFTA or the "side deal" on the environment is the issue of means, financial or otherwise, to encourage compliance addressed. This omission is especially glaring when one considers that NAFTA represents the materialization of the "trade not aid" principle for developing countries. This principle must be applied with some degree of finesse if the desired objective of environmentally sustainable economic development is to be achieved.

While the monitoring and enforcement of environmental practices and regulation is critical, it is arguable how effective using a trade sanction to attack an environmental problem can be. The effectiveness of these unrelated measures as a means to advance environmental goals is not proved. More to the point is attacking the problem head-on through domestic policies. In order to do this in the international arena, there should be some consideration to providing financial aid and technical assistance to use as needed in establishing effective enforcement capabilities and, if necessary, to assist those parties lagging behind to meet the incremental costs of compliance with accepted standards.

Parallel accords and/or new institutions might establish such financing mechanisms to ensure enforcement of environmental standards and assist small and medium-sized businesses to retrofit existing investments. It might also establish US-Canadian-Mexican cooperative frameworks among the ministries and departments of environment to provide Mexican officials with technical assistance in writing and enforcing regulations, training inspectors, and the like. Models for such a mechanism can be found in the Multilateral Fund, the GEF and the Cohesion Fund.

During the course of the side deal negotiations and surrounding the NAFTA debate a number of funding ideas were suggested, such as border transaction taxes and regional funding schemes. In late October 1993, some progress was made when the US administration announced that it had reached a deal with Mexico on a border environmental financing package which created a North American Development Bank. At least US$2.6 billion of the Bank's total capitalization of US$3 billion will be spent on border environmental infrastructure projects. This is clearly indicative of a movement to assist Mexico with the massive cleanup of its *maquiladora* border region. It would not necessarily have come about without the NAFTA or the subsequent environmental "side deal." However, some would argue that the driving force behind the US administration's announcement was to secure Congressional votes and support in anticipation of the November 17, 1993 vote on the NAFTA package.

Ideally, a development bank would be built into the trade agreement itself, and would be available to tackle a wide range of social and environmental issues. The issues that will arise as a result of North American Free Trade cannot necessarily be predicted, and the roadblocks to sustainable development will stretch beyond the 20 kilometre strip of land along the US-Mexico border, the *maquiladora*.

From a Canadian perspective, on March 18, 1992 the Canadian government announced the intensification of bilateral environmental cooperation with Mexico. Canada and Mexico reached agreement on a series of cooperation projects valued at CDN$1 million to reinforce environmental monitoring in Mexico. In the agreement, there is provision for a formal mechanism to continue the development of additional bilateral initiatives in the coming years. In fact, the Canadian assistance is largely being used to help the Mexican Ministry of the Environment formulate environmental regulations by hiring consultants, often Canadians. Although a small example, such influence at the front end of the process of environmental development will probably result in raised environmental standards for the Mexicans and provide Canadians with increased opportunities for exporting equipment and expertise to Mexico.

In many respects, from a Canadian perspective a NAFTA, with its side deals on environment and labour and its prospective Commission on Environmental Cooperation, begins to look somewhat like the EC 1992 agenda in breadth if not in depth. This route is necessary to establish a functional free trade zone, but also to promote sustainable development. However, a financial mechanism is necessary to raise the level of compliance that can realistically be expected from all Parties, provide the tools for that compliance, and thereby promote sustainable development. Bringing together advanced and less developed economies is an expensive proposition and it is time to admit that the resources necessary to bring together the economies of Mexico, Canada and the United States in a free trade agreement will not be brought about through the free market alone.

The NAFTA with its side agreement is, in large measure, a solid platform to work from. However, if this new North American regime is going to realize its true potential, those who are responsible for its implementation should now, at its inception, ensure that the issues of resources are adequately addressed in the further design of the institution. The bilateral initiatives already underway should be built on by canvassing segments of society beyond government, all of whom have a stake in a sustainable future.

VI   Conclusion: Looking to the Future

If one accepts that harmonization of non-economic policies is inevitable within free trade areas, one has to consider how to ensure that common standards are, at a minimum, maintained, or preferably increased, and that regulations are complied with. Policies that encourage developmental trade will more effectively incorporate the responsibilities associated with sustainable development and the costs and benefits of increased standards than will an adversarial approach.

The NAFTA and its parallel accords present the opportunity to promote sustainable development by adopting a new operating paradigm through the creation of a new tri-national institution with the power to adjudicate issues with such credibility so as to give them the equivalent of "direct affect" in the sense of the European Community. However, it stops short of providing the means to achieve the desired end.

Issues for the future go beyond the environment and embrace the impact of free trade with less developed nations on quality of life and issues of social justice, notably regional, generational and gender equity and even individual and collective identity. In fact, beyond the environmental dimension, the difference in the state of development between Canada, the United States and Mexico argues for an unprecedented social dimension to prevent what one author has termed "social dumping."[18] Issues of social justice, including culture, are the third "arm" of sustainable development.

Modern economies depend on the international economy and the globalization of trade as well as a healthy environment and access to the resources necessary to promote their prosperity. The trade and environment debate recognizes this interdependence and has been critical in advancing sustainable development and beginning a shift towards the true integration of environmental values into international economic objectives. In examining the linkages, it seems inevitable that the completion of this shift to include issues of social justice will, over time, result in coordination, harmonization, and community building that go well beyond NAFTA. A certain amount of sovereignty will be lost as a trade-off in the process.

North Americans must ask themselves how far they are prepared to go in this process and how much responsibility they are willing to bear. This is a necessary question if one engages in a comprehensive examination of liberalized trade through the prism of sustainable development. At the end of the day, North Americans must remind themselves that not only is there opportunity to be gained through generosity, but that what they are looking for fundamentally in promoting environmentally sustainable economic development is a world where the economy can develop in harmony with the environment, and where people can prosper in harmony with each other.

Endnotes

1   The statements and views expressed in this paper are those of the author in her personal capacity and do not necessarily reflect the views of the NRTEE or the Government of Canada. The author wishes to thank John Kirton, Jeremy Byatt, and in particular, the late Henry Richardson, for their thoughtful comments on earlier drafts of this paper.
2   In particular, this characteristic is visible in the numerous majority voting provisions throughout the Agreement.
3   It is worth noting that developmental trade does not only come associated with costs. It also provides great opportunities to capitalize on the imperatives of new technology and thus enhance long-term competitiveness in trading relationships. Cleaning up the environment is good economics in the long-term.
4   The Montreal Protocol on Substances that Deplete the Ozone Layer is one of the international environmental agreements that contain trade sanctions. It is the most well developed and is the subject of this paper because of its unique funding mechanism. This chapter will not discuss the world's major trade governing organization, the General Agreement on Tariffs and Trade (GATT), because it does not include any serious institutional mechanism to implement "developmental trade."

[5] These provisions might be inconsistent with the GATT principles of National Treatment and Most-Favoured Nation status, but they are unlikely to be challenged, in part because they are the result of tortuous multilateral negotiation and agreement on an issue which must urgently be addressed as a global environmental imperative.

[6] For more information see Robin Round, "At the Crossroads–The Multilateral Fund of the Montreal Protocol," A Report for Friends of the Earth International (London: Friends of the Earth, November 1992).

[7] As amended in 1990 in London, and most recently in 1991 in Copenhagen.

[8] In 1990, the EC agreed to establish a European Environmental Agency with the responsibility of monitoring the state of the environment throughout the Community. Member States' compliance with European environmental legislation will also be evident through uniform reporting procedures. There are also increasing calls for an EC Environmental Charter which would incorporate the PPP. The Charter would incorporate the following principles of sustainability: the presumption against pollution; the precautionary principle; the polluter pays principle, and freedom of environmental information. An enforceable EC Environmental Charter will depend upon the political will of the Community to truly integrate environmental protection into all aspects of its economic and political union goals.

[9] Article 171. Failure to pay these fines can result in the freezing of sizeable payments from the Community's Structural Fund.

[10] Article 130s(5). For example, Spain and Portugal secured a ten-year delay in implementing some of the provisions in the directive on large combustion plants.

[11] Article 130t, retained from the *Single European Act*.

[12] In that dispute, a GATT panel held that the US could not invoke its domestic *Marine Mammal Protection Act* (which prohibited the killing of a specified number of dolphins while fishing), in order to justify an embargo on Mexican tuna caught outside US jurisdiction in a manner which violated the provision of the Act. For a more detailed discussion on the reaction of the US to the GATT Panel ruling, see Sarah Richardson, "Trade, Environment and Competitiveness: An Overview," in Sarah Richardson and John Kirton, eds., *Trade, Environment and Competitiveness* (Ottawa: National Round Table on the Environment and the Economy, 1992), 267-374.

[13] See for example, Peter Gorrie, "Greens call protections hot air," *The Toronto Star*, February 7, 1993. Process standards in particular are very difficult to monitor at the border, especially in an environment of liberalized trade.

[14] In March 1988, Mexico enacted a comprehensive environmental protection law, the *Ecologic Equilibrium and Environmental Protection Act*. This legislation generally places Mexican environmental law on the same plane as the US and Canadian regimes. Poor enforcement is due in part to Mexican officials cautious not to discourage foreign investment in the *maquiladora*.

[15] Bob Davis, "Clash Looms over Scope of NAFTA Panel," *Wall Street Journal*, January 28, 1993.

[16] *North American Agreement on Environmental Cooperation*, August 13, 1993. Annex 34 of the Agreement limits the fine to a value no greater than US$20 million for the first year that the Agreement is in force. After that, any fine shall be no greater than .007 per cent of the total trade in goods between the Parties.

[17] See Annex 36A. See also John Saunders, "Canada Takes Euro-Style Approach to NAFTA: Analysts," *The Globe and Mail*, August 18, 1993.

[18] Peter Morici, "Trade Talks with Mexico: A Time for Realism" (Washington D.C.: NPA Committee on Changing International Realism, National Planning Association, 1991); Mexican wages are less than one-eighth of US levels and one author suggests that this offers Mexico a greater advantage in attracting new manufacturing plants than a 10 per cent or 20 per cent tariff. From a Canadian perspective, this gap is even greater. For example, one Toronto-based firm has a plant in Mexico where it pays workers $1.05 per hour and gets the same degree of productivity that it gets in its Toronto plant where workers are paid $14.00 per hour. Jonathan Ferguson, "The Winds of Trade," *The Toronto Star*, February 7, 1993.

Chapter 3

Pressing Global Limits: Trade as the Appropriation of Carrying Capacity

William E. Rees

William Rees is currently Professor and Director of the University of British Columbia's School of Community and Regional Planning. His planning and policy research focuses on the developmental implications of global change and the ecological conditions necessary for sustainable socioeconomic development. His most recent work on "ecological footprints and appropriated carrying capacity" estimates the natural capital requirements of the human economy and contributes to the emerging discipline of ecological economics. Rees serves on Canada's Public Advisory Committee for State of Environment Reporting (Environment Canada and Statistics Canada) and on the National Capital Commission Advisory Committee on Planning and Real Asset Management. He holds a Ph.D. in bio-ecology from the University of Toronto and his work on environment-economy relation-ships has taken him to dramatically different environments around the world, from the wilderness reaches of the Peruvian Andes and Arctic Canada to congested cities on almost every continent.

Abstract

This chapter examines "free trade" from the perspective of ecological economics and its implications for global carrying capacity. I use a novel approach to carrying capacity based on "ecological footprint" analysis to compare the scale of the economy with available natural capital stocks. This framework reveals serious negative ecological and ethical consequences of trade that are generally invisible to conventional monetary analyses.

Mainstream economic theory assumes a world "in which carrying capacity is infinitely expandable." Inter-regional trade is said to relieve local con-straints on growth, eliminating concerns about ecological carrying capacity. By contrast, I argue that any perceived increase in carrying capacity is illusion. In fact, by enabling all regions to exceed local limits simultaneously, by reducing the risks associated with depleting local natural capital, and by exposing regional ecological surpluses to global demand, unregulated international trade eventually reduces global carrying capacity, accelerating the encroachment of limits and increasing the risk of ecological collapse to all.

Moreover, ecological analysis shows that the average First World resident requires the productive output of four to six hectares of land to maintain his/her consumer lifestyle. However, there are only 1.7 hectares of productive land per capita on Earth. This means that industrialized countries "appropriate" a disproportionate share of global carrying capacity, much of it through commercial trade, effectively pre-empting developing economies from using their fair share. Indeed, accelerating global trends such as atmospheric change, ozone depletion, and soil erosion suggest that the one-quarter of humanity in the developed world has already appropriated the entire long-term carrying capacity of the ecosphere. If so, it is biophysically impossible for everyone in the world to enjoy current developed-country levels of consumption. There simply is not sufficient natural capital remaining both to support the present world population at developed-country material standards and to maintain the life-support functions of the ecosphere. These findings have serious moral and geopolitical implications for prevailing world development patterns.

Introduction and Purpose

Trade is indisputably effective at stimulating economic growth. More liberal trade is therefore a central element in most standard economic development models and in mainstream prescriptions for sustainable global development.[1] At the same time, excessive economic scale is already feared by many to be at the root of an emerging global ecological and social crisis. This trade-growth-environment conundrum is never far below the surface in the current discussions and debates over such formal trade agreements as the GATT and the NAFTA.

Most analyses of the ecological and social implications of liberalized trade, including those of most environmentalists, implicitly adopt the perspective of mainstream, market-oriented (neoclassical) economics.[2] Much of the current debate therefore focuses on economic efficiency issues, the pollution effects of increased production, and the implications of freer trade for local and national environmental standards. By contrast, this chapter examines trade-environment linkages through the double lens of ecological economics and a reformulation of the much neglected concept of human "carrying capacity." This novel perspective sheds new light on significant ecological and ethical implications of trade that are generally invisible to conventional analyses.[3] The major issue addressed here is the role of trade in accelerating the depletion of "natural capital" and the implications of this for geopolitical security and traditional models of development.

Contrasting Analytic Visions

Conventional Economic Logic

Neoclassical economics implicitly sees the economy as a self-regulating and self-sustaining, independent and isolated system whose productivity and growth are unconstrained by the environment. The dominant image is of a system in which "the flow of output is circular, self-renewing, and self-feeding"[4] and in which "complete reversibility" is the general rule.[5] Most economic textbooks feature a standard circular diagram of economic process as "a pendulum movement between production and consumption within a completely closed system."[6] In this conventional model, the value embodied in goods and services flows from firms to households in exchange for spending by households (national product). An equal value, reincarnated in factors of production, flows back to firms from households in exchange for wages, rents, profits, etc. (national income).

This "circular flow of exchange value" is the conceptual starting point for economic analysis.[7] In other words, economic models and the prescriptions they produce are based on the monetary value of market exchanges among different sectors of the economy. Significantly, there is no reference in the standard diagram to the linear physical flows of energy and material needed to sustain the circular flow of income. The money circle therefore cannot measure the linear throughput of real value. In effect, economists–and society in general–have come to confuse money, a mere symbol of wealth, with concrete wealth itself.[8] Indeed, conventional theory generally lacks representation of the material and energy stocks and flows, the physical structures, and the time-dependent processes necessary to describe the economy's "connectivity" to the ecosphere.[9]

Such excessive abstraction, combined with unbridled confidence in market dynamics and technology, has led many neoclassical economists to the belief that resource depletion is not a fundamental problem. Historical experience and empirical studies seem to show that rising prices for scarce resources automatically lead to conservation of the original resource and stimulate the search for more technologically advanced substitutes.[10] In a classic misinterpretation of thermodynamic laws, Barnett and Morse go so far as to argue that:

> Advances in fundamental science have made it possible to take advantage of the uniformity of energy/matter - a uniformity that makes it feasible, without preassignable limit, to escape the quantitative constraints imposed by the character of the earth's crust ... In a neo-Ricardian world, it seems, the particular resources with which one starts increasingly become a matter of indifference.[11]

Little wonder that resources

> are frequently omitted as variables in the production function ... or when included, the function is usually multiplicative so that, on paper at least, resources can approach zero while output remains constant if capital and labor increase in a compensatory fashion.[12]

The same conventional rationality argues that trade among nations benefits all trading partners. According to the orthodox theory of competition, "free trade results, inevitably, in increased living standards and increased productivity and efficiency through comparative advantage and gains from trade." Most importantly, the efficiency gains are assumed to be redistributed throughout the economy and are thus "translated into welfare gains for both trading partners."[13] Such assumed benefits help explain the prominent place of export-led development models in the quest for global sustainability –the developing world is deeply in need of welfare gains from trade, increased efficiency, or anything else.

This standard argument for unregulated trade is repeated dogmatically even though some of its key assumptions (e.g., capital immobility) are no longer valid. As Daly and Goodland[14] have argued, the belief that free trade is the best policy unless proved otherwise in particular cases is the "default position" among growth advocates in the current debates over such trade agreements as the GATT and the NAFTA. Serious consideration of the ecological and social case for some degree of regulated trade is lamentably absent in official circles. Indeed, until very recently, it has been difficult to find any discussion by mainstream economists of the potential negative impacts of economic globalization and trade on the environment, broadly defined.

Not surprisingly, many economists reject the concept of ecological carrying capacity. Some do acknowledge that certain countries may face carrying capacity limitations "...even if the rest of the world is poised for sustainable growth indefinitely without significant environmental or resource constraints."[15] However, a 1986 economists' committee report on population growth and economic development for the US National Research Council[16] is more typical: "...neither the word *nor the concept* of 'carrying capacity' played a role."[17]

As should already be apparent, the economists' case against carrying capacity stands in part on the twin pillars of market/or price-induced technological advances (which can increase the efficiency of resource use and substitute manufactured for natural capital), and inter-regional trade (which can relieve locally significant constraints on growth). Again, this vision of the global economy is one in which "the factors of production are [presumed to be] infinitely substitutable for one another," in which using any resource more intensively guarantees an increase in output,[18] and in which "there are no limits on the feasibility of expanding the supplies of [such] nonhuman agents of production."[19] As Daly[20] observes, our prevailing economic myth implicitly assumes a world in which "carrying capacity is infinitely expandable." Taylor[21] characterizes this economic vision as the "expansionist world view."

Economics as Human Ecology

Human ecology paints a dramatically different picture. From this perspective, the relationship of humankind to the ecosphere is similar to those of millions of other species with which we share the planet. Like all other organisms, human beings cannot exist in isolation from the ecosystems of which they are a part. Technological arrogance aside, humankind remains in a state of "obligate dependency" on the products and processes of the natural world.[22]

At the risk of sounding anthropocentric, the ecosphere functions in three ways to sustain the economic (and all other) activities of humankind.[23] First, the ecosphere produces or provides our material resources. Some of these, such as air, water, and food, we consume directly. Others serve as raw material inputs to the production of economic goods and services. Second, the ecosphere assimilates our wastes. "Waste" includes the organic, metabolic excreta and the dead bodies of plants and animals, as well as industrial metabolites and eventually the discarded manufactures themselves.[24] Third, the ecosphere provides certain services which benefit humankind. These include space and amenities for outdoor recreation, aesthetic enjoyment, and spiritual fulfilment. More fundamentally, however, biophysical systems perform life-support functions essential to life as we know it, such as maintaining atmospheric composition, stabilizing the climate, and regenerating the ozone layer. These three classes of functions define the ecological framework for the economy.

Much ecological analysis focuses on material, energy, and information flows in nature and the mechanisms that have evolved to "allocate" these flows among competing species; economics, meanwhile, is concerned with mechanisms to ensure the efficient allocation of energy, material, and information resources among competing sectors of the human economy. Thus, ecology and economics not only share semantic roots but have much the same substantive focus. Indeed, I have argued elsewhere that economics is really a theoretically deviant branch of human ecology.

Reaffirming its ecological roots would dramatically change the basis of economic analysis.[25] In contrast to conventional theory, ecological economics would, at the minimum, see the economy not in splendid isolation, but as an inextricably integrated, completely contained, and wholly dependent subsystem of the ecosphere. Far from being self-feeding, this economy is sustained entirely by low-entropy energy/matter (exergy)[26] produced by biophysical processes elsewhere or at earlier times in the ecosphere; and by the contemporary capacity of the ecosphere to assimilate the high-entropy (degraded) energy and material throughput of the economy instead of the circular flows of money, the conceptual starting point for analysis becomes the linear flows and transformations of matter and energy in the economy.

The Entropy Factor

Like all such transformations in nature, the latter are subject to the Second Law of Thermodynamics: every material transformation produces an increase in net entropy, a permanent degradation of available energy and the dissipation of matter (i.e., resource depletion and pollution). Thus, in thermodynamic terms, the ecologically relevant flows through the economy are unidirectional and irreversible:

> Just as an organism maintains its physical structure by a metabolic flow and is connected to the environment at both ends of its digestive tract, so too an economy requires a throughput, which must to some degree both deplete and pollute the environment.[27]

It should be self-evident that the quality of what comes out of this process differs from the quality of what goes in. Inputs to the economy are considered resources precisely because they possess properties that make them useful. We extract this "utility" in the production of goods or the provision of services. What is left is regarded as residuals or waste because this utility has been removed. In the case of energy, it is the potential or "availability" to do work that is irretrievably lost, dissipated as low-grade heat into the environment. The first law of thermodynamics–the conservation law–may tell us that we do not lose quantity but the second law dictates that we do lose quality, the capacity to perform useful work.

Failure to understand this reality is failure to distinguish between a lump of coal and the smoke and ashes left after its use. Contrary to the assertions of Barnett and Morse,[28] material uniformity does not represent freedom from "quantitative constraints." Quite the opposite–uniformity is a Second Law consequence of having used up all available energy/matter; at thermodynamic equilibrium, there is no potential for any process at all. It is steep gradients and different concentrations in nature that confer utility and the potential for work. Far from being "a matter of [increasing] indifference," the quality of resources with which one starts is an increasingly critical concern.

The Economy as Dissipative Structure

The modern formulation of the Second Law suggests that all highly-ordered complex systems develop and grow (increase their internal order) "at the expense of increasing the disorder at higher levels in the system's hierarchy."[29] In other words, complex systems maintain their internal order and remain in a dynamic non-equilibrium state through the continuous dissipation of available energy/matter extracted from their host environments. The reduced entropy of the local system is achieved at the cost of increased entropy of the global system within which the local system is imbedded. Because they feed upon and degrade available energy/matter from outside themselves, such self-organizing non-equilibrium systems are called dissipative structures.[30]

The human economy is one such highly ordered, dynamic, far-from-equilibrium dissipative structure. Its internal order and complexity continuously increase as it grows and develops, particularly through the formation of manufactured capital made from natural capital. However, because the economy is an open subsystem of the materially closed, non-growing ecosphere,[31] the increasing order (reduced entropy) of the former can be purchased only by increasing the disorder (entropy) of the latter. From this perspective, global ecological change is the thermodynamically inevitable result of human population growth and economic expansion. The material closure of the ecosphere means that the continued growth of the human enterprise can be "sustained" only by displacing other species from their habitats and by appropriating an ever greater share of the low entropy energy/matter continuously being formed by biophysical processes in the ecosphere.

The ecosphere, of course, is also a complex self-organizing dissipative structure. However, the ecosphere has evolved by tapping into the solar flux, an extra-planetary source of available energy. This means that the bounteous complexity of life on Earth (decreasing entropy) is made possible by the dissipation of solar energy (the increasing entropy of the sun). The solar system, the ecosphere, and the economy therefore exist in a nested systems hierarchy. However, while the ecosphere has no effect on the rate of solar decay (and the anticipated life of sun imposes no practical limit on the life of the ecosphere), the economy is capable of seriously undermining the ecosphere (and destabilization of the ecosphere would devastate the economy). This risk is magnified by systemic positive feedback among the three categories of human use of the ecosphere.

It should be clear from the above that acceptance of the entropy law and recognition that the economy is a subsystem of the ecosphere implies acceptance of limits to growth. Contrary to conventional wisdom, the industrial economy is ultimately constrained by finite stocks of high-quality ores and fossil hydrocarbons (produced by ancient biological processes), by the current rate of renewable resource formation (mostly by contemporary photosynthesis), and by the limited waste absorption capacity of ecosystems.

The Constant Natural Capital Stocks Criterion

Recognition that the economy is sustained by continuous flows of low-entropy energy and material resources extracted from both depletable and potentially renewable stocks of "natural capital" is a hallmark of ecological economics. Many of these stocks and flows are invisible to the prevailing system of prices and market incentives. Indeed, some stocks now seen to have immeasurable positive economic value have not previously been recognized by the economy at all. These critical "assets" (e.g., the ozone layer) maintain the life-support functions of the ecosphere. The risks associated with their depletion are unacceptable, and there may be no possibility for technological substitution. In this light, even some fairly conservative economists have noted that "conserving *what there* is could be a sound risk-averse strategy."[32]

Ecological economists are therefore debating various interpretations of a "constant capital stock" condition for sustainability.[33] Much of the discussion centers on the degree of substitutability of manufactured for natural capital. The most risk-averse position assumes low substitutability for most forms of essential self-producing natural capital and might be stated as follows. Each generation should inherit an adequate stock of self-producing natural assets alone no less than the stock of such assets inherited by the previous generation.[34]

This interpretation is compatible with Daly's[35] definition of "strong sustainability" and is the most relevant to considerations of human carrying capacity pursued below.

The constant capital stocks criterion implies, that for the foreseeable future, humankind must learn to live on the annual production (the "interest") generated by remaining stocks of essential natural capital, leaving the latter intact.[36] These sustainable flows are related to Hicksian (or "sustainable") income, the level of consumption that can be maintained from one period to the next without reducing real wealth (productive potential). Of course, if populations or material standards are increasing, capital stocks would have to be increased to satisfy rising demand.

Revisiting Carrying Capacity

Carrying capacity is the fundamental basis for demographic accounting.[37]

Ecological economics holds that carrying capacity, based on the productivity of both localized and open access forms of natural capital, is fundamental to demographic/resource analysis. Indeed, the discipline is preoccupied with whether the ecosphere has the capacity to continue supplying the material and energy demands of the economy unimpeded. From this perspective, two important analytic questions pertaining to economic scale appear self evident: first, how much productive natural capital is required to sustain the present human enterprise? and; second, how do anticipated requirements compare to available stocks of natural capital? These basic questions suggest a third more value-driven one: "How big should the economy be? That is, what is the scale of the economic subsystem that optimizes value, either for humans alone or for the biosphere as a whole?"[38] The rest of this chapter addresses the first two questions.[39]

Inverting Carrying Capacity:
Estimating the Natural Capital Requirements of the Economy[40]

Ecologists define "carrying capacity" as the population of a given species that be supported indefinitely in a defined habitat without permanently damaging the ecosystem upon which it is dependent. For a population of human beings living in place, carrying capacity could be interpreted as the maximum rates of resource consumption and waste discharge that could be sustained indefinitely in their home region without progressively impairing the functional integrity and productivity of essential ecosystems. The corresponding population would be a function of per capita rates of resource consumption and waste production (i.e., sustainable production divided by per capita demand).[41] The important point here is that a given thermodynamic throughput can support fewer people at high material standards or many more at subsistence levels.

Unfortunately, the standard definition of carrying capacity cannot easily be applied to humankind because (as economists are fond of pointing out) people do not live in isolated regions. Much of our consumption is supplied by inter-regional trade and every region exports some of its wastes in natural flows of air and water. Commercial trade and natural flows do not, however, alter the fact that finite stocks of natural capital are required to generate the resource flows required by any defined population, however widely dispersed those stocks might be. For sustainability, the natural capital needs of an economy must be understood as the minimal physical stocks required to produce the biophysical "goods and services" that this economy extracts from global flows without compromising future production, wherever on Earth these stocks are located.

Inverting the standard definition of carrying capacity suggests a way to estimate the natural capital requirements of a given population. Rather than asking what population a particular region can support sustainably, the question becomes: How much land in various categories is required to support the region's population indefinitely at a given material standard? As noted, the resource flows extracted by a defined population or economy represent carrying capacity "appropriated" from total global productivity.[42] To provide a first approximation of natural capital stocks, this "appropriated carrying capacity" (ACC)[43] can be represented as the corresponding area of land and water in various ecosystems required by participants in that economy to produce all the resources they consume and absorb all the wastes they emit indefinitely at current material standards with existing technology.

Preliminary data for industrial countries suggest that per capita primary consumption of food, wood products, fuel, waste-processing capacity, etc., coopts on a continuous basis several hectares of productive land, the exact area depending on individual material standard of living. This average per capita index can be used to estimate the total land area functionally required to support any given population. We call the resultant aggregate land area the total "ecological footprint" of the corresponding population on the Earth.

Cities as Exergy Sinks

> Capitalist production, by collecting the population in great centres, and causing an ever-increasing preponderance of town population, disturbs the metabolism of man and the earth...[44]

ACC analysis reveals that the land "consumed" by urban regions is typically at least an order of magnitude greater than that contained within the usual political boundaries or the associated built-up area. However brilliant its economic star, every city is an entropic black hole drawing on the material resources and productivity of a vast and scattered hinterland many times the size of the city itself. Indeed, urban industrial regions are sustained mainly on carrying capacity appropriated from distant elsewheres.

The lower Fraser Valley of British Columbia (Vancouver to Hope) serves as an example. For simplicity's sake, consider the ecological use of forested and arable land alone: assuming an average Canadian diet and current management practices, the land requirement for food production is approximately one hectare, for forest products 0.5 hectares, and for the absorption of CO_2 from fossil fuel combustion, an additional 3.0 to 4.0 hectares of forested land per capita. Thus, to support only the food, wood fibre, and fossil fuel demands of their present consumer lifestyle, the region's 1.7 million people require, conservatively, 8.5 million hectares of land in continuous production. The valley, however, is only about 400,000 hectares. Thus, our regional population "imports" the productive/absorptive capacity of about 21 times as much land for these functions as it actually occupies. (At about 425 people/km^2, the population density of the valley is comparable to that of the Netherlands or just less than twice that of the UK.)

Even with generally lower per capita consumption, European countries live far beyond their ecological means. For example, our estimate suggests that the Netherlands' population consumes the output of at least 14 times as much productive land as is contained within its own political boundaries for these same uses (approximately 110,000 km^2 for food and forestry products and 360,000 km^2 for energy) .[45]

While economists see cities as loci for intense socioeconomic interaction among individuals and firms and as engines of production and national economic growth, this preliminary analysis reveals that, in ecological terms, cities and urban regions are mostly not even where they appear to be. The city is a node of pure consumption dependent on low entropy resources and surplus waste absorption capacity produced by a extensive resource base somewhere else. While the latter may be spatially diffuse "the relevant knowledge is that it must be somewhere, it must be adequate, it must be available, and it must grow if the city grows."[46]

Trade and Global Carrying Capacity

If all human populations were able to live within their own regional carrying capacities (i.e., on the "interest" generated by natural capital within their home regions) the net effect would be global sustainability. However, no region exists as an independent unit–the reality is that the populations of all urban regions and many whole nations already exceed their territorial carrying capacities and depend on trade for survival. Such regions are running an unaccounted ecological deficit–their populations are appropriating carrying capacity from elsewhere. Unfortunately, prevailing economic logic and trade agreements ignore carrying capacity and sustainability considerations.[47] In these circumstances, the terms of trade may actually accelerate the depletion of essential natural capital thereby undermining global carrying capacity. Several subtle mechanisms are at work.[48]

Trade and Liebig's Law

In the middle of the last century, the German agro-chemist Justus von Liebig postulated the "Law (or Doctrine) of the Minimum" for plant growth. He observed that essential plant nutrients occur naturally in varying concentrations from superabundance to insufficiency in cultivated fields. However, he found that "it is by the minimum that the [growth of] crops are governed."[49]

This insight, that systems and processes are governed by that single necessary factor in least supply, led to the use of more specific fertilizers in agriculture. For example, if plant growth is stunted by the lack of phosphate, one need only fertilize with phosphate. The crop can now continue growing and accessing more of its required nutrients until some other factor becomes limiting. The next limiting factor for this crop might be nitrate, and then water, so still higher productivity will need more complex fertilizers, then irrigation, and so on.

However, there are ecological drawbacks. In nature, limiting factors serve inadvertently to regulate production systems. The shortage of only one essential requirement prevents plant growth from exhausting the entire resource base. The effect of chemical fertilization is to accelerate the depletion of successive components of the soil, a potentially renewable form of natural capital, while creating economic dependencies on non-renewable manufactured capital. This amounts to the short-circuiting of natural biological fuses.

The Law of the Minimum can also be applied to economic growth: economies seem to expand until they reach some limiting factor.[50] Thus, an economy might be stunted by inadequate human capital (e.g., labour and education); cultural capital (e.g., social institutions and political stability); human-made capital (e.g., plant, machinery, physical infrastructure); or natural capital (e.g., resources and biodiversity). Today, natural capital is emerging as a major bottleneck and more liberal trade is perceived as the best way to overcome related local limits.[51]

Unfortunately, unregulated trade acts like fertilizer: it can short-circuit ecological fuses which historically kept economic throughput in balance with local bioproductivity. Indeed, most economists support unrestricted trade precisely because it enables local economies to overcome any material barriers to growth. In this way trade contributes to the prevailing economic myth that "carrying capacity is infinitely expandable."

Trade and Spatial Discounting: Importing Carrying Capacity ...

Such "short-circuiting" is facilitated by urbanization and trade because these factors tend to distance people physically and psychologically from the ecosystems that support them. The resultant "spatial discounting" introduces systematic biases into peoples' valuation of place that affect their economic behaviour.[52]

The free exchange of ecological goods and services allows the population of any given region to grow beyond its local carrying capacity unknowingly and with apparent impunity. In the absence of negative feedback from the land on their economy or lifestyles, there is no direct incentive for such populations to maintain adequate local stocks of productive natural capital. For example, the ability to import food makes people less averse to the long-term risks associated with urbanization of locally limited agricultural land. If low-priced agricultural imports subsequently undermine local agriculture there is little resistance, even among farmers, to converting land to activities that yield higher short-term economic returns.

At the same time, the expanding network of trade-dependent regions may be drawing down "surplus" natural capital stocks everywhere. This is the direct result of global markets gaining access to local resources. In some cases, upward pressure on prices may encourage over-exploitation of scarce resources. Ironically, in a competitive market, downward pressure on prices may have the same effect as sellers compensate for reduced revenues through increased volume. Trade, therefore, only appears to increase carrying capacity. In fact, by encouraging all regions to exceed local limits, by reducing the perceived risk attached to local natural capital depletion, and by simultaneously exposing local surpluses to global demand,[53] uncontrolled trade accelerates natural capital depletion, reducing global carrying capacity and increasing the risk to everyone.

This situation applies not only to commercial trade but also to the unmonitored flows of goods and services provided by nature. This is a novel variant of the so-called "common property" problem. For example, northern urbanites are now dependent on the carbon sink, global heat transfer, and climate stabilization functions of tropical forests. There are many other variations on this theme from drift-net fishing to ozone depletion, each involving open access to, or shared dependency on, some form of threatened natural capital in the common pool.

... and Exporting Ecological Degradation

The importing of carrying capacity by wealthy industrialized countries may equate to exporting ecological and social malaise to the developing world. Many impoverished countries have little other than agricultural, fisheries, and forest products to offer world markets and current development models encourage the "modernization" and intensification of production of specialized commodities for export. Unfortunately, the consolidation of land and other scarce resources to produce luxury export crops often jeopardizes domestic staples production, contributing to local food shortages and malnutrition. The process also displaces thousands of small farmers, farm workers, and their families from the better agricultural lands. This concentrates wealth in relatively few hands while forcing the dislocated peasants either to eke out a subsistence existence on inferior land that should never go under the plough, or to migrate to already overcrowded cities.[54] Erosion, desertification, and deforestation in the countryside and debilitating social and environmental problems in burgeoning squatter settlements around many Third World cities are the frequent result.

The distancing of First World consumers from the negative impacts of their consumption only makes things easier for Third World elites, international capital, and transnational corporations, all of whom benefit from the expanding commodity trade. Meanwhile, the developing country itself becomes increasingly dependent on export earnings, much of which must go to pay off the original "development" loans.

Overall this pattern contributes to the net transfer of both wealth and sustainability from the poor to the rich within developing countries and from the poorest countries to the richest among the trading nations.[55] Ultimately, of course, the drain of debt servicing and downward pressure on prices in an increasingly competitive global market reduce the economic surpluses available for sound resource management, accelerating the erosion of the export regions' best lands and associated natural capital. The resultant capital liquidation both jeopardizes present levels of production and reduces the future potential for more sustainable forms of development.

Thermodynamic Imperialism: Trade as Appropriated Carrying Capacity

> The structure of trade, as we know it at present, is a curse from the perspective of sustainable development.[56]

As may already be apparent, the ecological perspective on trade and natural flows suggests a disturbing interpretation of the prospects for global development. Much of the industrial countries' wealth comes from the exploitation (and sometimes liquidation) of natural capital, not only within their own territories, but also within their former southern colonies. Colonialism, of course, involved the direct appropriation of extra-territorial carrying capacity but the same resource flows continue today in the form of commercial trade. (What used to require territorial occupation is now achieved through commerce.)

The point is that this persistent relationship is an inevitable consequence of thermodynamic law. The techno-economic growth and high material standards of developed countries require net transfers of negentropy to the industrial centre.[57] Indeed,

> industrial production and world trade are ... mutually reinforcing modes of exergy appropriation. To export industrial goods would be meaningless if the money gained could not be used to purchase new resources with higher exergy content. The "net order" thus appropriated by industry is as fundamental to its reproduction (as a synthetic "biomass") as food is to an organism.[58]

At the same time, consistent with the second law, less developed regions and countries "must experience a net increase in entropy as natural resources and traditional social structures are dismembered."[59]

These latter effects are not all confined to developing countries. The depletion of the northern cod stocks of Atlantic Canada and the temperate rainforests of British Columbia has been driven largely by export markets and is producing unprecedented socioeconomic stress in the human communities that have historically depended on these resources. Similarly, Canada's prairie soils have lost half their original organic matter and natural nutrients as a result of intensive agricultural practices and decades of grain exports to the world. All this while the economics of production agriculture depopulates the countryside.

Thus, to the extent that trade and the restructuring of rural economies displace people from productive landscapes to over-crowded cities, particularly in the South, to supply urban industrial regions, mainly in the North, they contribute to impoverishment, urban migration, and local ecological decay. Moreover, to the extent that the current international development model favours net transfers of wealth to the North and the depletion of natural capital in the South, this poverty and ecological decline is a chronic condition. The people of less developed countries cannot live simultaneously on carrying capacity (exergy) exported to the world's industrial heartlands.

The editors of *The Ecologist*[60] develop a similar argument in a recent issue dedicated entirely to the proposition that the prevailing international development model represents the effective "enclosure" of the global commons:

> The market economy has expanded primarily by enabling state and commercial interests to gain control of territory that has traditionally been used and cherished by others, and by transforming that territory–together with the people themselves–into expendable "resources" for exploitation.[61]

This supports both the present analysis and Hornborg's view that "the ecological and socioeconomic impoverishment of the periphery are two sides of the same coin ... "[62]

These parallel arguments suggests that for all the ebullient optimism of some development economists, many developing countries will not be able to follow northern industrial countries along their historical path to material well-being. There simply is not sufficient natural capital to support the present world population at northern material standards and also maintain the functional integrity of the ecosphere. In short, the world cannot safely expand its way to sustainability.[63] It is not merely a question of adequate resources for direct consumption. The world must also now come to appreciate that many remaining stocks of natural capital as diverse as forests, fossil hydrocarbons, and the ozone layer, are already fully committed in place providing unpriced life support services.

Although never stated in quite these terms, the appropriation of most of the world's carrying capacity by the urban industrial North (and reluctance to give it up) and the insistence by the South of its right to a fair share (and the threat to seize what it can through sheer growth in numbers and inefficient technologies) was really the only issue at the Earth Summit in Rio in June 1992.

Discussion and Conclusions

Breaking the Camel's Back: Will Unregulated Trade be the Final Straw?

There is accumulating evidence that we may not be far from the biophysical limits to global to carrying capacity. Nearly 40 per cent of terrestrial net primary productivity (photosynthesis) is already being "appropriated" by humans, one species among millions, and this fraction is steadily increasing.[64] If we take this percentage as an index of the human carrying capacity of the Earth and assume that a growing economy could come to appropriate 80 per cent of photosynthetic production before destroying the functional integrity of the ecosphere,[65] the earth will effectively go from half to completely full within the next doubling period–currently about 35 years.[66] In fact, this may be optimistic. Such seemingly persistent trends as ozone depletion, atmospheric change, deforestation, soil exhaustion and erosion, desertification, etc., signal both the breaching of critical waste absorption capacities and the depletion of critical natural capital stocks. In short, even the present human population with existing technologies and today's average (and highly inequitable) material standards, may be in excess of the long-term carrying capacity of Earth.

Additional evidence of the scale of the problem may be found by extrapolating the ecological standards enjoyed by people in the developed world to the global level. If the entire world population of 5.5 billion "consumed" productive land at the conservative rate used for our Fraser Valley example, the total requirement would be 27.5 billion hectares. In fact, the total land area of Earth is only just over 13 billion hectares of which only 8.8 billion hectares are productive cropland, pasture, or forest. The implications are twofold: first, it shows again that the rich countries–indeed, wealthy people everywhere–unconsciously appropriate far more than their fair share of global carrying capacity (much of it through trade); second, we would require an additional two Earths, assuming present technology and current efficiency levels, to provide for just the present world population at Canadians' ecological standard of living.

The disparity between anticipated demand for ecological goods and services and available supplies from remaining stocks of natural capital is a measure of the "sustainability gap" confronting global society.[67] The present analysis suggests that policies to reduce demand and redistribute wealth are more likely to succeed in closing this gap sustainably than are efforts to increase supplies. This conclusion presents a serious challenge to the Brundtland Commission requirement for sustainable development: "a five to ten-fold expansion of world industrial output by the time world population stabilizes [at twice the present level] sometime in the next century."[68] Such marked growth in material throughput is thermodynamically and ecologically unsustainable given the energy and other technologies likely to be widely available in the critical decades ahead. To the extent that unregulated trade is used to facilitate realization of this expansionist scenario, it may well become the economic straw that breaks the ecological camel's back.

Trade and Geopolitical Security

Homer-Dixon et al.[69] review the evidence that generally deteriorating ecological conditions and growing scarcities of renewable resources in coming decades will likely contribute to social instability and precipitate civil and international strife. Similarly, Gurr[70] argues that the persistent scarcity of essential resources in contemporary societies will "tend to create greater material inequalities within and among societies, intensify internal and international conflict, and [create] a shift from open toward more closed and authoritarian political institutions." His rationale is that economically advantaged groups are better able to use market forces and political influence, and if scarcity persists, "they will increasingly exert economic and political power to [retain] their absolute and relative advantages."[71]

The present analysis suggests that such geopolitical tensions may be exacerbated by the dependencies created through foreign trade. Populations that have come to rely on imports have no direct control over the natural capital stocks that sustain them from afar (and they may have destroyed much of their domestic natural capital). This raises a question as to the inherent stability of trading relationships in an era of global change. Are external sources secure if climate change, ozone depletion, or soil erosion reduce biological production or local populations lay claim to the land or export flows? Do prevailing management practices in export region "A" ensure adequate maintenance or enhancement of natural capital stocks critical to the survival of import regions "B" and "C"? How far will import-dependent countries go to protect their perceived right of access to economically, strategically, or functionally critical resources as demand increases and supply is eroded?

To the extent that inter-regional dependency threatens geopolitical security we have an argument for policies to enhance regional economic diversity, independence, and self-reliance, and to restrict trade to the exchange of true ecological surpluses. Needless to say, such prescriptions fly in the face of prevailing development rhetoric which calls for economic specialization, concentration of capital, unrestricted access to resources, freer markets, expanded trade, and material growth as the route to future prosperity.

The Way Ahead: Trade if Necessary, but Not Necessarily Trade

There can be no doubt that achieving sustainable development will require a sophisticated understanding of real-world human ecology. Today, however, the primary decision rules determining human material relationships with the rest of the ecosphere come from ecologically empty economic models. We would therefore be well advised to reassess these models in light of a key cybernetic theorem, Ashby's Law of Requisite Variety: The internal variety (diversity, complexity) of a managing system must correspond to the variety of the managed system if the manager is to maintain control.[72] As the global economy becomes increasingly coincident with the ecosphere, how can we hope to maintain control if our management models for the former remain unconscious of the essential "internal variety" of the latter?

While no comprehensive alternative development model based on the present analysis exists, it is certainly possible to speculate on the form it might take. The following qualities are all compatible with the need to restore ecological balance and social equity to development within a framework recognizing the relationship between regional and global carrying capacity. They also reflect the basic logic of ecological economics. Future global development policies should incorporate:

- Greater use of proper (full cost) pricing, "green" taxation, and other economic incentives to ensure a significant reallocation of resource revenue from income (consumption) to investment in restoration and maintenance of essential natural capital. Where applicable, conventional market economics can help to induce changes in individual behaviour and the shift to social values compatible with long-term sustainability.

- Emphasis on community responsibility and social capital formation to restore balance with the present weight on individual rights and private capital accumulation. To what extent can social caring capacity substitute for individually appropriated carrying capacity?

- Recognition in resource and property law that we may already have reached the point in some sectors where the exercise of private rights to economic benefits from the exploitation of natural capital may in impose greater costs on the public and, therefore, represents a net loss to society. Such uneconomic development might be associated, for example, with forestry where the value of non-market common-pool benefits and life-support functions destroyed through harvesting exceeds the resultant private income gains.

- Explicit promotion of cooperative activity to balance industrial society's current worship of competitive behaviour.[73]

- A restoration of balance from the present emphasis on global economic integration and inter-regional dependency toward intra-regional ecological balance and self-reliance. (If all regions were in ecological steady-state the aggregate effect would be global stability.) This position is compatible with Daly and Goodland's[74] recommended alternative "default position" on international trade, that we should strive "to reduce rather than increase the entanglement between nations."

- ◆ Examination of the emerging philosophy of bioregionalism as a potentially useful conceptual starting point for the articulation of a more geopolitically stable development pattern.

- ◆ Development and use of regional ecological (i.e., physical) accounts to assist (bio-)regions in computing their ecological footprints and monitoring their ecological/thermodynamic balance of trade.

- ◆ Regulation of commodity trade flows based on sustainable ecological surpluses and no net loss of natural capital stocks (i.e., sustainable rates of supply) rather than global market demand.

- ◆ Negotiation of a General Agreement on the Integrity of (Ecological) Assets (a GAIA agreement) to regulate economic activities affecting global life-support system, including patterns of commercial trade in ecologically significant commodities. (Such an agreement would set the ecological "bottom line" for such instruments as the GATT.)

- ◆ International agreements for the more equitable allocation of present wealth, essential natural capital, and related life-support functions to all the world's people. Initially this might involve such things as: the purchase of development rights to tropical forests by the industrial nations to conserve their carbon sink, biodiversity, heat distribution, etc., values, and to compensate tropical peoples for development benefits foregone; global markets in tradable emissions permits for access to the ecosphere's available CO_2 uptake capacity. (Following initial allocated to all countries on a population or per capita basis, trade in such permits would also result in wealth transfers from rich to poor.)

As noted, most of these suggestions oppose the current development rhetoric with its emphasis on more liberal trade, economic integration, centralization, globalization, specialization, deregulation, competition, and the primacy of material growth. Nevertheless, if the analytic framework developed in this paper is valid, movement along these contrary lines may be essential to making significant progress on humankind-environment reconciliation.

Endnotes

[1] See WCED, *Our Common Future* (Oxford: Oxford University Press, 1987).

[2] The most significant exception is H. Daly and R. Goodland, *An Ecological-Economic Assessment of Deregulation of International Commerce Under GATT*, Discussion draft (Washington,D.C.: The World Bank, 1993).

[3] For present purposes, interregional "trade" is broadly defined to include both commercial transactions and the natural biogeochemical cycling of air, water, and essential nutrients.

[4] R. Heilbroner and L. Thurow, *The Economic Problem* (New York: Prentice-Hall, 1981), 135.

[5] N. Georgescu-Roegen, "Energy and Economic Myths," *Southern Economic Journal* 41 (3) (1975), 347-381.

[6] N. Georgescu-Roegen, *The Entropy Law and the Economic Process* (Cambridge, Massachusetts: Harvard University Press, 1971). Georgescu-Roegen's 1971 and 1975 contributions provide a comprehensive critique of the mechanical "perpetual motion" concept of the economy.

[7] H. Daly, "Sustainable Development: From Concept and Theory Towards Operational Principles," *Population and Development Review* 16 (1990); H. Daly, "The Circular Flow of Exchange Value and the Linear Throughput of Matter-Energy: A Case of Misplaced Concreteness," *Steady-State Economics* (2nd ed., Washington, D.C.: Island Press, 1991).

[8] Daly, *Steady-State Economics*, 197 defines this "money fetishism" as "applying the characteristics of money, the token and measure of wealth, to concrete wealth itself.   Thus, if money can grow forever at compound interest, then, presumably, so can wealth; if money flows in a circle, then, presumably, so does output."

[9] P. Christensen, "Driving Forces, Increasing Returns and Ecological Sustainability,"in R. Costanza, ed., *Ecological Economics: The Science and Management of Sustainability* (New York: Columbia University Press, 1991), 5.

[10] H. Barnett and C. Morse, *Scarcity and Growth: The Economics of Natural Resource Scarcity* (Baltimore: Johns Hopkins Press, 1963); P. Dasgupta and D. Heal, *Economic Theory and Exhaustible Resources* (Cambridge and New York: Cambridge University Press, 1979).

[11] Barnett and Morse, *Scarcity and Growth:The Economics of Natural Resource Scarcity*, 11. This assertion seems to be based on the First Law of Thermodynamics (the law of conservation of matter and energy) but ignores completely the Second Law.

[12] Daly, *Steady-State Economics*.

[13] Brenda Leith, "Emerging Trade Agreements and Their Impact on Agriculture," Chapter 7 in this Volume.

[14] Daly and Goodland, *An Ecological-Economic Assessment of Deregulation of International Commerce Under GATT*.

[15] R. Muscat, "Carrying Capacity and Rapid Population Growth: Definition, Cases, and Consequences," in D. Mahar, ed., *Rapid Population Growth and Human Carrying Capacity: Two Perspectives* . Staff Working Papers #690 (Population and Development Series, #15) (Washington, D.C.: The World Bank, 1985), 6.

[16] National Research Council (Committee on Population), *Report of the Working Group on Population Growth and Economic Development* (Washington, D.C.: National Academy Press, 1986).

[17] G. Hardin, "Paramount Positions in Ecological Economics," in Costanza, ed., *Ecological Economics: The Science and Management of Sustainability* 54. Original emphasis.

[18] J. Kirchner, G. Leduc, R. Goodland, and J. Drake, "Carrying Capacity, Population Growth, and Sustainable Development," in Mahar, ed., *Rapid Population Growth and Human Carrying Capacity.*

[19] W. Nordhaus and J. Tobin, "Is Growth Obsolete?" in M. Moss, ed., *The Measurement of Economic and Social Performance* (New York: Columbia University Press for National Bureau of Economic Research, 1973), 522.

[20] H. Daly, "Comments on Population Growth and Economic Development," *Population and Development Review* 12 (1986), 593-585.

[21] D. Taylor, "Disagreeing on the Basics: Environmental Debates Reflect Competing World Views," *Alternatives* 3 (18) (1992), 26-33.

[22] W. Rees, *Sustainable Development and the Biosphere*, Teilhard Studies Number 23, American Teilhard Association for the Study of Man, or: "The Ecology of Sustainable Development," *The Ecologist* 20 (1) (1990), 18-23.

[23] M. Jacobs, *The Green Economy* (London: Pluto Press, 1991), Chapter 1.

[24] These latter categories are unique products of human ecology. See R. Ayres, "Industrial Metabolism and Global Change," *International Social Science Journal* 121 (1989), 363-373.

[25] W. Rees, "Ecological Footprints and Appropriated Carrying Capacity: What Urban Economics Leaves Out," *Environment and Urbanization* 4 (2) (1992), 121-130; W. Rees and M. Wackernagel, "Ecological Footprints and Appropriated Carrying Capacity: Measuring the Natural Capital Requirements of the Human Economy," Forthcoming in C. Folke, M. Hammer, A-M. Jansson, and R. Costanza, eds., *Investing in Natural Capital* (Washington, D.C.: Island Press, 1994). (Originally an invited plenary paper to the Second Meeting of the International Society for Ecological Economics on Investing in Natural Capital, Stockholm, Sweden: 3-6 August, 1992).

[26] Low-entropy energy/matter, negentropy, unbound energy, available energy, and exergy are often used synonymously in the literature. "Exergy" is more commonly used in Europe. All terms refer to the potential of high-grade energy to do useful work. This potential is a measure of the difference between a high-grade energy source and low-grade background conditions. In the case of matter (e.g. mineral deposits) it measures concentration relative to background.

[27] H. Daly, "Steady-State Economics: Concepts, Questions, Policies," *Gaia* 6 (1992), 333.

[28] Barnett and Morse, *Scarcity and Growth: The Economics of Natural Resource Scarcity.*

[29] E. Schneider and J. Kay, "Life as a Manifestation of the Second Law of Thermodynamics," *International Journal of Mathematical and Computer Modelling* (in press).

[30] G. Nicolis and I. Prigogine, *Self-Organization in Non-Equilibrium Systems* (J. Wiley and Sons, 1977).

[31] Daly, "Steady-State Economics: Concepts, Questions, Policies."

[32] D. Pearce, E. Barbier and A. Markandya *Sustainable Development: Economics and Environment in the Third World* (Aldershot: Edward Algar, 1990), 7. Emphasis added.

[33] R. Costanza and H. Daly, "Natural Capital and Sustainable Development." Paper prepared for the CEARC Workshop on Natural Capital. Vancouver, BC, 15-16 March 1990 (Ottawa: Canadian Environmental Assessment Research Council); Daly, "Sustainable Development: From Concept and Theory Towards Operational Principles"; D. Pearce, A. Markandya and E. Barbier, *Blueprint for a Green Economy* (London: Earthscan Publications, 1989); D. Pearce et al., *Sustainable Development: Economics and Environment in the Third World;* J. Pezzey, "Economic Analysis of Sustainable Growth and Sustainable Development," Environment Department Working Paper No. 15. (Washington, D.C.: World Bank, 1989); W. Rees, "Understanding Sustainable Development: Natural Capital and the New World Order," *Journal of American Planning Association* (forthcoming).

[34] The major alternative interpretation refers to maintaining a constant aggregate stock of human-made and natural capital. Pearce et al., *Blueprint for a Green Economy.*

[35] Daly, "Sustainable Development: From Concept and Theory Towards Operational Principles."

[36] Rees, "Sustainable Development and the Biosphere," Teilhard Studies Number 23; "The Ecology of Sustainable Development," 18-23.

[37] Hardin, "Paramount Positions in Ecological Economics," 54.

[38] Daly, "Steady-State Economics: Concepts, Questions, Policies," 336.

[39] Mainstream macro-analysis essentially ignores all questions pertaining to appropriate scale.

[40] The following sections are liberally adapted from Rees, "Understanding Sustainable Development: Natural Capital and the New World Order," and Rees, "Natural Capital in Relation to Regional/Global Concepts of Carrying Capacity," In *Ecological Economics–Emergence of a New Development Paradigm* (Ottawa: University of Ottawa, Institute for Research on Environment and Economy and Canadian International Development Agency, 1993); and Rees and Wackernagel, "Ecological Footprints and Appropriated Carrying Capacity."

[41] This formulation is a variation of Hardin's "Third Law of Human Ecology:" (Total human impact on the ecosphere) = (Population) x (Per capita impact). Early

versions of this law date from Ehrlich and Holdren who also recognized that
human impact is a product of population, affluence (consumption), and technology: I=PAT: P. Ehrlich and J. Holdren, "Impact of Population Growth," *Science*
171 (1971), 1212-1217; J. Holdren and P. Ehrlich, "Human Population and the
Global Environment," *American Scientist* 62 (1974), 282-292.

[42] P. Vitousek, P. Ehrlich, A. Ehrlich and P. Matson, "Human Appropriation of the
Products of Photosynthesis," *Bioscience* 36 (1986), 368-374.

[43] "Carrying capacity" is used slightly inaccurately here, but seems to transmit
meaning better than a more accurate term such as "appropriated bioproductive
flows."

[44] K. Marx, *Capital* (I) (London: 1970), 505.

[45] Using data from World Resources Institute, *World Resources* 1992-93 (New York:
Oxford Universtiy Press, 1992). The Reijksinstituut voor Volksgezondheid en
Milieuhygiene in the Netherlands suggests that for food production alone that
country appropriates 170,000 to 240,000 km2 of agricultural land, 5-7 times the
area of domestic agricultural land (RIVM, cited in D. Meadows and J. Randers,
Beyond the Limits (Toronto: McClelland & Stewart 1992).)

[46] R. Overby, "The Urban Economic Environmental Challenge: Improvement of
Human Welfare by Building and Managing Urban Ecosystems," Paper presented
in Hong Kong to the POLMET 85 Urban Environment Conference (Washington,
D.C.: The World Bank, 1985). Emphasis added.

[47] As this is being written, the major political preoccupation at every level of
government in Canada (and in many other countries) is how to control the fiscal
deficit. Although arguably more threatening to security in the long run, the
ecological deficit is unmeasured and unknown to economic planners and decision-makers.

[48] Less subtly, keep in mind that the whole purpose of trade is to relieve local
constraints and increase the potential for economic growth. Thus, at a minimum,
to the extent that trade-induced growth increases material consumption and
pollution it must necessarily increase the pressures on natural capital.

[49] J. von Liebig, *Natural Laws of Husbandry*, Translated by John Blyth (New York: D.
Appleton and Company, 1863), 207.

[50] M. Wackernagel and W. Rees, "Perceptual and Structural Barriers to Investing in
a Natural Capital," Paper presented to the Second Meeting of the International
Society for Ecological Economics on Investing in Natural Capital, Stockholm,
Sweden, 3-6 August 1992 (Vancouver: UBC School of Community and Regional
Planning, 1992).

[51] W. Catton, *Overshoot: the Ecological Basis of Revolutionary Change* (Urbana: The
University of Illinois Press, 1980), 158.

[52] B. Hannon, "Sense of Place: Geographic Discounting by People, Animals, and
Plants," Paper presented to the Second Meeting of the International Society for
Ecological Economics on Investing in Natural Capital, Stockholm, Sweden: 3-6
August 1992; G. Daily and P. Ehrlich, "Population, Sustainability, and Earth's
Carrying Capacity," *BioScience* 42 (10) (1992), 761-771.

[53] Such surpluses might otherwise represent a global "safety net".

[54] In theory, the wealth generated by exporting local carrying capacity is supposed to "trickle down" to ordinary people, enabling them to purchase staple foods imported from more efficient producers at a lower cost than they could grow it themselves. However, trickle-down development theory is largely discredited and the benefits of the so-called green revolution are increasingly called into question. See, for example, *The Ecologist* 21(2) (March/April 1991) on the role of international development in "promoting world hunger."

[55] The latter transfers reached tens of billions of dollars annually in the late 1980s.

[56] T. Haavelmo and S. Hansen, "On the Strategy of Trying to Reduce Economic Inequality by Expanding the Scale of Human Activity," in R. Goodland, H. Daly, and S. El Serafy, eds., *Environmentally Sustainable Ecological Development: Building on Brundtland* (Paris: UNESCO, 1991), 46.

[57] Remember, manufactured capital can only be sustained by flows of natural capital.

[58] A. Hornborg, "Machine Fetishism, Value, and the Image of Unlimited Goods: Toward a Thermodynamics of Imperialism," *Man* 27 (1) (1992), 9. Original emphasis.

[59] A. Hornborg, "Codifying Complexity: Towards an Economy of Incommensurable Values," Paper presented to the Second Meeting of the International Society for Ecological Economics on Investing in Natural Capital, (Stockholm, Sweden: 3-6 August, 1992).

[60] "Whose Common Future?" *The Ecologist* 22(3), (A special issue on the enclosure of the global commons, July/August 1992).

[61] Ibid., 131.

[62] Hornborg, "Codifying Complexity."

[63] See also Haavelmo and Hansen, "On the Strategy of Trying to Reduce Economic Inequality by Expanding the Scale of Human Activity"; R. Goodland and H. Daly, "Why Northern Income Growth Is Not the Solution to Southern Poverty," *Ecological Economics* 8 (1993), 85-101.

[64] Vitousek et al., "Human Appropriation of the Products of Photosynthesis."

[65] This is a dubious assumption at best. In a finite ecosphere, significant expansion of human populations and the material economy can only occur through the "dissipation" of other species and ecosystems.

[66] H. Daly, "From Empty World Economics to Full World Economics: Recognizing an Historical Turning Point in Economic Development," in R. Goodland, H. Daly, and S. El Serafy, eds., *Environmentally Sustainable Ecological Development: Building on Brundtland*, Environment Working Paper No. 46 (Washington, D.C.: World Bank, July 1991) .

[67] Rees and Wackernagel, "Ecological Footprints and Appropriated Carrying Capacity."

[68] WCED, *Our Common Future*, 213.

[69] T. Homer-Dixon, J. Boutwell and G. Rathjens, "Environmental Change and Violent Conflict," *Scientific American* (February 1993), 38-45.

[70] T. Gurr, "On the Political Consequences of Scarcity and Economic Decline," *International Studies Quarterly* 29 (1985), 51-75.

[71] Ibid., 58.

[72] Or, in Stafford Beer's more colourful terms: "We cannot regulate our interaction with any aspect of reality that our model of reality does not include because we cannot by definition be conscious of it." S. Beer, "I Said, You Are Gods," *Teilhard Review* 15 (2) (1981), 90.

[73] A general shift in values away from the material and the individual toward the intangible and the community may be essential for sustainable development in a finite world.

[74] Daly and Goodland, *An Ecological-Economic Assessment of Deregulation of International Commerce Under GATT.*

CHAPTER 4

TRADE AND SUSTAINABLE DEVELOPMENT: FRIENDS OR ENEMIES?

David Runnalls

David Runnalls is the President of Runnalls Research Associates and Senior Advisor to the President of the International Development Research Centre. He is also Senior Advisor to the Administrator of the United Nations Development Programme. Previously, he was Director of the Environment and Sustainable Development Programme at the Institute for Research on Public Policy in Ottawa. Runnalls was also the Director of the North American Office of the International Institute for Environment and Development IIED, an international non-governmental organization which specializes in policy research, technical assistance and information dissemination on issues related to environment, natural resource management and the economic development of the Third World. Educated at the University of Toronto and Columbia University, Runnalls is the author of a number of papers and articles on sustainable development. He has served as a consultant to the United Nations Environment Programme, the World Bank, the OECD, the Asian Development Bank, the Canadian International Development Agency, the National Film Board of Canada and the United States Agency for International Development.

The report of the World Commission on Environment and Development demonstrated graphically that the earth's economy and its ecology are now so closely interlocked that policies in one area which ignore the other are bound for failure.

The earth's population now stands at about 5½ billion. More than 1½ billion of these live in absolute poverty with few demands on the environment. Yet even now the earth's natural systems are near the breaking point with deforestation approaching 20 million hectares per year, an area of Africa the size of all of India subject to desertification, the destruction of the ozone layer and climate change over the next fifty years greater than that experienced over the past 10,000.

The demographers tell us that we will reach the 10 billion mark somewhere near the middle of the next century. Brundtland estimated that simply to provide everyone with a current southern European life style would require food production to triple, energy use to quintuple and raw material use to increase by roughly the same amount. With current systems of production, consumption and income distribution, this would lead to ecological catastrophe.

Seen against this background, the Brundtland solution, sustainable development, is a radical prescription. It implies a new form of development that is far more energy and raw material efficient. It implies dramatic changes in income distribution, both North and South and within countries. It implies living off the interest of our natural capital, rather than running down the capital itself. It requires economic systems which take account of the needs of future generations. And it requires a complete change in the way governments, the private sector and individuals make decisions. For only if the environment becomes a factor in every economic decision, before that decision is taken, can the world move toward more sustainable forms of development.

Sustainable development has become a popular concept because it appears to present a set of win/win solutions rather than the more traditional either/or choices of conventional environmental politics. This is also its weakness, allowing it to be hijacked by all manner of governments, corporations and interest groups and transformed into business as usual with a bit more thought given to the environment early on in the process.

This in turn makes a number of groups unhappy with the term. Many environmentalists view it as a fig leaf behind which all manner of shady economic interests can hide. Many developing countries, on the other hand, view it as a stalking horse for the North to impede their future development by attaching all sorts of environmental conditions to their development process.

It was these sorts of suspicions which dogged the United Nations Earth Summit in 1992. Rather than choosing the win/win scenario of sustainable development, the delegates to the first Preparatory Committee for the summit chose the 1972 formula of environment and development. This left the whole process bogged down in a fight over two agendas. The Northern agenda looked very familiar to us in Canada–climate change, ozone depletion, deforestation, biodiversity and marine pollution. The Southern agenda looked very familiar to anyone who took part in the North/South debates of the 1970s and 1980s–debt, increased access to financial resources on concessional terms, technology transfer. At its worst, Rio became a debate not about environment and development, but about environment *versus* development. As a result, little of immediate benefit was accomplished.

And yet conditions in much of the developing world continue to worsen for the very poor. And ecological conditions also continue to deteriorate globally. The need for more sustainable forms of development is greater than ever.

No matter how it is defined, the transition to sustainable development will be expensive. The Rio Secretariat estimated its cost at no less than $625 billion per year. One quarter of this–$125 billion or so, would come from the developed countries in the form of resource transfers.

Even if one adopts a completely different concept of sustainability (the Rio figures represent a pretty conventional scaling up of present patterns), there is no doubt that it will be costly. And there is no doubt that sums of that magnitude will not come exclusively, or even largely, from parsimonious northern parliaments. Most aid advocates reckon that we will be lucky to hold our own over the next five years or so. Private capital will make up some of the difference but it brings its own forms of problems in the governance of multinational corporations, the fact that it flows to relatively few, relatively well-off developing countries, and that it carries its own environmental baggage.

The only remaining large scale source of finance available to the Third World is in market access. According to the Pakistani economist Mahbub ul Haq, tariffs, quotas and other trade restrictions cost the developing world up to $500 billions per year in lost revenue.

But as the other chapters in this volume clearly indicate, freer trade can carry a substantial ecological price unless it is accompanied by measures to internalize costs, minimize predatory pricing, and allow countries to take measures which they deem prudent to protect their natural resources and environment from the potential damage caused by increased trade.

Unfortunately the trade/environment debate may be heading down the same path as the environment/development debate. Instead of trade and the environment, we are now in danger of arguing about trade *versus* environment.

In order to see whether trade policies could be designed to support sustainable development, the International Institute for Sustainable Development in Winnipeg brought together a group of nine people, broadly representative of the environment and trade communities and of the developed and developing worlds. We met several times over the course of a year and exchanged numerous drafts and comments in between.

We found, not surprisingly, that there is no integrated approach to formulating trade, environment, and development policies. Accordingly, we developed the following principles to fill that void. We are under no illusions that the adoption of these principles will instantly make free trade environmentally friendly, but we feel that they represent a significant step in bringing the trade and environment communities closer together in support of sustainable development.

Principles for Trade and Sustainable Development

I   Goal

These principles are intended to guide trade and trade-related environment and development policies, practices and agreements, to help ensure that they work to achieve sustainable development.

II   Points of Departure

The growing realization that the earth's environment and economy are linked is transforming international relations, and creating a demand for sustainable development. Of the many new sets of issues this raises, one– the multifaceted linkages connecting trade, environment and development–has only recently received serious attention. The relationships which encompass these sectors are evolving rapidly in response to structural changes in the world's economies, in particular in response to the declining relevance of national boundaries for production and investment decisions, and to the growing recognition of the imperative of environmental protection.

Global and regional trade agreements, environmental policies and accords, structural adjustment and lending policies and national and multilateral development efforts all have spillover effects beyond their own policy spheres. Repercussions from these effects often come back full circle, to impede or improve the achievement of the original policy goals. As this is better appreciated, the need for an integrated approach to formulating trade, environment and development policies, at both national and international levels, becomes increasingly obvious. In each sphere, sustainable development must become a primary goal.

> Sustainable development is development that meets the needs of the present without compromising the ability of future generations to meet their own needs. It contains within it two key concepts: the concept of "needs," in particular the essential needs of the world's poor, to which overriding priority should be given; and the idea of limitations imposed by the state of technology and social organization on the environment's ability to meet present and future needs.

We embrace this Brundtland Commission definition and note the seven strategic imperatives it identified for sustainable development: reviving growth; changing the quality of growth; meeting essential needs for jobs, food, energy, water, and sanitation; ensuring a sustainable level of population; conserving and enhancing the resource base; reorienting technology and managing risk; and merging environment and economics in decision-making.

The principles that follow take this definition of sustainable development as their starting point, along with three key assumptions:

> *Need for Poverty Alleviation.* Sustainable development cannot be achieved worldwide while massive poverty persists. Poverty alleviation is a central objective of development, and a key concern for environment policies. Wealth created by trade is an essential means to achieving this end. In the developing world, combating poverty and achieving sustainability depends on the growth of per capita income, on its distribution, on appropriate domestic policies, and on international policies that support them. Worldwide, economic growth, continued economic reforms, and a substantial increase in the transfer of financial resources and technology from rich to poor countries are vital for achieving poverty alleviation.

> *Importance of Environmental Policies.* Domestic and international environmental policies are of paramount importance for all aspects of

sustainable development. These policies rely principally on cost internalization as a means of achieving environmental protection. As internalization progresses, the risk that economic activities–including trade and development–may contribute to environmental degradation is reduced. Until that risk is eliminated, through considerable improvement in environmental policies and cost internalization, the environmental repercussions of trade and development policies will need to be considered and addressed, in ways that are consistent with the continued promotion of sustainable development.

Role of Trade Liberalization. Barriers to trade can create impediments to the achievement of sustainable development, particularly for developing countries, and trade liberalization is an important component of progress toward sustainable development for all countries. Developed country import barriers make poverty alleviation more difficult for exporting countries, and may cause them to accelerate rates of natural resource exploitation by preventing diversification. As well, countries with relatively closed trading systems often pay heavily to protect inefficient domestic producers, and tend to have poor access to environmental technologies. The contribution of trade liberalization to sustainable development is promoted by policies that respect environmental and social policy goals.

III   Principles

Efficiency and Cost Internalization

Efficiency is a common interest for environment, development and trade policies. An activity is efficient if it uses the minimum amount of resources to achieve a given output, or alternatively, achieves maximum output from a given amount of resources. Increased efficiency is the raison d'etre for trade liberalization.

Internalization of environmental costs is essential to achieve efficiency. Despite the substantial practical difficulties this entails, high priority should be attached to its implementation. As costs are progressively internalized the contribution of all economic activity, including trade, to the efficient utilization of resources is enhanced .

Environmentalists, development specialists and trade economists share a common interest in promoting efficiency. More efficient production reduces the drain on scarce resources such as raw materials and energy, and limits the demands placed on the regenerative capacity of the environment. It should be noted in this connection that preventing environmental damage and minimizing waste is generally more efficient than engaging in remedial cleanup and restoration. Efficient environmental protection policies lower the cost of attaining environmental quality, thereby making resources available for other purposes, including additional environmental protection. Efficient use of land, labour and capital is also the heart of development efforts to combat poverty and satisfy human needs. Allowing the most efficient producers to provide the world's goods and services is the main rationale for an open trading system.

Efficient resource use requires that the prices paid by producers for inputs, and by consumers for final goods and services, accurately reflect their full costs. In fact, most goods are not priced to reflect full costs (the magnitude of the distortion will vary from case to case), but this is difficult to rectify. There are technical difficulties in evaluating unpaid environmental costs and designing instruments to deal with them. As well, some groups resist change because they benefit from these distortions, even though their net effect on the community at large may be seriously damaging both economically and environmentally.

One common source of price distortions is the failure to attach costs to environmental externalities. Producers and consumers rely upon many materials and services from the natural environment, including the capacity of soils, rivers, lakes, oceans and the atmosphere to receive their wastes. These resources are also needed to sustain life itself, as well as for aesthetic and spiritual fulfillment. At some point, however, the regenerative capacity of renewable resources may be impaired by over-harvesting, or the waste going into an ecosystem may exceed its capacity for harmless absorption. The resulting environmental damage imposes costs, often on large segments of the community. Prices that fail to incorporate these costs lead to inefficient use–most notably, excessive consumption–of environmental resources. Since the resulting environmental costs tend to be borne by large numbers of people, and are often long-lasting, government action is generally required to achieve the internalization of environmental externalities.

Some environmental externalities are international. Often these externalities are negative, as in the case of acid rain. However, price distortions of this type also include the "free" environmental services "exported" to the rest of the world by countries which, for example, preserve their forests, including tropical rainforests. Internalizing these positive externalities might involve international payments from the rest of the world for such things as preservation of biodiversity, and for carbon-sink services which counter global warming trends. In tropical countries, globally valuable biological resources are frequently in the care of indigenous peoples and subsistence farmers. Some forms of international internalization might consist of assistance for these groups, in recognition of their services to the world at large, in the form of payments, capacity-building initiatives, or other appropriate measures.

Import restrictions are another important cause of price distortion in developed and developing countries which, like other price distortions, can result in negative environmental and social impacts. Protectionism in developed countries including tariffs that rise with the degree of processing and therefore discourage local processing of raw materials blocks exports and prevents value being added locally. The direct environmental effect is often to force countries to over-intensively exploit their natural resources and eat away at natural capital stocks. Protectionism also helps to perpetuate poverty in developing countries by narrowing options for employment and income generation, and thus confounds progress on health problems such as inadequate sewage treatment, and poverty-driven environmental problems such as the felling of trees for firewood or charcoal, and slash-and-burn clearing of forests to provide jobs and food. Price distortions created by import barriers can be reduced or eliminated by trade liberalization.

Price distortions due to environmental externalities, in contrast, are corrected by "full cost internalization" that is, by policies that cause external costs to be incorporated into the prices of goods and services. Polluting firms, and consumers of polluting products, should bear the costs of pollution prevention and cleanup in accordance with the "polluter pays principle." This provides incentives for firms to alter their production methods and for consumers to switch to alternative products, thereby safeguarding the environment and increasing efficiency. It also avoids trade and investment distortions, which occur when goods and services are sold at less than their full costs.

That said, there are formidable problems in identifying and valuing the costs of using environmental resources and allocating costs to particular goods. But that only underscores how urgently those problems need to be addressed. Broadly speaking, the problems can be divided into three groups. First, consensus is only beginning to emerge on essential concepts, definitions, measurement techniques, data needs and methods of analysis, and further research is urgently needed. Even where the theory is fairly clear, there is often disagreement as to how internalization should be put into practice. Frequently the process is further complicated by poorly-defined property rights to environmental resources. Many countries have limited experience with addressing such complexities, and limited human, technical and financial resources with which to do so. For developing countries, special consideration should be given, in terms of longer time frames and assistance for implementation.

Second, in the course of internalizing costs, producers fear there will be inadequate offsetting gains in efficiency, and that they will lose business to competitors facing less onerous requirements. It is not yet clear to what extent these fears are in fact valid, as evidence on this issue remains inconclusive. For example, given the trend to stricter environmental regulation worldwide, and growing "green" demand in major markets, companies that have a head start in adjusting production processes to environmental demands may in fact gain market share as cost internalization proceeds elsewhere. Nevertheless, competitive concerns are likely to remain, at least in the early stages of cost internalization. In instances in which it can be demonstrated that competitive forces are contributing to continued underpricing of specific products–for example, those produced by extractive industries the acceptance of cost internalization would be aided by an internationally negotiated and coordinated schedule for internalizing the locally determined costs. Once a good faith effort had been made, however, a failure to agree on such a schedule would not be a justification for postponing cost internalization. Ultimately, each government can, at least, ensure that environmental resources within its national boundaries are not misused because of a failure to internalize costs.

Third, cost internalization is not an adequate approach to dealing with environmental costs stemming from irreplaceable losses, such as species extinction or lasting damage to the regenerative capacity of renewable resources. These problems are discussed in more detail below, under the principle of Environmental Integrity.

Despite these considerable complications and challenges, it is evident that cost internalization based on the polluter pays principle must play a central role in efforts to improve efficiency, improve the management of natural resources and promote worldwide sustainable development.

Equity

Equity relates to the distribution both within and between generations of physical and natural capital, as well as knowledge and technology. In the transition to sustainability additional obligations should be assumed by those, primarily in the developed world, who have used resources in the past in a manner which limits the options of current generations, particularly in developing countries. Trade liberalization can contribute to greater equity through the dismantling of trade barriers that harm developing countries.

While domestic equity is a fundamental goal of governments, policies to achieve it are hard to implement. In seeking to promote greater equity it is possible to strive for growth to generate additional resources for distribution, or to seek better distribution of existing resources, but the two are not mutually exclusive. While there may be trade-offs in the short run, success in the long run depends on pursuing both policies simultaneously.

Inequity and poverty contribute significantly to environmental degradation and political instability, particularly in developing countries. When basic needs are not met, the poor have no choice but to live off whatever environmental resources are available. At the same time, past use of natural resources already limits the choices available to present generations, particularly in developing countries. Faced with these limitations, and having limited financial, administrative and technical capacity to deal with problems of environment and development, many developing countries will require transfers of technology and financial resources. Failing such assistance, they may be unable to adequately protect their environmental resources, including many which are of global significance.

The substantial investment needed for sustainable development requires new and additional external resources in developing countries far in excess of conceivable increases in traditional foreign aid. Increased trade and investment flows, the result of more open borders in both developed and developing countries, together with appropriate domestic policies in developing countries, are the best alternative for increasing incomes in poorer countries by the magnitudes necessary to achieve sustainable development.

Protected markets in the developed world must be opened to goods and services from developing countries. Continued protection contributes to the perpetuation of poverty in developing countries, and may also result in unsustainable depletion of their natural resources in the absence of other options for alleviating poverty. Other measures to achieve equity and poverty alleviation include strengthening developing country capacity to develop indigenous technologies and to manage environmental resources, and creating mechanisms for the accelerated transfer of existing clean technologies. Continued progress in resolving the debt crisis is also important, as is an increase in transfers of financial resources. At the same time, developing countries must adopt policies which ensure that the additional resources are used in ways that are efficient, alleviate poverty and foster sustainable practices.

Just as past use of resources limits the choices of present generations, current patterns of use, such as significant use of nonrenewable resources, or use of renewable resources beyond their capacity to regenerate, may limit the choices of future generations, creating issues of inter-generational equity. In the interests of inter-generational equity, the combined stock of human-made and natural capital should not be depleted. If future generations are to be at least as well-off as are present ones, trade and development policies and programmes which involve environmental change should be accompanied by a compensating development of more efficient technologies, increased knowledge, better infrastructure or improved social systems. At the same time, it must be recognized that there are limits to the extent to which increases in human-made capital can compensate for losses of environmental resources. Many such resources meet needs that cannot be met by augmented stocks of human-made capital, such as the life-support services provided by the ozone layer, and a variety of spiritual and aesthetic needs.

Environmental Integrity

Trade and development should respect and help maintain environmental integrity. This involves recognition of the impact of human activities on ecological systems. It requires respect for limits to the regenerative capacity of ecosystems, actions to avoid irreversible harm to plant and animal populations and species, and protection for valued areas. Many aspects of the environment for example, species survival or the effective functioning of biological food chains have values which cannot be adequately captured by methods of cost internalization, highlighting the need for other policy instruments.

Progress in achieving cost internalization would go a long way towards ensuring that development and trade policies take account of and address environmental consequences. At the same time, there are limitations to cost internalization. It is not useful in cases where the environmental losses are irreplaceable, as in the case of species extinction, since it is difficult to price something for which there is no substitute. Furthermore, it cannot accurately reflect costs to future generations, since we have no way of knowing what value they will attach to environmental resources. Nor is cost internalization necessarily useful when costs are extremely high; the magnitude of the future costs involved in ozone depletion, for example, may be so great that for practical reasons the chemicals contributing to the problem should simply be phased out, rather than priced accurately.

There are three types of threats to environmental integrity requiring special conservation measures which may have potential trade impacts: first, actions which seriously damage the regenerative capacity of ecosystems such as fisheries and forests that are vulnerable to irreversible depletion; second, actions which lead to irreplaceable losses, such as extinction of species and loss of biological diversity; and third, actions which threaten valued areas such as designated parklands or sites of internationally recognized ecological, cultural or historical significance.

Moral and existence values are among the grounds for special conservation and management measures. Such values refer to, for example, the humane treatment of animals and the desire to know that a species exists even if it does not serve material human needs. They may also refer to an inherent right of a species to exist. Moral and existence values will be strongly affected by cultural traditions, income levels, and other factors.

Measures to protect environmental integrity may represent an important exception to normal trade rules, whether in the context of trade agreements or environmental agreements. They may take the form of trade bans or quantitative restrictions. It is therefore important to be clear as to just what is allowed by current trade rules. Under existing multilateral (GATT) trade rules a country is free to take a variety of measures to protect its own environment, provided that the measures meet the non-discrimination and national treatment requirements aimed at preventing protectionist abuse (some adjustment of the rules may be necessary to allow countries to give temporary financial assistance for the purpose of promoting the introduction of environmentally friendly production processes). In contrast, when the issue involves the integrity of the environment outside the country's borders–that is, in other countries or in the global commons–there is a continuing debate concerning the extent to which the trading rules should permit unilateral trade actions such as bans and restrictions. In such cases of "extrajurisdictional" environmental problems, depending on how GATT's Article XX is interpreted, there may be a need to revise the rules to allow special measures to protect environmental integrity.[1]

Historically, few of the more than 150 international environment agreements have contained trade provisions. Provisions allowing for restrictions on imports and exports are included in treaties to protect the ozone layer, preserve endangered species and limit the trade and transport of hazardous products and wastes. Trade provisions may also be included in new international agreements to address ecological concerns about climate change, biodiversity, desertification and forests, especially if their inclusion reduces the risk of unilaterally imposed trade barriers. Including trade measures in environmental agreements requires not only safeguards against protectionist abuse, but also a careful consideration of their likely effectiveness and the availability of equally effective alternative policies.

Subsidiarity

Subsidiarity recognizes that action will occur at different levels of jurisdiction, depending on the nature of issues. It assigns priority to the lowest jurisdictional level of action consistent with effectiveness. International policies should be adopted only when this is more effective than policy action by individual countries or jurisdictions within countries.

Environmental policies can reflect differences in environmental conditions or development priorities. This may lead to different environmental standards within countries or among groups of countries, involving both higher and lower standards than those applied elsewhere. In the absence of agreements voluntarily accepted by all affected countries and where the environmental consequences remain within domestic jurisdictions, other countries should not use economic sanctions or other coercive measures to try to eliminate differences in standards. Where there are significant transborder environmental impacts, solutions (including international environmental agreements, the formulation of international standards, incentives for voluntary upgrading of standards and the possible use of trade measures) should be sought multilaterally.

In essence, subsidiarity represents no more than a general principle of good governance: decisions should be taken as close as possible to the affected public, at the lowest level of jurisdiction encompassing all those affected. It follows from the recognition that diversity, tolerance and decentralization are among the attributes of a good society. In the context of trade and sustainable development, where issues of global dimension have significant and varied effects at the local level, it has particular relevance.

Variations in environmental policies from one jurisdiction to the next can arise from one or more of three principal sources: differences in environmental conditions; differences in priorities according to the resources available for environmental protection and cleanup; and differences in values. Certain emissions might be more harmful in some environments than others, since different ecosystems respond differently to pollutants. As well, some societies might strive for greater levels of environmental quality than others. It is important to recognize this diversity in an international structure of agreements and practices which is stable, equitable and reflects differences in environmental conditions and priorities.

This is not to deny that harmonization can play an important role as a principled approach to achieving international cooperation by ensuring that essential differences respect a common framework. It may focus on laws, technical standards, emission standards, ambient environmental quality, or procedural requirements.

There are nevertheless two major concerns with harmonization of environmental standards. Many developed countries fear that they will be prevented from adopting standards sufficiently rigorous to deal with the heavy burdens their economic activities impose on the environment and to meet the high demand for environmental quality among their citizens. Developing countries in contrast are concerned that they cannot afford to meet environmentally-based process standards designed for the conditions of developed countries, and that as a result their exports to those countries will be penalized. Both sets of concerns can be met by agreements which allow a diversity of environmental quality standards supplemented, where feasible, by negotiated minimum process standards. Frameworks for establishing minimum standards should be agreed on by all affected countries, and will need to recognize and address the transitional difficulties that might be faced by lower standard countries, particularly developing countries. Another concern with harmonization–that it may stifle innovation–can be dealt with by designing standards which specify desired environmental results, rather than particular production technologies.

While subsidiarity implies a fair degree of discretion in the setting of environmental standards, it does not extend the argument for tolerance to the case where lower product or production standards result in significant transborder effects. At that point, the standards in question may become a matter of international concern. On the other hand, where a country adopts product standards for environment, health and safety high enough to have trade effects, it should at a minimum notify and be available to consult with its affected trading partners. (A requirement to this effect already applies to signatories to the GATT Code on Technical Barriers to Trade.) The discretion accorded policy-makers under the principle of Subsidiarity is also limited by the need to respect the principle of Environmental Integrity.

Subsidiarity requires an important element of cooperation in international affairs. Where a country suffers competitive disadvantages from lower standards abroad, imposing higher trade barriers or granting subsidies to domestic producers are not viable solutions. However, there may be cases for temporary protection, according to multilaterally agreed guidelines, in situations where the introduction or tightening of environmental measures leads to a sudden increase in imports that threatens to injure a domestic industry. More generally, the most effective solution will be to offer incentives for upward convergence of standards, involving some of the elements of capacity-building and technical and financial resource transfers discussed under the principle of Equity. The responsibility of countries seeking higher environmental standards abroad to seek them multilaterally, shunning coercive measures, is matched by an obligation on the part of other countries to cooperate in such efforts.

International Cooperation

*Sustainable development requires strengthening international systems of coopera-
tion at all levels, encompassing environment, development and trade policies.
Where disputes arise, the procedures for handling them must be capable of
addressing the interests of the environment, development and the economy together.
This may involve changes to existing rules, changes to existing dispute settlement
mechanisms, or the creation of new mechanisms.*

*The most desirable forms of international cooperation will avoid conflicts, through
international efforts at development and environmental protection, and by improving the functioning of the global trading system. When international disputes do
arise, they must be resolved internationally. This requires open, effective and
impartial dispute settlement procedures that protect the interests of weaker countries against the use of coercive political and economic power by more powerful
countries. Unilateral action on transboundary environmental issues an option
generally available only to a few large countries should be considered only when all
possible avenues of cooperative action have been pursued. Trade sanctions are the
least desirable policy option, signifying failure by all the parties concerned.*

Increasingly, countries cannot achieve their own environmental goals
without regional or global environmental agreements. For development,
additional international action is needed in particular to ensure technology
transfer, capital flows and improved market access. Trade policies are
international by definition and should be developed within a cooperative
multilateral framework.

While the goals of trade, environment and development are compatible in
principle, in practice conflicts will inevitably occur. These must be resolved
internationally without resort to economic or political coercion. Respect for
the principle of non-discrimination in trade represents an essential step in
this direction. The rules which existing dispute settlement mechanisms for
trade interpret might require adjustment to ensure that the interests of the
environment are more adequately addressed. As well, existing mechanisms
might include more expertise in environment and development matters,
and new mechanisms might be established for the treatment of conflicts
primarily related to these areas.

In a world free of the traditional cold-war political tensions, and characterized by increasingly globalized economic activity, attention is now more

than ever focused on the ability of countries to compete with each other in the international marketplace. To capture the full benefits of competition, however, there must be cooperation; countries must subscribe to a rules-based international trading system which defines the conditions of competition in world markets. Making such a system work for sustainable development will require new forms of cooperation in some areas. For example, the introduction of sustainable practices for the production of internationally traded commodities with significant environmental impacts may require innovative new joint regimes involving both producers and consumers.

In some cases, countries may need to exchange some national sovereignty for global progress on sustainable development. Historically, there are many examples of countries making such exchanges for progress on global issues, but it has only occurred when the countries involved have seen it to be in their best interests. Countries signing a multilateral treaty, or subscribing to international organizations such as the International Telecommunications Union, are usually making such a "deal." This type of international cooperation will be critical to achieving sustainable development in today's context. Progress on climate change, biodiversity and sustainable forestry practices can only come about with the sustained cooperation of developing countries. Such cooperation is unlikely to be forthcoming if these countries feel they are being victimized by unilateral trade sanctions undertaken by large economic powers, in the absence of internationally agreed rules for their use.

The best forms of cooperation will involve proactive measures to improve human well-being and the environment internationally, and to improve the functioning of the global trading system. These measures might include more initiatives aimed at technology sharing, capacity building, transfers of resources and debt relief, an opening of protected markets, and cooperative cost internalization. Progress in these areas of cooperation will address the root causes of many apparent trade-environment conflicts, in particular large disparities in technical capacity for environmental management and a lack of resources to invest in environmental protection. Cooperation may also take the form of multilateral agreements on the environment. Countries in a position to exercise leadership in dealing with environmental issues should do so by devoting the time and energy needed to achieve such multilateral accords.

Science and Precaution

In the development of policies intended to reconcile trade, environment and development interests science, in particular ecological science and the science of complex systems, can provide the basis for many necessary decisions, including the suitability of health, safety and environmental standards.

Action to address certain problems, however, will still have to be taken in the face of uncertainty and scientific disagreement, particularly where mistakes may have very serious consequences. It is therefore also essential in certain instances to adopt a precautionary and adaptive approach that seeks the prevention and easing of environmental stress well before conclusive evidence concerning damage exists, and which adapts policy as new scientific information becomes available.

Science is the basis for much of what we know about the environment. Since understanding ecological processes is central to valuing environmental services and costing environmental damage, science is also a fundamental prerequisite for cost internalization measures. It therefore is an underpinning of environmental policy and should form the basis of any measures taken to protect the natural environment. Science must underlie any trade measures which seek to protect environment and health.

Our understanding of ecosystems is still highly uncertain. They are characterized by thresholds, critical points beyond which all relationships change dramatically, triggered by events such as extinction of a critical species in a food chain or an overloading of pollutants beyond the point of assimilative capacity. They are often unforgiving of errors in modeling and forecast. Many times, the resulting environmental change cannot be easily reversed, if at all.

Inherent uncertainty, coupled with the reality of threshold effects and irreversibility, argues for a precautionary approach to rules and standards. There must be a margin of safety that prevents inevitable errors from having catastrophic effects. How wide the margin of safety should be will at times be controversial, and the danger exists that the precautionary approach could open the door to costly misjudgement, or abuse for protectionist purposes. At the same time, it is obvious that there are circumstances in which a lack of scientific certainty should not be used as a justification for a lack of action to prevent potentially serious environmental damage.

The principle of precaution presents policy-makers with several operational challenges. To begin, it is difficult to define the appropriate level of precaution. Given the risks of global warming, for example, and the uncertainty in scientific understanding of it, what is the appropriate policy? Such decisions must involve an element of judgement, based on a balancing of the magnitude of the potential environmental damage and the risk of its occurrence, against the cost of preventing it. Fortunately, prevention can have spin-off benefits which lower its long-run cost; many of the measures involved in preventing global warming, for example, are improvements in efficiency, and encourage the development of new technologies which make economic sense in their own right.

Openness

Greater openness will significantly improve environmental, trade and development policies. Just as access to information is essential for effective participation by producers and consumers in markets, public participation, including open and timely access to information, is essential for the formulation and practical implementation of environmental policies. It is also important in minimizing the risk of "protectionist capture," that is, that trade policies will be manipulated to favour inefficient producers at the expense of others.

While it is widely recognized that openness and accountability should be enshrined in domestic processes, this is much less true at the international level. Attitudes and institutional procedures are lagging behind the changing nature of international relationships, characterized by among other things the increasing globalization of economic activity, and our increasing awareness of serious environmental problems which cannot be adequately addressed at the national level. Since action by individual governments will often have significant international effects, there is a need for internationally agreed criteria and mechanisms of public participation, access to information and accountability at the international level.

Openness comprises two basic elements: first, timely, easy and full access to information for all those affected; and second, public participation in the decision-making process by among others environmental and development NGOs, industry groups and scientists. While structures for openness are increasingly evident in dealing with problems at the national level, there has not been a comparable development for issues of an international nature. As people worldwide devote increasing attention to such issues, there is a need to find forms of participation appropriate to the different international organizations and negotiations.

National and international rule-making and dispute settlement should be transparent, seeking, when appropriate, scientific and technical advice on environmental and developmental impacts and soliciting the views of the public, including specialists in relevant areas to the dispute settlement process. Transparency and the opportunity for interested members of the public to make submissions are also important when trade issues are involved. At a minimum, adjudicating panels should entertain written submissions from non-governmental organizations, and panel decisions should be published with a minimum of delay.

IV   Applying the Principles

The forgoing trade and sustainable development principles are more than simply a code of good will. They imply significant changes in the way trade, and trade-related environment and development policies are formulated and implemented. The next steps, on which IISD and others are now working, are to clarify the nature of those changes, looking at the development of existing institutions and agreements as well as the creation of new forms of cooperation, and at mapping out a new global research agenda.

The primary audience for such work, and for the principles themselves, is those who are responsible for effecting change: policy-makers within governments, and the multilateral institutions of which they are constituent parts. As well, the principles are aimed at the wider policy community which influences the decisions of governments, including environmental and development NGOs, the business community, academia and the media. The end goal is not only institutional change, but also the requisite accompanying change in the behaviour of individual decision-makers.

The principles cover a wide range of policy areas. They may be applied to trade agreements, both multilateral and regional, as well as to trade-related environment and development initiatives, such as accords on the global commons, structural adjustment plans and domestic and international policies for official development assistance. In all these areas they are both a model for future action and a benchmark by which existing policies may be measured.

Implementing the principles will take time; progress in some areas will depend critically on progress in others. There needs to be, for example, cooperative effort to build capacity for sound science and cost internalization in some countries, as well as technology sharing and increased financial transfers as laid out in Agenda 21. There may also need to be special concessions during a period of implementation. Some models for this approach already exist, including the Montreal Protocol and the Biodiversity Convention.

It will be tempting in some cases to pick and choose principles that serve the needs of the moment or the interests of the drafters in formulating trade, environment and development policies. The results of such a partial approach are not likely to serve any of these needs or interests in the long run. The principles are an interdependent and mutually reinforcing whole, and must be taken as such if they are to help achieve sustainable development.

The realities of international economic and environmental interdependence demand the type of cooperative approach embodied by these principles, involving not only the building of mutual understanding and trust but also a degree of flexibilty and acceptance of the fact that no group is going to achieve all of its demands. The search for consensus, though difficult, is well worth the effort. In the end, effective international response to problems of trade and sustainable development can only be achieved on the basis of commonly-recognized interests and principles.

Endnotes

[1] While such measures could include unilateral trade restrictions, a distinction must be made between unilateral measures taken within the context of internationally agreed criteria, and those taken outside of that context. When we speak of trade rules permitting unilateral actions to protect environmental integrity, we are referring to the former.

MEMBERS OF THE IISD WORKING GROUP ON PRINCIPLES
FOR TRADE AND SUSTAINABLE DEVELOPMENT

The members of the Working Group all served in their capacities as individuals. None of the material in this document should in any way be attributed to their affiliated organizations.

Richard Blackhurst is Director of Economic Research at the General Agreement on Tariffs and Trade (GATT). Since joining the GATT Secretariat in 1974, he has also been an Adjunct Professor at the Graduate Institute of International Studies in Geneva.

Janine Ferretti is Executive Director of Pollution Probe, Toronto. She is a member of Canada's International Trade Advisory Committee, and a member of the Ontario Round Table on the Environment and the Economy.

Arthur J. Hanson is President and CEO of IISD, Winnipeg. He was Professor and Director of the School for Resource and Environmental Studies at Dalhousie University, and a staff member of the Ford Foundation. Other positions have included serving as Chair of the Canadian Environmental Assessment Research Council and Director of the Environmental Management Development Project in Indonesia.

Nurul Islam is Senior Policy Advisor at the International Food Policy Research Institute, Washington, D.C. Previously, he was Assistant Director-General at the U.N.'s Food and Agricultural Organization, and served as Deputy Chairman/Minister in the Planning Ministry of the Government of Bangladesh. He was also Fellow at Saint Anthony's College, Oxford, and at The Economic Growth Centre, Yale.

Konrad von Moltke is Senior Fellow at the World Wildlife Fund, Washington, D.C., and Senior Fellow at the Institute for International Environmental Governance at Dartmouth College, New Hampshire. He was founding Director of the Institute for European Environmental Policy.

H.E. Rubens Ricupero is Brazil's Minister for the Environment and the Legal Amazon Region and, formerly, Ambassador to the United States. He served as Brazil's Representative to the GATT, and as the Chairman of GATT's Contracting Parties he undertook, in 1991, at the request of the GATT Council, consultations for the reactivation of the GATT Group on Environmental Measures and International Trade. At the UNCED in Rio de Janeiro, he was the Coordinator of the Contact Group on Finance which drafted Chapter 33 of Agenda 21.

David Runnalls is Senior Advisor to the President of the International Development Research Centre, Ottawa. With Barbara Ward, he was one of the founders of the International Institute for Environment and Development. He is a member of the Council of The World Conservation Union (IUCN) and of the Ontario Round Table on the Environment and the Economy.

H.E. Mohamed Sahnoun is Pearson Fellow at the International Development Research Centre, Ottawa, and Board Member of IISD. He was Special Advisor to the Secretary-General, U.N. Conference on Environment and Development, and was a member of the Brundtland Commission. He was previously Special Representative of the Secretary-General of the U.N. for Somalia; Chief of the Algerian Permanent Mission to the U.N.; Deputy Secretary-General, Arab League; and Deputy Secretary-General, Organization of African Unity.

Erna Witoelar is founder and first Executive Director of WALHI, the Indonesian Environmental Forum. She was a member of the Advisory Group on Industry and Development to the Brundtland Commission, and of the Commission on Developing Countries and Global Change, and is former President of the Indonesian Consumer's Association. She is currently President of the International Organization of Consumers' Unions.

PART II

TRADE AND ENVIRONMENT

SOME CASE STUDIES

CHAPTER 5

THE ENVIRONMENTAL IMPLICATIONS OF NAFTA: A LEGAL ANALYSIS

Michelle Swenarchuk

Michelle Swenarchuk is Executive Director of the Canadian Environmental Law Association, and a senior practitioner of law in the fields of environmental protection, trade, aboriginal rights, labour, administrative, and aviation law. As Counsel to the Association, she has represented individuals and environmental groups on issues including forest management, environmental assessment, contaminated lands, land use, and aboriginal rights. She has also participated in law reform and consultations with governments regarding a broad range of environmental and legal issues. Swenarchuk has analyzed and spoken widely on the environmental impacts of free trade agreements since 1988. In 1992 and 1993, she coordinated a team of enviromental lawyers, trade experts, and economists, in conducting a study of the environmental implications of trade agreements (GATT, the Uruguay Round GATT Proposals, the Canada-US Agreement, and NAFTA) for the Ontario Ministry of the Environment and Energy. She also coordinated and edited studies of the NAFTA environmental side agreement, and the impacts of free trade agreements on water resources

This article is adapted from Chapter 4 of *The Environmental Implications of Trade Agreements* prepared under contract for the Ontario Ministry of Environment and Energy by the Canadian Environmental Law Association, Toronto, 1993. © Queen's Printer for Ontario, 1993

Introduction

This chapter provides a detailed examination of the wording of the North American Free Trade Agreement (NAFTA) that has potential impacts on the environment, and on environmental protection strategies. In it, we consider its implications for certain international environmental agreements; resource conservation; environmental standard-setting; investment; and dispute settlement.

Since the wording of NAFTA frequently echoes provisions of the General Agreement on Tariffs and Trade (GATT), the Canada-US Free Trade Agreement (FTA), and trade panel decisions, relevant provisions from these sources are identified to assist in understanding NAFTA's potential impacts.

II Preamble and Objectives

The preamble to the agreement includes three statements in support of environmental protection. The Parties resolve to:

- Undertake (other goals) in a manner consistent with environmental protection and conservation;
- Promote sustainable development;
- Strengthen the development and enforcement of environmental laws and regulations...

Unfortunately, as Canadian negotiators report,[1] the preamble is not enforceable; in the case of a conflict between one of its terms and a substantive provision of the agreement, the substantive provision will prevail. In contrast, the objectives of the agreement, which largely relate to promoting an increase in trade and do not refer to environmental goals, are enforceable; the provisions of the agreement are to be interpreted in the light of these objectives. (Art. 102)

III International Environmental and Conservation Agreements

The agreement provides that with regard to three environmental international agreements, their obligations will prevail over the NAFTA in the event of conflict. This precedence is qualified by the requirement that a Party which relies on the environmental agreement must chose among "equally effective and reasonably available means of complying with such" agreement, "the alternative that is the least inconsistent with the other provisions of this Agreement" (Art. 104). In the event of a dispute proceeding to a trade dispute panel, this "least NAFTA inconsistent" test will permit panel members to decide whether the path of compliance chosen by a government is acceptable under NAFTA.

The three environmental agreements named include the *Convention on the International Trade in Endangered Species of Wild Fauna and Flora (CITES)*, the

Montreal Protocol on Substances that Deplete the Ozone Layer and the *Basel Convention on the Control of Transboundary Movement of Hazardous Wastes and Their Disposal*[2] (when it comes into force for the three countries). In addition, two bilateral agreements have been included: the Canada-US agreement regarding transboundary hazardous waste movements, and the US-Mexico agreement for cooperation regarding environmental cleanup in the border area. (Annex 104.1)

The *CITES* trade provisions include the requirement of export and import permits, or outright bans in trade, for specified species of plants or animals. This convention is in force and 110 countries are party to it.

Trade provisions of the *Basel Convention* include the right to prohibit the importation of specified hazardous wastes for disposal and the prohibition of export without prior informed consent. Parties are not to permit the export of wastes to a non-party. There is still some uncertainty over the precise criteria by which to evaluate a chemical as severely restricted or banned. This convention is in force for countries, including Canada, that have ratified it.

The *Montreal Protocol on Substances that Deplete the Ozone Layer*, negotiated in 1989 and amended since, established a schedule for reduction by stages of production and consumption of ozone depleting substances. The substances are used in products such as refrigerators, air conditioners, and fire extinguishers. The Protocol urges Parties to discourage trade in the products on the list to achieve the target of eliminating the production and consumption of controlled substances by the year 2000.

Parties are also to consider the feasibility of restricting or banning imports from non-parties of products produced with, but not containing, controlled substances listed in Annex A to the Protocol. Specifically, with regard to trade with non-parties, the most likely source of trade disputes, the Protocol sets specific dates after which imports from and exports to non-parties, will be banned. The import ban on the Protocol's Annex A substances was effective January 11, 1991; the export ban of Annex A substances was effective January 1, 1993. The substances added in the London amendment (Annex B) were banned effective January 1, 1993. A fourth meeting of the parties to the Protocol took place on November 23-25, 1992. At that meeting a phase-out date of 1996 was agreed to for CFCs, carbon tetrachloride and methyl chloroform. Halons will be phased out by 1994. This last round of amendments came into force on January 1, 1994.

There have been no trade dispute panel decisions based on a conflict between a trade agreement (GATT or the FTA) and an international environmental agreement. However, the possibility exists, particularly from GATT members who are not parties to the environmental agreement in question. Article 104 does not preclude challenges under NAFTA, but does limit a trade panel hearing a dispute concerning one of the specified agreements to an examination of whether the measure in question was the least-NAFTA-inconsistent one available.

IV Provisions Regarding Trade in Resources

Like GATT and the FTA, the NAFTA prescribes free trade in resources by limiting the rights of governments to enact measures restricting such trade. Chapter 3 (National Treatment and Market Access for Goods) and Chapter 6 (Energy and Basic Petrochemicals) contain these provisions.

Parties may not increase duties or adopt new ones, with some exceptions (Art. 302). Parties may not "adopt or maintain any prohibition or restriction on the importation of any good of another Party or on the exportation or sale for export of any good destined for" the other Party, except in accordance with GATT Article XI, which is incorporated into the NAFTA (Art. 309). This prohibition includes export and import price requirements. GATT Article XI permits restrictions through "duties, taxes or other charges whether made effective through quotas, import or export licences or other measures" but Article 315 of NAFTA limits this right; such measures are permissable only if also applied to all other Parties to NAFTA and to domestic consumption of the good.

Canadian exceptions to these requirements regarding resources include the right to maintain controls on exports of raw logs and some unprocessed fish, some agricultural products including imports of grain from the US, and preferential grain freight rates (Annex 301.3).

NAFTA also limits the powers available under GATT XI:2(a) regarding temporary export restrictions to prevent shortages of food and other essential materials; and under GATT XX(g)(i)(j) which includes measures for conservation of natural resources, a domestic two-price system for essential materials, and acquisition of products in short supply.

Specifically, Parties may not reduce the proportion of their production of a given product that is exported below the amount available to another Party in the previous 36 months "or such other representative period as the Parties may agree" (Art. 315). This provision, the "proportionality clause" like Article 409 of the Canada-US FTA, effectively prevents a "Canadians first" policy for all natural resources even in times of shortage. Mexico is exempt from this provision (Annex 315).

4.1   Water[3]

There is no clause in the agreement exempting water exports from these provisions and they are therefore also subject to these requirements. Specifically, water is subject to the same requirements of National Treatment of goods as other goods (Art. 301). Nor is there any wording in the NAFTA or pertinent Tariff definitions limiting the definition of water to bottled water. Rather, water appears as item 22.01 in the NAFTA tariff heading as follows:

> Waters, including natural or artificial mineral waters and aerated waters, not containing added sugar or other sweetening matter nor flavoured, ice and snow.[4]

More complete definitions of water exist in the Canadian Customs Tariffs, Revenue Canada Customs and Excise, and in the "Harmonized Commodity Description and Coding System Explanatory Notes," considered to be the official Canadian nomenclature for tariff goods. From the Explanatory Notes, one may conclude that:

> This heading (22.01) covers: (A) Ordinary natural water of all kinds (other than sea water - see heading 25.01)[5]

The federal government has argued that this tariff heading does not cover water in river systems as this was not considered a "good" in the commercial sense; further, they have cited the tariff chapter heading, "Beverages, Spirits and Vinegar," to support the view that only bottled water is covered by the heading. However, the interpretation rules accompanying the tariff schedule indicate that such chapter titles are provided "for ease of reference only" and that for legal purposes, classification shall be determined according to the terms of the headings and relative Section or Chapter Notes[6]

As Jamie Linton notes,

It has been upheld by recognized and respected Canadian experts in international trade and resource law that naturally-flowing water is indeed covered under tariff heading 22.01. Even the Ottawa law firm that the federal government referenced in the water-trade debate of 1988 has acknowledged this:

"A review of the various Tariff Items in Chapter 22 .... reveals that Chapter 22 is directed at beverages. However, nothing in the wording of Tariff Item 22.01 suggests that the word 'waters' is restricted to waters used as a beverage or waters that are not of large scale quantities such as would be required for a diversion.

.... In conclusion, it is my opinion that any water, other than sea water, would be classifiable under Tariff Item 22.01 regardless of the quantity of water imported and regardless of its use."[7]

Despite parallel wording in the Canada-US FTA, the federal government included an apparent exemption of water from that agreement in its implementing legislation. Specifically, Section 7 of the *Canada-US Free Trade Agreement Implementation Act*[8] reads:

(1) For greater certainty, nothing in this Act or the Agreement, except Article 401 of the Agreement, applies to water.

(2) In this section, "water" means natural surface and ground water in liquid, gaseous or solid state, but does not include water packaged as a beverage or in tanks.

Article 401 of the FTA refers to the elimination of customs duties on goods.

Gordon Ritchie, Deputy Chief Negotiator for Canada during the FTA negotiations, has argued that the US accepted that exemption, given the wording of the US implementing legislation, and that water is therefore excluded from the ambit of the FTA.[9] By implication, Canadians could protect water from the requirements of NAFTA by including such an exemption in the NAFTA implementing legislation. Such a purported exemption has been included in Section 7 of Bill C-115, *An Act to Implement the North American Free Trade Agreement.*

For such an exemption to be effective would require that the terms of domestic legislation prevail, in instances of conflict, over the terms of the international agreement. Canadian courts will not apply an international treaty obligation to override federal or provincial legislation. Nor will they apply an international treaty unless it has been enacted into law by the appropriate legislative body.[10]

However, in contrast, trade dispute panels, which derive their jurisdictional powers from the trade agreements, are not bound by such domestic legal considerations. In the normal course of their deliberations, they frequently determine whether a given domestic law is consistent with the trade agreement in question.[11] When such a discrepancy is found, the country whose law has been found in conflict is expected to change the law in accordance with the finding of the panel.[12] NAFTA provides in Article 2018 that such action should normally follow upon a dispute panel decision.[13] It is through this process that the provisions of trade agreements may, in fact, take precedence over domestic legislation.

Finally, with regard to the question of water exports, there is no mention of an acceptance of the exclusion of water from the ambit of the FTA in the US implementing legislation, entitled the *United States-Canada Free-Trade Agreement Implementation Act of 1988.*[14] Rather, the section referred to by Ritchie reads as follows:

> Section 101(b) CONDITIONS FOR ENTRY INTO FORCE OF THE AGREE-MENT.– At such time as the President determines that Canada has taken measures necessary to comply with the obligations of the Agreement, the President is authorized to exchange notes with the Government of Canada providing for the entry into force, on or after January 1, 1989, of the Agreement with respect to the United States.

This lack of an explicit exemption for water from the FTA and NAFTA contrasts with the exemptions that do exist for raw log export prohibitions and some exports of unprocessed fish. Had the Parties intended an exemption for water, it is reasonable to assume that it would have been included: its absence raises the inference that an exemption for water was not intended by the Parties.

A further difficulty arises if Canadians accept the argument that the American implementing legislation takes precedence over the wording of the FTA, since the US statute includes this provision:

> Section 102 (a) UNITED STATES LAWS TO PREVAIL IN CONFLICT.–No provision of the Agreement, nor the application of any such provision to any person or circumstance, which is in conflict with any law of the United States shall have effect.

One may conclude from this section that the US government does not consider itself bound by the FTA provisions at all. In fact, both parties have, through their use of the dispute panels, accepted the jurisdiction of the panels to review domestic laws in the light of the FTA provisions.[15]

This precedence of the FTA wording in trade panel decisions removes any basis for the argument that water has been excluded from the Agreement. It seems clear that should a dispute panel adjudicate on this issue in the future, it will find that water is a good within the terms of the FTA and NAFTA. It follows that management of Canadian water resources is subject to the same FTA-induced constraints that affect all natural resources.

4.2   Energy and Basic Petrochemicals

The same scheme for restricting GATT-based import/export control measures is explicitly outlined with regard to energy and basic petrochemical products in the NAFTA (Arts. 603 to 606). However, Mexico is exempt from Article 605, the proportionality clause (Annex 605) and has reserved to the Mexican state many elements of the energy sector, including electricity as a public service and nuclear energy. Private sector participation in services related to energy production will be allowed (Annex 602.3).

NAFTA permits the continuation of incentives for oil and gas exploration and development, as does the Canada-US FTA (Art. 608). NAFTA also permits requirements relating to the Hibernia project, that certain goods and services be sourced in Newfoundland and in Canada, and that the project operator use "best efforts" to achieve specific Canadian and Newfoundland content levels. Canada may also require the transfer of technology to a Canadian company in connection with Hibernia (Annex I, p. I-C-28).

NAFTA gives the terms of the International Energy Program, by which Canada is obliged to share petroleum resources with the US in times of shortage, precedence over the NAFTA (Annex 608.2) "as between Canada and the United States." Since the IEP binds all members of the International Energy Agency, an OECD body, and includes strictly defined triggering mechanisms, a shortage in the US alone may not be sufficient to invoke the IEP requirements.

V   Provisions Regarding Environmental Standard-Setting

5.1   Sanitary and Phytosanitary Standards (SPS)

This section is subject to the overall requirement that the federal government ensure compliance by the provinces (Art. 105) and by non-governmental standard-setting bodies such as the Canadian Standards Council, and Canadian Standards Association (Art. 711). This assumption of federal power is new, and did not form part of the Canada-US Free Trade Agreement.

SPS measures are defined broadly and include plant and animal health standards, including pesticides, and as they apply to humans, food additives. Also included are product-related processing or production methods; testing procedures; statistical methods; sampling procedures; risk assessment methods; packaging and labelling related to food safety; and quarantine requirements (Definition, 7-43 to 7-44).

Although the word "harmonization" is not used, the chapter outlines a comprehensive approach to the harmonization of these standards by a group of international bodies, including the Codex Alimentarius Commission, the International Office of Epizootics, the International Plant Protection Convention, and the North American Plant Protection Organization (Art. 713).

5.1.1 Sovereignty over SPS Measures

In Article 712, the rights of each country to set its own SPS standards are detailed, together with the qualifications on that right. Countries have the right to adopt any SPS standards necessary to protect human, animal or plant life or health within their own territory, including measures more stringent than international standards, and may establish their own "appropriate level of protection" (Art. 712, Paras. 1,2; Art. 715). They must do so in accordance with the procedures and rules established by the SPS subchapter. Qualifications on this apparently wide power include the need to use "scientific principles," risk assessment, non-discrimination between goods of different parties, application only to the extent necessary to achieve its appropriate level of protection, and no measures that have the effect of creating a disguised restriction on trade.

The wording of these qualifications, some of which echo previous trade panel decisions and standards, requires detailed examination.

a. "in its territory" (Art. 712 para. 1)
A country is limited to enacting only those SPS measures that have effects within its territory. This section effectively codifies the decision in the much criticized GATT tuna-dolphin ruling, in which the US *Marine Mammal Protection Act* was found incompatible with GATT. It could limit the right of Canada to take protective measures regarding animals or plants that are located outside Canada, but affect health or the environment within Canada. Measures regarding migratory birds and anadromous fish like salmon could be affected.

Since the definition of an SPS measure includes "product-related processing or production method," the wording also raises the issue of extra-territorial impacts of, for example, a ban on import of products to Canada if they contain residues of a pesticide banned for use here.

b. "based on scientific principles" (Art. 712, para. 3)
Although consideration of scientific evidence of environmental and human health impacts is fundamental in environmental standard-setting, differing interpretations of any given set of scientific data commonly exist and judgements must be made regarding which interpretation will be relied on.

Policy-makers need to exercise judgement based on many factors in setting standards. Scientific evidence or "principles" are not determinative of the questions. Even after considering the scientific evidence, standard setters still need to decide what level of protection will be set.

David Wirth's comments on the GATT Uruguay Round inclusion of "scientific justification" for SPS standards applies also to the NAFTA wording of "scientific principles":

> ... the Dunkel Draft's "scientific justification" test inappropriately confuses scientific conclusions with social policy choices. While scientific analysis

can assist in the technical means for attaining a given level of protection, the choice of level to be achieved reflects societal values as to which science provides little, if any guidance. For instance, a risk assessment may help in setting a standard designed to limit the probability that an individual will develop cancer after a lifetime of exposure to a particular chemical substance to no more than one chance in a million. By contrast, the choice of the one-in-a-million goal–as opposed to, say, zero or one-in-a-thousand– is one of public policy. There is also a risk that the Dunkel "scientific justification" test could be interpreted to require a causal connection between exposures and effects, a highly inappropriate standard for environmental and public health decision-making where scientific uncertainties abound and an approach that is inconsistent with many of our domestic environmental and health and safety laws.[16]

c. "based on a risk assessment, as appropriate to the circumstances" (Art. 712, para. 3)

As defined in the NAFTA, risk assessment requires an evaluation of the potential that an unwanted pest will become established within a territory, and its potential associated biological and economic consequences, or the potential for adverse health effects on human or animal health of an additive, contaminant, toxin or disease-causing organism (7-43).

Numerous issues arise from this wording. The definition suggests that a risk/benefit analysis, involving a balancing of health impacts against economic factors is not required in each risk assessment. However, "economic feasibility" is a factor to be considered in setting SPS standards (Art. 712, para. 5). This appears to introduce the balancing requirement, as well as adding the uncertainty of "technical ... feasibility." These requirements raise the issue of whose assessment of technical and economic feasibility counts. They may provide a basis for a producer who wishes to export into Canada to argue that an SPS standard is insupportable if compliance with it is not feasible for his particular business.

That standards must be "based on" risk assessment also raises the issue of what kind of legal standard will be applied by trade panels in examining whether a measure is "based on" risk assessment; and to what extent measures will need to be "dictated" by the results of the risk assessments.

Risk assessments must be "appropriate to the circumstances," but when they would be "appropriate" is similarly unclear. The issue of the role of risk assessment and risk benefit analysis is not a new one to Canada in relation to trade agreements.

The current Canadian law regarding the standard for registration of pesticide, regulations passed pursuant to the *Canadian Pest Control Products Act,*[17] requires consideration of scientific evidence regarding whether a pesticide may be registered in Canada, but is a health-based standard. The Minister of Agriculture may refuse to register a pest control product if he is of the opinion that the use of the pesticide "would lead to an unacceptable risk of harm to ... public health, plants, animals or the environment."[18]

In contrast, under the US *Federal Insecticide, Fungicide and Rodenticide Act (FIFRA),*[19] the US EPA must make a threshold finding regarding whether the pesticide in question causes "unreasonable adverse effects on the environment," prior to exercising its regulatory authority to register a pesticide (*FIFRA*, s.3(c)(5)). The EPA may not refuse to register a pesticide for a given use unless the risks of that use outweigh its benefits (s. 2(bb)). The Act defines "unreasonable adverse effects on the environment" to mean:

> any unreasonable risk to man or the environment, taking into account the economic, social and environmental costs and benefits of the use of any pesticide.

Because the Canadian standards do not require health risks to be weighed against economic benefits, the Canadian standards for pesticide registration are arguably more strict than those of the US.

The Canada-US FTA required the harmonization of pesticide standards including "working toward equivalence in ... the process for risk-benefit assessment" (FTA Annex 708.1, Schedule 7).

Canada did conduct a Pesticide Registration Review, which recommended that regulatory decisions be made using a *risk management* approach, involving an evaluation of efficacy, risk assessment and, when appropriate, value assessment. This approach is different from formalized quantitative risk-benefit analysis which numerically weighs risks against benefits. Although "risk management" includes an evaluation of the scientific data package in order to determine the risk of harm to human health, safety or the environment, it entails regulatory decisions of a qualitative nature based on the totality of the evidence.

The recommended changes, if implemented, will provide a Canadian scheme which, like the current Canadian scheme, differs from the NAFTA emphasis on risk assessment. The potential for trade-based challenges to the Canadian scheme exists.

d. "necessary"

SPS measures to be taken are those *"necessary"* for the protection of human, animal or plant life or health, and they can be applied only to the extent *"necessary* to achieve (an) appropriate level of protection, taking into account technical and economic feasibility."

The use of the term "necessary" echoes the wording of Article XX of the GATT which permits measures that are non-discriminatory and are not disguised restrictions on trade if they are:

> (b) *necessary* to protect human, animal or plant life or health.

An extensive jurisprudence exists under GATT Article XX regarding measures assessed by trade dispute panels for their consistency with GATT.[20] According to Wirth:

> ... I am unaware of a single GATT panel report that turns on the interpretation of this word where the measure in question was held to be consistent with the GATT. The panel reports articulate, variously, a "least GATT-inconsistent" or a "least trade restrictive" test. Quite obviously, the word "necessary" has been interpreted to give dispute settlement panels a roving commission to second-guess domestic measures and to substitute their own judgment as to the desirability of a particular regulatory measure, an analytical approach that in practice virtually assures that a measure whose consistency with the agreement in question turns on this test will not pass muster. And, unlike domestic courts, dispute settlement panels have only one remedy: a conclusion that a particular action is or is not consistent with the regime.[21]

Reviewing the history of what he calls the "mutating 'necessary' test," Steve Charnovitz notes that the term "necessary" received little attention at the meetings where the GATT was drafted, but documentation indicates that disputes under Article XX(b) were to be resolved on the basis of a scientific test.[22] The Canadian government used this reasoning in its intervention in a US court proceeding involving a challenge of a US EPA rule banning the manufacture, importation, processing, and distribution in commerce of most asbestos-containing products.[23] Canada argued that the ban was not supported by sufficient evidence to prove it was "necessary" within the meaning of the GATT and Canada-US FTA, and that the availability of less stringent measures meant the ban constituted an unnecessary obstacle to trade.

The "least GATT inconsistent test," based on the premise that a health-based standard can be considered "necessary" only if there are no alternative measures less inconsistent with the GATT that could be reasonably employed, originated with the *Thai Cigarette* case.[24] The same type of analysis was used by trade panels which found that the Canadian *Fisheries Act* Regulation examined in the *Salmon and Herring* case[25] was inconsistent with the GATT and FTA.

A similar test is apparent regarding NAFTA's degree of protection for trade actions taken in accordance with the named international environmental agreements. In the event of inconsistency between the NAFTA and the specific agreements, parties are obliged to choose "among equally effective and reasonably available means of complying with such obligations ... the alternative that is the least inconsistent with the other provisions" of NAFTA (Art. 104).

A "least trade restrictive test" was used in defining "necessary" by a GATT panel in the *US Beer Case*[26] in a disturbing analysis. The issue in the case was whether state laws requiring that alcoholic beverages be imported by carriers authorized to operate within particular states could be justified under GATT Article XX (d).

The panel decided:

> ... the United States has not demonstrated that the common carrier requirement is the least trade restrictive enforcement measure available to the various states and that less restrictive measures, e.g. record-keeping requirements of retailers and importers, are not sufficient for tax administration purposes (Id at 5.52).[27]

Further, the panel found justification for its conclusion in holding that since "not all fifty states of the United States maintain common carrier requirements ... some states have found alternative, and *possibly* less trade restrictive, and GATT-inconsistent ways of enforcing *their* tax laws." (Emphasis added).

Charnovitz comments that:

> In other words, the panel concludes that the mere existence of unharmonized states laws shows that alternative methods are available for enforcement.[28]

Panel members did not consider all the possible reasons why such differences might exist: differing tax goals, alcohol policy objectives, effectiveness of various measures in different states, etc.

The "least trade restrictive" test is proposed as the standard to be utilized in the GATT-Uruguay Round proposals regarding the "Standards Code" and the "SPS Decision" on product standards and regulations.

In the light of these increasingly restrictive interpretations of the "necessary" test in trade jurisprudence, the inclusion of this term in the SPS "Basic Rights and Obligations" clause may be expected to act as a significant barrier to a country or province that wishes to set an SPS standard different than those set by the named international standard setters.

e. "disguised restriction on trade"
In applying the tests noted above, trade dispute panels are essentially inquiring into whether the measures in question are "bona fide" environmental protection measures or whether they can, in the opinion of the panel members, be characterized as "disguised restrictions on trade." NAFTA prohibits a party from utilizing an SPS standard "with a view to, or with the effect of, creating a disguised restriction to trade between the Parties" (Art. 712, para. 6), underlining the power of the panels to conduct their inquiries on this basis. The inclusion of "with the effect of" casts the net widely; as with the tests enumerated above, it constitutes a severe restriction on Parties' rights to set their own standards.

f. "in accordance with this Subchapter" and "Notwithstanding any other provision of this Subchapter" (Art. 712, Paras. 1 and 2)
These two paragraphs permit parties to establish SPS measures more stringent than international standards and to establish their appropriate level of protection provided the measures are established in accordance with the SPS subchapter of NAFTA. The establishment of the appropriate levels of protection are protected from challenges based on other sections of the SPS chapter, but not necessarily from challenges based on other sections of

the agreement; such protection would have flowed if the wording in question were "Notwithstanding any other provision of this agreement ..."

In summary, the wording of the NAFTA which establishes Parties' rights and obligations regarding SPS measures contains considerable uncertainty and in the light of previous trade panel decisions, significant constraints on the rights of Parties to set standards different from international standards.

The overall approach to the use of international standards is to be based on use of "equivalence" of standards, which the Parties will attempt to achieve without reducing the level of protection of health. (Art. 714, para. 1). Each party is entitled to establish its "appropriate level of protection," and in doing so, "should take into account the objective of minimizing negative trade effects" (Art. 715, para. 3). The introduction of a trade objective into the decision-making process for establishing levels of protection is another indication of the primacy of trade considerations in the agreement, but the use of "should" rather than "shall" in the section reduces the likelihood of a successful trade challenge to an SPS standard on this basis alone.

Parties "shall" consider economic factors when establishing the chosen levels of protection, including "the relative cost-effectiveness of alternative approaches to limiting risks" (Art. 715, para. 2 (c)).

Parties "should" consider other parties' proposed or actual SPS standards in developing new ones (Art. 714, para. 4), may establish provisional measures prior to receiving sufficient scientific evidence to complete its risk assessment, and may, at the request of another Party, phase in the implementation of the measure (Art. 715).

5.1.2 NAFTA Processes for Developing SPS Standards

Federal government standard setters are required, when proposing to adopt or modify an SPS measure, to provide notice to other parties and consider any comments they may wish to submit. Federal authorities are also required to "seek, through appropriate measures, to ensure" that provincial governments follow the same process (Art. 718). Presumably, in Canada, the "appropriate measures" would entail federal-provincial consultation. If Ontario agrees to these procedures, more resources may be required at the provincial level.

Overall, the inclusion of this requirement not only for the adoption of new SPS measures but also regarding modification of current ones may mean a significant degree of involvement of foreign governments in the standard-setting process in Canada. If the NAFTA is implemented and countries throughout the hemisphere accede, the resource implications of the notice and consultation requirements may become considerable.

The agreement also provides for a Committee on Sanitary and Phyto-sanitary Measures, with representatives from each country, to "facilitate the enhancement of food safety and improvement of SPS conditions in the territories" of the three countries, using consultations between the Parties and with experts (Art. 722).

International Bodies named as SPS Harmonizers include Codex Alimentarius, the International Office of Epizootics, the International Plant Protection Convention, and the North American Plant Protection Organization.

Public access to all these bodies is very limited. The Codex restricts public access to those who are associate members. The International Office of Epizootics and International Plant Protection Convention permit no public access. The North American Plant Protection Organization permits repre-sentatives of national or international organizations and agricultural groups concerned with plant health to attend meetings.

5.2   Standards: Technical Barriers to Trade (TBT) (Standards-related measures)

This section of NAFTA applies to standards-related measures (SRMs) other than sanitary and phytosanitary measures (Art.901) and includes a wide range of environmental standards. Examples include regulations regarding auto emissions, pulp and paper effluent, hazardous waste management, fisheries, conservation, etc.

The federal government is not required to ensure compliance of provincial governments with this chapter, but it is required to seek compliance "through appropriate measures," as it is with regard to notice requirements for provincial SPS measures (Art. 902).

5.2.1 Basic Rights and Obligations Regarding Standards-Related Measures

As is true with regard to SPS standards, the intent of this chapter is to establish a comprehensive approach to harmonization of technical standards, including those pertaining to environmental and consumer protection and human, plant, and animal health. A broader right is left to the individual parties to set their own standards than is true of SPS standards, but it remains a qualified right.

Specifically, parties may establish levels of protection as they consider appropriate (Art. 904, para. 2), and may set standards higher than those of international standards (Art. 905, para. 3). They may not set standards with the intention or effect of creating an unnecessary obstacle to trade; this requirement echoes GATT Article XX. Such an obstacle will be deemed not to be created if:

> the demonstrable purpose of such measure is to achieve a legitimate objective; and
> such measure does not operate to exclude goods of another Party that meet that legitimate objective (Art. 904, para. 4).

Significantly, the definition of "legitimate objective" includes safety, protection of human, animal, or plant life or health, the environment or consumers, and sustainable development (Art. 915). Although the FTA includes "health, safety, essential security, the environment, or consumer interests" as legitimate domestic objectives (FTA Article 609), NAFTA is the first trade agreement to include "sustainable development" in the definition. This has the potential to provide protection for a broad range of differing standards, if in the event of challenge, trade dispute panels interpret the provision liberally.

5.2.2 Qualifications

However, as the right to set appropriate levels of protection operates "Notwithstanding any other provision of this Chapter" (Art. 904, para. 2) and not "Notwithstanding any other provision of this *Agreement*," the use of the "Nullification and Impairment of Benefits" provision to challenge a standard still exists. In fact, this is made explicit in Annex 2004 which permits a challenger of a TBT measure to go to dispute settlement based on this wording even if the measure in question is consistent with the terms of NAFTA. This Annex provides that parties may challenge a standard that is *consistent* with NAFTA if it "nullifie(s) or impair(s)" a benefit the party "reasonably" expected to gain under NAFTA.

Similarly, the wide protection given to protective measures would presumably not extend to resource export bans as a conservation measure, even as a component of sustainable development or environmental protection. Such actions would contravene provisions of Chapters 3 and 6 rather than provisions within this Chapter.

The question remaining is whether, given this limitation, these provisions would have led to a different result in such disputes as the Canadian *Salmon and Herring Case* and more broadly, whether these provisions will provide a higher level of environmental protection than has occurred in trade decisions based on GATT Article XX (b) and (g) as interpreted also under the Canada-US Free-Trade Agreement.

5.2.3 NAFTA Technical Barriers Procedures

The parties have committed to working jointly to "enhance" environmental and health and safety levels through making their standards compatible, and may use risk assessment in standard-setting (Art. 906 and 907). They will also seek to make conformity assessment compatible and cooperative amongst the three countries (Art. 908). Federal authorities will be required to provide notice and opportunities for comment to other parties when proposing a new or modified standard.

Article 909, paragraph 6 provides:

> Where a Party allows non-governmental persons in its territory to be present during the process of development of standards-related measures, it shall also allow non-governmental persons from the territories of the other Parties to be present.

This would appear to give broad rights of consultation to "stakeholders" in all three countries to become involved in standard-setting in the other countries.

Although this chapter is not subject to Article 105, which requires that the federal government "ensure" compliance by provincial governments, it clearly envisions a considerable right of involvement by other governments in provincial practices concerning standard-setting. This is to be achieved by the federal governments through "appropriate measures" at the provincial level. These rights include rights of notification of new or amended standards (Art. 909, paras. 2 and 3), and changed application of standards (para. 7) and permitting participation by non-governmental persons from other territories as specified for federal standard-setting. Environmental protection is an area of shared provincial and federal jurisdiction in Canada. The possibility of constitutional disagreements exists, should provincial governments decline to cooperate with any federal attempts to obtain compliance with these provisions.

The policy and resource implications of these requirements are very significant. They may involve considerable expense. In an era when environmental decision-making often involves multi-stakeholder processes, it provides a basis for non-Canadian businesses to require inclusion in these processes. Canadians will have the same rights in foreign processes. Though it presumably provides the same rights to other foreign citizens and citizen groups, few will have the financial resources to utilize the right. It will mainly benefit large multinational corporations, with their financial and locational advantages.

The Parties have committed to establishing a Committee on Standards-Related Measures and a series of sub-committees, with mandates that include many subjects important in environmental protection. These include:

- Land Transportation and Automotive Standards Subcommittees, whose mandate will include emissions and environmental pollution levels and transportation of dangerous goods (Art. 913, para. 5 and related Annexes)
- packaging and labelling
- accreditation of conformity assessment bodies
- chemical hazard classification and communications
- enforcement programs
- good laboratory practices
- good manufacturing practices

- ◆ criteria for assessment of environmental hazards of goods
- ◆ risk assessment methodologies
- ◆ testing of chemicals, including industrial and agricultural chemicals, pharmaceuticals and biologicals.

Although the agreement internationalizes consultation where it now exists, it provides no rights of public access to these new committee processes, and no provision of information to the public. In this sense, it is likely to foster disputes between Canadian environmentalists and their provincial and federal governments if, in contrast to current Canadian processes, environmentalists find themselves shut out of standards decision-making.

The overall sweep of the harmonization initiatives in the TBT chapter, as in the SPS chapter, will potentially result in a very different approach to standard-setting from the one now used in Canada.

VI Investment

In the public debate concerning NAFTA, concern has been expressed that free trade with Mexico will permit corporations to move investment to the jurisdictions that have the lowest levels of environmental protection, including Mexico and some American state jurisdictions. In response to this concern, environmentalists called for provisions in the NAFTA to prevent such moves. This was not achieved, and the "Investment" chapter merely discourages government policies designed to foster the practice. Specifically, Article 1114, paragraph 2 states:

> The Parties recognize that it is inappropriate to encourage investment by relaxing domestic health, safety or environmental measures. Accordingly, a Party should not waive or otherwise derogate from, or offer to waive or otherwise derogate from, such measures as an encouragement for the establishment, acquisition, expansion, or retention in its territory of an investment or an investor. If a Party considers that another Party has offered such an encouragement, it may request consultations with the other Party and the two Parties shall consult with a view to avoiding any such encouragement.

The agreement does not prohibit encouragement of investment through relaxing of environmental issues, nor would a Party apparently have recourse to a trade dispute panel to raise such an issue. The clause provides for consultations only. Nor does it prevent shifts in investment due to existing differences in environmental standards and enforcement.

VII Intellectual Property Rights

The NAFTA provides protection for intellectual property, an issue excluded from the Canada-US FTA. Environmental concerns arise from the provisions regarding patenting of life forms, and the possible long-term effects on agriculture and biodiversity. The agreement permits exclusions from patentability for inventions when:

> necessary to protect *ordre public* or morality, including to protect human, animal or plant life or health or to avoid serious prejudice to nature or the environment, provided that the exclusion is not based solely on the ground that the Party prohibits commercial exploitation in its territory of the subject matter of the patent (Art. 1709).

Parties may also exclude from patentability treatments for health, "plants and animals other than micro-organisms" and "essentially biological processes for the production of plants or animals." However, Parties are required to provide for the protection of plant varieties through patents, an effective scheme of *sui generis* protection, or both (Art. 1709).

Canadians are currently most familiar with the impacts on pharmaceuticals, and the move to longer patent protection of drugs, justified by the federal government in terms of the future requirements of the Intellectual Property section of NAFTA. The federal government has also passed plant breeders' rights protection. However, concerns have been expressed regarding the environmental impacts, particularly on agriculture, of these provisions and of future implications of life forms patentability.

As one analyst has argued:[29]

> ... the legislative history in industrialized countries shows clearly that plant variety rights lead to exclusive monopoly rights over microbials and then animals. In a technology where fish and insect genes are inserted into crop plants and human genes are inserted into mice, pigs, sheep and goats, the "natural barriers" between–not only species–but biological kingdoms are broken down. Life is homogenized.

Further,

> Life form patents will result in farmers being denied their traditional rights
> to save seed [because] planting seeds without paying royalties is making an
> unauthorized copy of a patented product. Farmers will be forced to pay
> royalties for every seed and farm animal derived from patented stock,
> forced to become more dependent on fertilizers, pesticides, herbicides, and
> the machinery made by the same companies who collected the traditional
> seeds in the first place and now sell back the chemically-dependent
> derivatives.[30]

Pat Mooney also argues that the leading companies in private biotechnology research are predominantly pharmaceutical manufacturers, which
are also leading pesticide and seed companies. They concentrate on
producing pesticide-resistant plant varieties, to be produced with the use of
their herbicides. The environment would be better protected by the
development of pest-resistant plant species which could lead to a reduced
use of pesticides in agriculture.

VIII Dispute Settlement Processes

As in the US-Canada Agreement, all parties are entitled to retain their
antidumping and countervailing duties laws, and to amend them in a
manner consistent with GATT and the free-trade principles of NAFTA (Art.
1902). Domestic judicial review of decisions made under these laws is
replaced by binational panel review (Art. 1904). The parties intend further
consultations including on the "potential for more effective rules and
disciplines concerning the use of government subsidies" (Art. 1907).[31]

As noted above, further dispute processes are provided in Chapter 20 to be
used for trade disputes including claims of nullification and impairment of
benefits (Art. 2004, Annex 2004). Thus, dispute panels may hear complaints
that measures *"that (are) not inconsistent with this Agreement"* but deprive a
party of a benefit it could have reasonably expected to accrue to it; subject
areas for which the right exists include most provisions regarding trade in
goods (Part 2 of NAFTA), the Technical Barriers to Trade section, and
intellectual property.

Unlike the Canada-US FTA, certain dispute provisions of the NAFTA apply
specifically to disputes involving environmental issues. Though complain-

ing parties can generally use the NAFTA dispute process or the GATT one, a responding Party may require that the NAFTA process be used if it involves issues of sanitary or phytosanitary standards, or other standards-related measures (Art. 2005, para. 3, 4).

In such challenges, the Party asserting that an SPS measure or other standards-related measure is inconsistent with their respective chapters of NAFTA will have the onus of showing the inconsistency (Arts. 723, para. 4, and 914, para. 4). This provides more support for the standards provisions than occur in disputes where GATT Article XX is invoked to defend an environmental standard. Whether the effect of the provision is significant remains to be seen. Normally, the onus of proof only plays a determinative role in legal cases that are evenly balanced, and trade disputes have not, to date, demonstrated such a fine balancing of evidence and law.

Scientific review boards may be convened, at the request of a trade panel (with the agreement of the parties) or at the request of a party "on any factual issues concerning environmental, health, safety or other scientific matters" raised by a party (Art. 2015). Such panel members are to be selected from "highly qualified, independent experts" after consultations with the parties and scientific bodies. Parties may provide comments to the science board and comments on its report to the panel. The panel is required to take its report into account.

However, as in Canada-US disputes, no public access to the entire process is permitted, nor is there any opportunity for public notice or participation:

> The panel's hearings, deliberations and initial report, and all written submissions to and communications with the panel shall be confidential (Art. 2012, para. 1).

Panels are not to disclose which panellists are associated with majority and minority opinions (Art. 2017, para. 3). As noted above, NAFTA also specifies what actions Parties should take after a dispute panel decision has been reached: normally, the elimination of the contested measure, or compensation to the complaining party (Art. 2018).

The NAFTA dispute provisions may result in more positive consideration of environmental concerns in dispute processes. It is to be hoped, for example, that scientific panels will be more receptive to the need for resource conservation measures than dispute panels have been in the past. However, the impact of the provisions will only be as strong as the wording of the substantive provisions that will be interpreted in each trade dispute.

The dispute processes depart radically from processes common to the Canadian legal system: public trials, citizens' rights of intervention, attribution of majority and minority judicial reasoning, and accessibility for all levels of government.

Given that national and provincial rights to set standards are qualified, subsidies issues have not been resolved, and the resource-sharing language of the agreement is like that of the Canada-US FTA, important limitations on environmental protection powers have been perpetuated in NAFTA.

IX Supplementary Agreements

The Bush administration negotiated NAFTA, and the Clinton administration adopted it, with the addition of the negotiation of two "side agreements," on labour and environmental questions.[32] The *North American Agreement on Environmental Cooperation* was promoted by President Clinton as a means to ensure that free trade with Mexico would not lead to a lowering of American environmental standards. However, in the view of Canadian environmentalists, it failed to provide that protection.[33]

The provisions of the environmental side agreement do not take precedence over the terms of NAFTA, and therefore, the identified environmental problems of NAFTA will flow, unimpeded, as the free trade accord is implemented.

The enforcement provisions of the side agreement ultimately may permit the use of trade sanctions or fines against a government found to have failed to enforce its environmental laws. However, the process of invoking sanctions or fines is long, tortuous, subject to political control from the three federal environment ministers, and is secretive. It falls far short of the process desired by environmentalists.

As noted by Zen Makuch and Scott Sinclair:

> The process takes place behind closed doors and permits only NAFTA
> Parties (not provincial governments or citizens) to participate. It is to be
> conducted in the absence of proper legal procedures and without adequate
> opportunities to collect evidence or call expert witnesses. The evidentiary
> requirements which must be met in order to successfully penalise a
> government for not enforcing its environmental laws appear to be insur-
> mountable. Finally, the dispute resolution process will provide little
> incentive to deter environmental destruction since polluters will not be
> liable for any of the penalties handed out at the completion of the process.[34]

In Canada, the only laws that can be enforced by the process are federal ones,
since the provinces are not bound by the agreement. Since provincial laws
form a large part of Canadian environmental regulation, the ambit of the
agreement is narrow. Laws whose purpose is the protection of natural
resources are also excluded from its ambit.

Enhanced cooperation among the three federal governments will be provided by the Commission for Environmental Cooperation, which is limited
to conducting research and writing reports. It will be funded by the three
governments, and dependent on them for programme approval. Little real
public involvement in its activities will be permitted.

In conclusion, the NAFTA environmental side agreement may lead to better
environmental cooperation among federal governments, but is unlikely to
contribute to effective enforcement of environmental protection regimes in
the three countries.

X   Conclusion

- The NAFTA perpetuates the environmental problems of the Canada-
  US Free Trade Agreement, and creates new ones.

- Although it provides partial protection to trade actions taken pursuant to three international environmental agreements, the protection
  is limited.

- The agreement does not prevent countries from lowering
  environmental standards or enforcement in order to attract investment.

- NAFTA continues the problems regarding strategies for resource conservation that flow from the requirements for national treatment, the "proportionality clause" and trade panel decisions under GATT and the US-Canada FTA. These barriers to conservation policies affect all Canadian resources including water.

- The agreement establishes a new approach to environmental standard-setting, different from current Canadian and Ontario practice. Many standards are to be set by unaccountable international bodies and no provisions for public participation in the processes exist in the NAFTA. The rights of national and provincial governments to set more stringent standards are qualified. NAFTA codifies tests used by previous trade panels, such as the "necessity" test, that have led to the loss of environmental standards. Notice and consultation requirements for the federal and Ontario governments may have considerable resource implications.

- Canada-US subsidy disputes have not been addressed or resolved in NAFTA.

- The NAFTA dispute processes are secret and provide no right of access to provincial governments and to the public.

Endnotes

1 Ron Davidson, External Affairs and International Trade, communication to member of environmental group, September 14, 1992, Ottawa.
2 The US, Canada, and Mexico are all parties to the *Montreal Protocol* and have ratified the London amendments. They have all also signed and ratified *CITES*. All three have signed the *Basel Convention*, and Canada and Mexico have ratified it. The US has not yet ratified this convention.
3 For an analysis of the economic issues related to water export see Bruce Campbell, "Globalization, Trade Agreements and Sustainability," *The Environmental Implications of Trade Agreements*, prepared by the Canadian Environmental Law Association for the Ontario Ministry of Environment and Energy (Toronto: Queen's Printer for Ontario, 1993), 7-63.
4 Canada, *An Act to Implement the NAFTA Schedule, Part A, Schedule I to the Customs Tariff;* Jamie Linton, *NAFTA and Water Exports*, A Submission to the Cabinet Committee on NAFTA of the Government of the Province of Ontario (Ottawa: April 1993), 124.

[5] Cited in Canadian Centre for Policy Alternatives (CPPA), *Which Way for the Americas, Analysis of NAFTA Proposals and the Impact on Canada* (Ottawa: 1992).

[6] "General Rules for the Interpretation of the Harmonized System," listed in NAFTA, Schedule Part A, 8, in Linton, *NAFTA and Water Exports* 2.

[7] Ibid., 3.

[8] *Canada-US Free Trade Implementation Act*, R.S.C. 1988, Chapter C-106.

[9] Gordon Ritchie, *The Toronto Star*, February 11, 1993, and personal communication, February 15, 1993.

[10] See Peter Hogg, *Constitutional Law of Canada* 3rd ed. (Toronto: Carswell, 1992), especially Chapter 11. In discussing the implementation of treaties within the Canadian federal system, Hogg concludes that the courts of Canada "will not give effect to a treaty unless it has been enacted into law by the appropriate legislative body." Instead, Canadian courts "will apply the law laid down by statute or common law, even if it is inconsistent with a treaty which is binding upon Canada." Further, he notes that "where the language of a statute is clearly and unmistakably inconsistent with a treaty or other rule of international law, then there is no room for interpreting it into conformity with the international rule and the statute must be applied as it stands." The current state of Canadian domestic law appears to be as follows: an international treaty obligation that is inconsistent with valid federal or provincial legislation will not override the federal or provincial legislation.

[11] For example, see the *Salmon and Herring* case, the *US Beer* case, both discussed below, and the *Tuna-Dolphin* case: *United States - Restrictions on Imports of Tuna, GATT Doc. DS21/R, 3rd. September 1991.*

[12] Countries do not always comply. The US for example continues to negotiate with Mexico in the wake of the GATT panel decision in the *Tuna-Dolphin* case. Penalties for non-compliance include withdrawal of the benefits and concessions negotiated under the trade agreement.

[13] NAFTA article 2018 specifies:

> 1. On receipt of the final report of a panel, the disputing Parties shall agree on the resolution of the dispute, which normally shall conform with the determinations and recommendations of the panel, and shall notify their Sections of the Secretariat of any agreed resolution of any dispute.

Wherever possible, the resolution shall be non-implementation or removal of a measure not conforming with this Agreement or causing nullification or impairment in the sense of Annex 2004 or, failing such a resolution, compensation.

[14] *United States-Canada Free Trade Implementation Act of 1988*, Pub.L. 100-449, 19 USCA para. 2112 nt. (West 1980 & Supp. 1993).

[15] For a further discussion of this issue see Scott Sinclair, "The Use of US Trade Remedy Laws: Impacts on Ontario Environmental Protection Strategies," in *The Environmental Implications of Trade Agreements* (Toronto: 1993), 167-194.

[16] David A. Wirth, *Statement and Testimony before the House Committee on Science, Space, and Technology*, Washington, D.C., September 30, 1992.

[17] *Pest Control Products Act*, R.S.C. P-10, s.1.

[18] *Pest Control Products Regulations*, s.18, CRC C. 1253 as amended.

[19] *Federal Insecticide, Fungicide, and Rodenticide Act*, 7 U.S.C.A. paras. 136-136y, (West 1980 & Supp. 1993).

[20] Wirth, *Statement and Testimony*.

[21] Ibid., 10-11.

[22] Steve Charnovitz, "Reconsidering the Debate on 'GATT and the Environment'," Paper prepared for the Ottawa Conference on International Trade and Sustainable Development, 1992.

[23] *Corrosion Proof Fittings* v. *EPA*, 947 F.2d 1201 (5th Cir. 1991); Brief for Amicus Curiae Government of Canada at 16-19).

[24] *Thailand - Restrictions on Importation of and Internal Taxes on Cigarettes*, GATT Doc. 375/200 (Thai Cigarette Case).

[25] Canada-US Trade Commission Panel, *In the Matter of Canada's Landing Requirement for Pacific Coast Salmon and Herring*, 1989, (Salmon and Herring Case).

[26] *United States - Measures Affecting Alcoholic and Malt Beverages*, GATT Doc. DS23/R, February 1992 (US Beer Case).

[27] Ibid. at 5.52.

[28] Charnovitz, "Reconsidering the Debate, " 15.

[29] Pat Mooney, quoted in Canadian Centre for Policy Alternatives, *Which Way for the Americas*: Analysis of NAFTA Proposals and the Impact on Canada (Ottawa: The Centre, 1992), 39-40.

[30] Ibid., 40.

[31] See Scott Sinclair, "The Use of US Trade Remedy Laws: Impacts on Ontario Environmental Protection Strategies" and Sinclair, "The Use of US Trade Remedy Laws: Case Study of The Softwood Lumber Disputes," in *The Environmental Implications of Trade Agreements*, 167-221, for a discussion of binational panel reviews under the FTA.

[32] *North American Agreement on Labor Cooperation* (Ottawa: Final Draft, September 13, 1993); *North American Agreement on Environmental Cooperation* (Ottawa: Final Draft, September 13, 1993).

[33] Canadian Environmental Law Association, *The Environmental Implications of the NAFTA Environmental Side Agreement*, (1993). Prepared by Zen Makuch and Scott Sinclair.

[34] Ibid.

CHAPTER 6

HARMONIZATION AND RISK ASSESSMENT IN THE NORTH AMERICAN FREE TRADE AGREEMENT

David Bennett

David Bennett is a member of the Fire Brigades' Union (UK) as well as a member of the Communications, Energy, and Paperworkers' Union of Canada (CEP). He is a graduate of Cambridge University and holds a Ph.D. from McGill University. After working as a fire fighter, he was employed as a labour instructor for the Workers' Educational Association in the United Kingdom where his main work was in instructing health, safety, and bargaining courses for the Trades Union Congress. Since 1980, he has worked for the Canadian Labour Congress (CLC) in union education, health and safety and, most recently, as National Director, Health, Safety & Environment Department. He was the author of the CLC's pioneering environmental education course and has written several books, pamphlets, and articles on health, safety and environment.

The proposed North American Free Trade Agreement (NAFTA) has been held up as the most "green" trade agreement ever concluded. There are a large number of provisions concerning the environment and some, on the face of it, enable the three signing Parties (Canada, Mexico and the US) to implement "any" standards or measures that they consider appropriate (see, e.g., Articles 712.1 and 2 and 904.1 and 2).

On the other hand, critics of the agreement contend that it will result in the "downward harmonization" of standards in several areas, including:

- public health and safety, including environmental health;
- occupational health and safety;
- environmental protection; and
- consumer protection.

This chapter will argue that the latter contention is quite correct: the NAFTA is hedged in by so many stipulations concerning the framing, implementation and review of standards that, so far as environmental well-being is concerned, the agreement "dies the death of a thousand qualifications." Further, the modes of standard-making are so new and different that what appears to be a mere trade agreement is, in effect, "a new Constitution for Canada," endorsed by the federal government without the public being aware of the enormous consequences of the NAFTA for the governance of Canada.

However, the ways in which the NAFTA will have an impact on Canada are not clear, simply because the text of the NAFTA is not clear. The NAFTA is, in a general way, anti-environmental; but the unclarities in the text make it difficult to gauge the ways in which the three signing Parties will move to implement its provisions.

The relevant chapters in the NAFTA are Chapter 7 on Agriculture, in particular, Section B–Sanitary and Phytosanitary Measures and Part III, Technical Barriers to Trade, Chapter 9, Standards-Related Measures. Since Chapter 7 is concerned with agriculture, this could give the impression that the scope of the chapter is limited to agricultural products and their relationship to human health and animal feedstuffs. Since Chapter 9 is the only chapter under Part III, this could give the well-founded impression that Chapter 9 is concerned only with the impact of standards on trade, rather than with communal and environmental well-being.

The two chapters have been interpreted as mutually exclusive,[1] with Chapter 7 pertaining to food and foodstuffs, while Chapter 9 covers all the remaining manufacturing and agricultural standards. This interpretation is hard to substantiate, at least in a rigid fashion. In the September 6, 1992 draft of the NAFTA, Chapter 7 applied to agricultural trade *and* to sanitary and phytosanitary measures. In the October 7, 1992 draft, the reference to sanitary and phytosanitary measures was dropped (Article 701) and the reference to agricultural trade is restricted to Section A (Agriculture), by implication excluding Section B (Sanitary and Phytosanitary Measures). The language of Chapter 7, Section B remains, however, largely the same, despite a different numbering of the Articles of the Section, which concerns the protection of "human, animal or plant life or health" (Article 713). Further, "animal" includes *wild* fauna and "plant" includes *wild* flora (Article 724: *Definitions*), making it clear that the chapter has a wide environmental and human focus. On the other hand, the definition of a sanitary or phytosanitary measure clearly has an agricultural focus (Article

724) since there is no specific reference to the threat of contaminants to animal or plant life. Contaminants are mentioned in reference to human or animal life or health in relation to food and feedstuffs.

A similar overlap or confusion arises when we look at Chapter 9. Article 901: *Scope* states that the chapter applies to any standards-related measures other than those covered by Chapter 7, Sub-chapter B. Yet Article 904 specifically includes human, animal and plant life and health in the scope of standards-related measures, as well as safety, the environment and consumers. This is confirmed in Article 915: *Definitions,* where a "legitimate objective" includes the protection of human, animal or plant life or health, as well as safety, the environment, consumers and, interestingly, sustainable development. This has been noted by the Government of Canada.[2]

There are also specific linkages and cross references between the two chapters. For instance, Annex 704.3 of the September text sets up Working Groups to review the operation of grade quality standards regarding agricultural goods. These Working Groups are to be coordinated with the Committee on Standards-Related Measures established under Chapter 9.[3] Further, disputes over standards in relation to trade will involve "risk assessment methodologies agreed on by those Parties" (Article 714.2[a]) and there is provision in Chapter 9 for attempting to achieve such agreement (i.e., harmonization).

The thrust of the two chapters is similar in many ways. Under Article 755, each party *shall* use relevant international standards, guidelines or recommendations with the objective of making its sanitary and phytosanitary measures equivalent or identical to those of the other Parties. The language of Article 905: *Use of International Standards* is similar.[4]

Article 714: *Equivalence* requires that, without reducing levels of protection, the Parties pursue, to the greatest extent practicable, the equivalence of their respective sanitary or phytosanitary standards. Article 722 sets up a Committee on Sanitary and Phytosanitary Measures to address equivalency issues. Of course, such protection levels may already be low and trade-offs of protection levels between Parties are evidently permitted, otherwise the article would have required the highest common factor. There is similar language in Article 906.2, with the aim of facilitating trade in goods and services between Parties.

Beyond these points, the thrust of the two chapters becomes confusing, in two main respects:

(1) the role of risk assessment; and

(2) the extent of the obligations of the Parties in regard to their provinces and states.

Article 712.3 requires sanitary or phytosanitary measures to be based on scientific principles and on a risk assessment. Further, the measures must be applied only to the extent necessary to achieve an appropriate level of protection "taking into account technical and economic feasibility" suggesting a further cost-benefit exercise after the risk assessment. (Compare Article 904.4.) This is confirmed in Article 715.2(c) in which the Parties are required to consider the relative cost-effectiveness of alternative approaches to limiting risks.

On the other hand, Article 907 says only that the Parties *may* conduct a risk assessment in pursuing their legitimate objectives. At worst, the text of the NAFTA is contradictory in that human, animal and plant health are covered in both Chapters 7 and 9, yet the former requires risk assessment while the latter leaves it optional.

The role of provincial and state governments is also unclear. Article 105 (Extent of Obligations) of Chapter 1 (Objectives) requires that the Parties ensure that all necessary measures are taken to ensure observance of the provisions of the Agreement by state and provincial governments. This is to be taken to include local governments according to the Definitions in Chapter 2. Chapter 9 is not subject to Article 105; there is an apparently weaker requirement to "seek to ensure" (Article 902.2) observance by state or provincial governments of the key Articles 904-908.

Article 105 has been taken to mean that the NAFTA requires the government to force the provinces to comply with the terms of the Agreement, even in areas of exclusive provincial jurisdiction.[5] Thus, provincial powers would disappear, not merely by default in the event of a failure to challenge specific provisions, but by the NAFTA superseding the Constitution. This does not seem to be right. It is hard to see how the NAFTA could be a *formal* threat in such areas as workplace health and safety, where provincial jurisdiction is explicit and entrenched.

The problem arises in those areas of jurisdiction which are concurrent (shared) or undefined or in those areas where federal powers to regulate foreign trade supersede *de facto* intra-provincial powers to regulate commerce. The problem is compounded by the evident overlap in the scope of Chapters 7 and 9.

The scope of harmonization also differs in the two chapters. Chapter 7 (Article 714) talks of harmonization in terms of "equivalence"[6] but the Committee on Standards-Related Measures in Chapter 9 (Article 913.2[b]) refers to the "compatibility" of standards-related measures which, according to the definition (Article 915), is slightly weaker than equivalence or identity. Neither non-governmental organizations (NGOs) nor representatives of provincial/state governments are given any status or mention in the consultations sponsored by the committees.[7] Nor do such representatives have any status on the (secret) NAFTA dispute settlement panels.

There are a number of topics which the Committee under Chapter 9 *may* deal with and these include:

◆ chemical hazard classification and communication;
◆ enforcement programs;
◆ assessment of the potential environmental hazards of goods;
◆ chemical testing "guidelines"; and
◆ risk assessment methodologies.

While there is no explicit reference to harmonization or standardization, it is clear from the context that the object of "addressing" (Article 913.5[b]) such topics is to produce uniform standards throughout the NAFTA signatories.

Should there be either a "downward harmonization" or a gravitation to US standards (the US being the dominant NAFTA partner), Canada would suffer an erosion of its national workplace right-to-know law, Workplace Hazardous Materials Information System (WHMIS), and it would suffer some erosion of chemical testing requirements. For instance, even though the proposed Notification of New Substances Regulations (1993) under the *Canadian Environmental Protection Act (CEPA)* have been eroded from the levels agreed in 1986[8] under pressure from Canadian business, they are still arguably stronger than those under the US *Toxic Substances Control Act*. On consumer issues, the threat to Canada is less severe.

The main threat is the near-exclusive reliance in the NAFTA on risk assessment methodologies. While risk assessment is not defined in the NAFTA, it evidently means the specialized technique used in the registration or licensing of agricultural pesticides, which is a main concern of Chapter 7. There have been many devastating criticisms of risk assessment,[9] but the main one is this. Risk assessment starts from the (usually unstated) premise that environmental detriments are acceptable or innocent unless there is some good scientific reason to limit them. Risk assessment methods, which rest heavily on statistical techniques and computations, are then used to calculate risk. Some level of risk is then deemed to be unacceptable and measures are then proposed (risk management) to reduce the risk to the acceptable level–but only to a degree commensurate with the risk calculated and accepted.

The nature of the data and the assumptions used in the risk assessment process almost always ensure that the risks are assessed as minimal or that they are too uncertain or controversial for risk reduction to be justified. Even when the risk assessment procedure has scientific integrity, it is still a conservative technique, resulting in minimal action to reduce environmental detriments. The main criticism is not that risk assessment is bad science but it is only one of a number of scientific techniques that can be used to justify environmental protection measures.[10] There is no warrant to the claim that the only "good science" of environmental protection must be based on risk assessment procedures, yet this is what is assumed in the NAFTA, particularly in Chapter 7. Risk assessment has been used to minimize protection measures, for example, in the case of dioxins[11] and cadmium compounds.[12]

There is one common misperception of risk assessment. Unlike the *Federal Insecticide, Fungicide and Rodenticide Act (FIFRA)* in the US, the Canadian *Pest Control Products Act (PCPA)* is not a "risk-benefit statute." From this fact, it is then inferred that Canada's pesticide registration regime is more stringent than the US. This is not correct. Risk assessment techniques are used under *PCPA* with legitimacy, since the Act does not specify the criteria whereby a product will be granted or refused registration. The result is the *PCPA* is as permissive as *FIFRA*: *all* products that go through the registration process are granted registration. If they are particularly hazardous, use-restrictions are stipulated, which are hard to enforce and, in practice, unenforced. Nor are the rules about what data have to be submitted to the regulatory authority enshrined in law so that, even if there were criteria for registration, they could not be consistently applied except by arbitrary *fiat*.

Trouble would arise if the Parties to the NAFTA tried to strengthen their pesticide regimes (e.g., by progressively refusing registration to the most dangerous chemical pesticides, using criteria of hazard in a systematic way).[13] This would be incompatible with the risk assessment requirements of Chapter 7 of the NAFTA since it would eschew current risk assessment methodologies in favour of hazard reduction techniques which, however else they may utilize the notion of risk, certainly do not rely on risk assessment calculations of the conventional sort. Thus, it has been argued persuasively that pollution prevention measures such as Toxic Substances Use Reduction (TUR) are incompatible with the retrogressive techniques of quantitative risk assessment.[14] It also seems clear that any "parallel agreement" to improve environmental practice or worker health standards would run counter to the conservative provisions and methodologies of the NAFTA. The stagnation and obsolescence of environmental standards is perhaps more of a danger than their decline through downward harmonization.

In all, the NAFTA poses a threat to progressive environmental protection measures because of its overriding concern that regulations must not be framed in such a way or with such a rationale as to interfere with free trade and the rights of free traders. While risk assessment may be a legitimate technique, it functions as the ideology of international deregulation.

In Canada, inter-provincial harmonization of occupational health and safety standards has already begun. This would be no bad thing if it were not for the fact that there is pressure from the NAFTA to harmonize such standardization downwards.

Environment Canada is at least considering the standardization of risk assessment methodologies, though it would be likely to pursue such a project in ways not specifically required or suggested in Chapter 9 of the NAFTA.

Internationally, the standardization of hazard categories and hazard threshold values has already begun, as regards both environmental health and the protection of the physical environment. It is likely that this has been influenced more by the GATT, which contains pressures similar to those of the NAFTA, than by the aura of high international standards which arose from the UNCED Conference in Rio, Brazil in June 1992 and, in particular, one of its principal documents, Agenda 21.[15]

Endnotes

[1] "The NAFTA Does Not Measure Up on the Environment and Consumer Health and Safety," *Public Citizen* (Washington, D.C.: n.d.), 2.
[2] "North American Free Trade Agreement, An Overview and Description," *Government of Canada* (August 1992), 7.
[3] This Annex has apparently disappeared from the October draft (which is itself not the final authenticated text) unless it is to be one of the "Other Working Groups" of Annex 2001.2. The references to the text of the NAFTA in this piece are from the version of October 7, 1992. For greater clarity, here is a table of comparison of selected article numbers in the NAFTA texts:

October 7, 1992	September 6, 1992
701	701
712	754
713	755
714	756
715	757
718	760
722	764
724	766
—	Annex 704.3

The Erratum/Notes on Pages 1-8 of Part 1 of the October 1992 draft also change the definitions of standards-related terminology from both the September and October texts (Article 915). See also the Notes on Chapter 22.
[4] The role of international standards in national standard-setting is not included in the scope of this article; nor is that of "non-governmental standardizing bodies." However, it is worth noting the language of Article 711: "Each party shall ensure that any non-governmental entity on which it relies in applying a sanitary or phytosanitary measures acts in a manner consistent with the Section." Thus, the Parties have not merely to *adopt* a standard which meets the requirements of the NAFTA, they have to ensure that standard-making bodies actually frame them according to the NAFTA rules. As usual, the corresponding language in Chapter 9 is weaker: the Parties have only to "seek to ensure" observance of Article 904-908 by standardizing bodies.

We can easily envisage a situation in which, under the guise of the work of "technical experts" from the three Parties on standardizing bodies, wide-ranging

environmental standards are framed which are then legislated by being incorporated *en bloc* into national regulations. The normal political debate and democratic process are then entirely bypassed.

[5] See Maude Barlow, "NAFTA Will Sap Provincial Powers," *The Globe and Mail*,
March 15, 1993.

[6] This provision builds on the requirement to work towards equivalence in the
Schedules to Chapter 7 (Agriculture) of the Canada-US Free Trade Agreement.

[7] *The Public Citizen* claims that state level representatives may be included in the
consultations, but that consumer and environmental advocates have no role.
Possibly, *The Public Citizen* was relying on an earlier draft of the NAFTA texts in
making this claim.   Article 913.4(a)(i) includes a reference to consulting "as
appropriate" with representatives of non-governmental bodies, but the intention
seems to be to consider including representatives of standardizing bodies. The
discrepancies between Chapter 7 and 9 may be explained in part by: (1) there
were two different sets of negotiations for the two chapters; and (2) the Parties
were insufficiently aware that the scope of federal authority in the three countries
differs both *within* the two chapters and in the linkages between them.

[8] See the "Final Report of the Environmental Contaminants Act Consultative
Committee," (Ottawa: October 1986).

[9] See Robert Ginsburg, "Quantitative Risk Assessment and the Illusion of Safety,"
New Solutions 3(2) (Winter 1993), 8-15.

[10] See, e.g., "Ontario Ministry of the Environment Scoring System for Assessing
Environmental Contaminants," (March 1990); "Candidate Substances List for
Bans and Phase-Outs," Ontario Ministry of the Environment (April 1992); and "A
Critique of the Ontario Hazard Assessment System," Canadian Labour Congress
(Ottawa: August 1992).

[11] Mary H. O'Brien, "Alternatives to Risk Assessment: The Example of Dioxin,"
New Solutions 3(2) (Winter 1993), 39-42.

[12] See Bob Davis, "When Science Enters the Political Arena," *The Globe and Mail*,
August 10, 1992, reprinted from the *The Wall Street Journal*.

[13] See David Bennett, "Pesticide Reduction, A Case Study from Canada," *New
Solutions* 2(2) (Fall 1991), 59-63.

[14] Ginsburg, "Quantitative Risk Assessment and the Illusion of Safety," 13-14.

[15] Agenda 21 is non-binding. Chapter 19 (The Environmentally Sound Management of Toxic Chemicals) includes provisions for a standardized international
system of chemical classification.

CHAPTER 7

EMERGING TRADE AGREEMENTS AND THEIR IMPACT ON AGRICULTURE

Brenda Leith

Brenda Leith is an Assistant Professor of Economics and Environmental and Resource Studies at Trent University. Her research is primarily in the area of renewable resource policy with an emphasis on the efficiency and equity implications of policy reform. Leith has written on distribution issues as they relate to fishery policies, waste management reform and agriculture under free trade.

> Tragically, as long as the political system insists on a zero price for resources that have real value, the pollution crisis will become worse.
> Michael Rothschild, *Bionomics* (1990)

Trade, Environment and Efficiency

To a worrisome degree, free trade has become the blunt instrument with which Canada is to be bludgeoned into accepting fiscal responsibility, institutional reform and technological change. Examinations of the nature of these reforms or the requirements for achieving technological change are noticeably absent as insight gives way to exhortation. Few people doubt that Canada requires massive institutional reforms. Using trade as the instrument of this change, however, has serious implications for the environmental, economic and social integrity of the country.

Canada has, along with most countries in the developed world, struggled for decades to achieve an adequate social policy to ensure the protection of common property and publicly owned natural resources. At the core of this struggle is the difficulty, in the context of a market economy, of establishing the social value of resources that do not have market prices. Among the values that are not captured in privately efficient markets are social and cultural values of equity, intergenerational justice, resource security and environmental protection. Moreover, market economies can deliver socially efficient outcomes only while the markets themselves are efficient. While many argue that the market economy, imperfect as it may be, is the best alternative, many social and economic advances in industrial societies have arisen from policies that explicitly bypass market outcomes. Canada enjoys the social and economic benefits of guaranteed health care and public education. While current estimates suggest that Canada achieves universal health care at a cost about 40 per cent less than health care costs in the United States, publicly funded medical care came into being because Canadians accept the principle that equity and social justice dictate universal access to health care. The current crisis in health care in the United States is a timely and instructive demonstration of the effect of reliance on market forces to achieve non-market outcomes. The link between investment in non-market capital and the returns in the form of lower production costs cannot be captured in a model which focuses only on increasing current output. Indeed, failure to incorporate the cost of non-market resources must be detrimental to long-term production costs. In the Atlantic cod fishery, where policy linked social payments to participation in the fishery, declines in the fish stocks forced people onto social assistance where they could qualify only through active participation in fishing. Any positive trade-offs between current production and preservation of the fish stocks have long since been exhausted and Canadians are now feeling the effects of a policy that effectively placed a zero value on this resource capital. Participation in the North American Free Trade Agreement (NAFTA) brings into question not only the advisability of export driven economic policies but also the ability of Canadians to value and invest in non-market resources.

Trade Theory and Social Welfare

In the orthodox theory of competition, free trade results, inevitably, in increased living standards and increased productivity and efficiency through comparative advantage and gains from trade. While this model is convenient for capturing the theoretical implication of trade, it is seriously inadequate as an analytic representation of the practical outcomes of trade. The sanguine expectation of mutual gains from trade can be justified only under a set of assumptions that have little relation to the economy as it exists in practice.

Assumption 1: In theory, trade gains come from access to larger markets, economies of scale and increased efficiency. High value-added industries will displace low wage inefficient industries in countries with relatively high labour costs.

Assumption 2: Models that look exclusively at trade flows ignore significant detrimental effects: Changes in stocks, both capital and resource will be neglected unless these stocks have a market price.

Assumption 3: The standard theory assumes that markets are perfectly competitive. This eliminates a role for government in creating comparative advantage. Social efficiency always coincides with private efficiency.

Assumption 4: Assuming perfect competition, efficiency gains are translated into welfare gains, for both trading partners, as the gains from increased efficiency are redistributed throughout the economy, leading to an increasing demand for goods from trading partners.

These assumptions are crucial to the argument that trade agreements are, by definition, socially beneficial. These results are not, of course, unknown to advocates of NAFTA and it is significant that the current rhetoric of free trade emphasizes not potential gains, but the inevitability of globalization. Canadians have been told endlessly that they must be more efficient and more productive or face the prospect of degenerating into Third World economic status. Those who conjure the grim spectre of globalization and offer it free trade as the cure ignore the trade-offs between gains from institutional reform and the potential for long-term losses of Canadian resources under NAFTA. Even under the most dire consequences of globalization, Canada holds an insuperable comparative advantage while it maintains the ability to protect resources, an advantage that will only become more valuable in the future.

Trade Theory Reconsidered

In reality, both the Canada-US Free Trade Agreement (FTA) and NAFTA are only superficially about trade.[1]

It is apparent that lowering trade barriers is not the primary objective of NAFTA. If the agreement is, in fact, a vehicle for institutional reform, legitimate questions arise about the efficacy of NAFTA as a device of policy reform. While the economic discourse of free trade is remarkably silent on the subject, trade theory itself suggests several consequences that may be crucial to understanding the institutional consequences of NAFTA.

Implication 1: The standard theory of comparative advantage assumes full employment; those who lose their jobs because of a comparative disadvantage in labour costs secure jobs in expanding export industries.

Trade data on FTA show that exports have risen while total manufacturing has fallen. Imports serve a larger share of the domestic market. Based on comparative advantage, there is little that Canadian agriculture would produce in a trade agreement between Mexico and the US. Ultimately, Canada faces a geographical disadvantage that, if efficiency is the sole criterion, suggests that Canada should import most of its agricultural commodities. Issues of food security and cultural integrity, while not easily embraced in trade theory, are nevertheless vital components in evaluating the consequences of NAFTA.

Implication 2: Economic models incorporating the standard theory to analyze impacts of free trade look exclusively at changes in trade flows.

While the objective of NAFTA is not to increase trade by lowering tariff barriers, the cost of the agreement will still include the cost of equating welfare with exports. National treatment, whereby all producers would enjoy equal access to all public programmes, implies the inability to pursue nationalist social policy in any sector that engages in trade. Such policies as preserving resource stocks for future generations or protecting the environment to a degree that differs significantly from the United States may become untenable under NAFTA.

Implication 3: Under imperfect competition, industrial strategies, tariff barriers and subsidies are viable, indeed, optimal government activities.[2]

There is abundant evidence that, in the absence of perfect competition, government intervention is justified and may, indeed, be necessary. The European Community and Japan provide compelling evidence of the social and economic value of industrial strategies. Moreover, Canadians should not overlook the Canadian-US Auto Pact in assessing the potential role for government in creating comparative advantage. Policy intervention exists in all economies and the grim prognosticators of globalization who urge Canadians to become more productive, plan consensually, think strategically, fail to acknowledge that all these activities are most successful within the context of cooperative agreements that are outside the scope of free market economics. The real danger in embracing the dictates of unrestricted trade may lie in abandoning social control in favour of an entirely ephemeral level playing field which may, in fact, be nothing more than an unimpeded slippery slope.

Implication 4: Comparative advantage, in a model of perfect competition, implies a relative abundance of some resource. Gains from trade emerge as resources are reallocated in response to scarcity. In reality, comparative advantage may be a policy-induced phenomenon that will not respond to resource reallocation.

For Canada, both the United States and Mexico may foster comparative advantage with labour laws, less redistribution of wealth to labour or indifferent environmental compliance. The important link between increasing standards of living and increasing markets for export derives from the increasing purchasing power of those who hold the relatively abundant resources. According to trade theory, jobs lost today in Canada are regained by increased employment in exporting industries.

This link between efficiency and increased welfare assumes that there are adequate redistribution mechanisms in place and that the economic implications of scarcity will adjust relative prices so that mutual gains emerge. Policy-induced comparative advantage implies the annexation of gains by one of the trading partners.

Agriculture, Economics and Equity

The ramifications of globalization for agriculture are of particular importance in Canada both because institutional reform will have a significant impact on the agriculture sector and because, as an exporter, Canadian agriculture is particularly vulnerable to the institutional practices of other countries.

Governments have traditionally protected agriculture from the market effects of uncertainty. The objectives of agriculture policy are generally to stabilize farming incomes, guarantee an adequate return to agriculture, and to provide a secure supply of essential commodities to society. There is a growing conviction that policy has failed abysmally in meeting any of these objectives. Indeed, there is a widely held perception that government intervention in agriculture is misplaced. Moreover, many arguments used to justify laissez-faire agriculture are critical in the wider NAFTA debate because the perceived needs in agriculture coincide with the changes predicted under the North American Free Trade Agreement.

Policy Reform

Current direct support programmes cost Canadians $7.5 billion per year while 23 per cent of Canada's 280,000 farms face financial crisis.

That Canada can no longer afford to support inefficient family farms is virtually a creed among those who cite institutional incentives for maintaining inefficient farming operations. Agriculture is particularly vulnerable to the prescription of NAFTA as the vehicle of institutional change because the institutional reforms may well be dictated by the parameters of the national treatment doctrine. While specialization and economies of scale are consistent with institutional practices in US agriculture, it is not clear that this policy direction is either efficient or socially desirable.

Advocates of agriculture reform cite endless chilling statistics suggesting that Canadian agriculture policies have failed. Statistics that suggest policy failure are equally attractive to proponents of free trade who view NAFTA as a means to reform public spending. However, evidence that the current crisis in Canadian agriculture is generated by an inefficient production technology or that changing this technology will eliminate the need for public intervention is noticeably absent. In the US, where large-scale industrial agriculture predominates, farm debt grew from $53 billion to $216 billion between 1970 and 1983. In 1982, interest payments on agricultural debt accounted for 98.9 per cent of farm incomes. It is naive and dangerous to ascribe problems in agriculture solely to ineffective agricultural policies. Indeed, Canadian interest rate policies and surplus production among agricultural exporters have combined, in the last decade, to put enormous pressure on Canadian farmers. These pressures cannot be reduced by abandoning farmers to the vicissitudes of international intervention in commodity markets. Indeed, a compelling argument can be made for increasing support to farms that face the devastating consequences of international trade wars in commodities.

Policy Reform under NAFTA

In 1990, it cost the Canadian taxpayer $115,000 for every job saved in the agriculture sector. This compares to $13,000 - $20,000 in the US.

This type of comparison is critical in appreciating the profound effect the national treatment may have on Canada. In a political system that denounces reliance on a social safety net, it should not be surprising that US agricultural policy tends to produce indirect support programmes. It is misleading and potentially dangerous to assume that levels of direct aid are an adequate or even relevant measure of intervention in the US. Within the agriculture sector, estimates for both Canada and the United States suggest that between 20 and 50 per cent of farm incomes are derived from the public. While political and social conventions dictate how public support is delivered, national treatment implies an equivalence that may threaten Canadian institutions in particular. There is abundant evidence that agriculture in the US absorbs a vast amount of public funding. The mechanism for delivering this funding is, however, often obscure, making negotiations on relative levels of agricultural support difficult and uncertain. The inability to compare effective rather than apparent policy may be the biggest threat to Canada's ability to negotiate an equitable partnership in a continental market.

Policy Reform and Consumer Prices

There is a widespread belief that all Canadians would benefit from the removal of import restrictions, lowering of commodity prices and the introduction of efficiency into farming. As the cost of agricultural support programmes has risen, advocates of policy reform emphasize the link between unwanted agricultural production, increased costs of farming and increased consumer costs. The implication is clear: price supports have lead to overproduction, escalation in costs and losses to consumers. If price supports are reduced, the result will be less overproduction, lower costs and lower consumer prices.

Moreover, the assumption that falling commodity prices at the farm level would benefit consumers has little empirical support. The evidence of the 1980s, when producer prices fell dramatically as a result of international commodity price wars, does not support the notion that falling prices are passed along to consumers. In fact, the main beneficiaries of abolishing farm support systems may be multinational commodity processors. In the US, the value received at the farm level declined by 6 per cent between 1980 and 1987. Farmers received approximately 25 per cent of the $380 billion spent on food.

The fundamental hypothesis of the theory of gains from trade is that increases in efficiency are translated into lower prices which benefit consumers. The market power of multinational corporations in agriculture suggests that decreasing trade barriers may not lead to decreasing prices and may, indeed, encourage increased concentration of power among a few international commodity processors.

The threats of globalization are advanced by many trade advocates to suggest the inevitability of NAFTA and other trade agreements. Implicit in the link between trade agreements and competitiveness is that the institutional and industrial changes that occur will be socially beneficial. However, the cost of such a passive approach to policy may be especially onerous in agriculture where the assumption that market price signals scarcity is particularly inappropriate. Without the medium of competitive prices, trade agreements may fail to produce expected efficiency gains while imposing all the costs associated with the effects of export-driven agricultural policy. Measuring standards of living solely in terms of increased trade flows ignores quality of life and protection of social, cultural and physical environments in determining social welfare. The implicit assumption that increased export production is equivalent to increased social welfare obscures the real structural adjustments that Canada must face in a global economy. Canada's ability to cope with technological change depends on its ability to improve education and training and actively address the long-term consequences of unemployment. The social and economic consequences of unemployment will not be improved by free trade unless Canada adopts an aggressive approach to training, education and technology.

Efficiency and Economies of Scale

Proposals for policy reform in agriculture are strongly grounded in the assumption that agricultural production is distinguished by economies of scale. When production is characterized by scale economies, costs decrease as the size of the production unit expands. Proponents of policy reform suggest that in a misguided attempt to protect the family farm, Canadian agricultural policies undermine the market forces that would expand production. They conclude that Canada can no longer afford to support inefficient family farming operations. Economic theory does predict that some of Canada's agriculture policies provide a disincentive to adopt new technology. However, this is not, itself, proof of economies of scale. For

Canadian farmers, anticipating a continental market for agricultural products under NAFTA, unexamined acceptance of the assertion that Canada subsidizes inefficient farming operations will have a significant impact in future negotiations. If, indeed, agriculture is characterized by economies of scale, reliance on a trade model of perfect competition will, almost certainly, distort both the incentives for trade protection and the benefits of trade liberalization.

Assumption 1: Competitive output markets provide market prices that reflect scarcity and indicate efficient production cost.

Specialization leads to increased efficiency, inevitably, from the economies of scale that characterize farming. As a consequence of the existence of economies of scale, productivity gains will be evident in any move towards large scale monoculture.

Assumption 2: Competitive input markets signal the efficient production technology.

Productivity in the agriculture sector most often refers to labour productivity. If all input prices are competitive then all inputs are used efficiently and there is no trade-off between labour productivity and efficient input use.

Assumption 3: Comparative advantage determines the output of the agriculture sector in a free trade context.

Free trade encourages specialization in export industries, ignoring social, cultural and environmental costs and benefits in favour of private efficiency considerations of exporters. Private efficiency is equivalent to social welfare to the degree that prices are competitive and include all the costs of production.

Implications

While agriculture is one sector where significant trade barriers exist, it is difficult to predict the effects of NAFTA because trade theory under increasing returns to scale and imperfect competition produces contradictory implications under competing assumptions. At best, it is possible to examine some of the distortions that characterize agriculture in the United States and Canada.

Implication 1: Small farming operations rely heavily on labour to produce output. However, industrial agriculture, in the US, has a politically generated comparative advantage, which does not reflect true economic efficiency.

> Price supports, energy and equipment loans, direct payments, export controls–marketing agreement and tax write offs–all have been designed to work chiefly to the benefit of the largest, usually corporate, farmers and have done so for 40 years.[3]

In the US, 40 per cent of the $9.3 billion dollars spent in 1990 on supporting grain, rice and cotton growers was received by 5 per cent of the farms. Similarly, 10 per cent of the wheat farms received 43 per cent of government payments in 1993.[4] In this context, trade liberalization may not reduce the size of Canadian agriculture subsidies but merely transfer them away from individual farmers towards corporate agriculture.

Implication 2: Productivity, narrowly defined to mean labour productivity, obscures the trade-offs among ecological productivity, resource conservation, energy efficiency and labour productivity. When energy and technology use are subsidized, using labour productivity as a measure of total productivity leads to inefficient reallocations of inputs away from labour to be measured as productivity gains. A true measure of productivity requires that all inputs be used efficiently and this measure of social efficiency includes the environmental and biological costs of monoculture production: land erosion, overmechanization, soil exhaustion, and excessive reliance on pesticides. Social values such as cultural preservation, food security and land preservation are all components of the social cost of agriculture.

Moreover, US agriculture policy not only provides incentives to specialize but, in fact, penalizes farmers who would prefer to rotate crops in the interest of soil conservation. Acreage, taken out of subsidized crops for one year, would be ineligible for federal subsidies for the next five years. With competitiveness as the sole criterion of welfare gain, Canadian farmers may be forced to pursue specialization to a degree that is inconsistent with long term ecological considerations.

Implication 3: Profit maximization when prices do not reflect the social and environmental costs of production leads to unsustainable land use and social welfare losses. Essentially, a policy that encourages current production, at the expense of future environmental damage, places a zero value not only on future resource stocks but on the future of farming itself.

The hallmark of virtually every environmental issue facing Canada is the damage that results when markets fail to internalize the social costs of environmental degradation. The reversion to a social policy that ignores environmental effects of intensive agriculture in favour of exports may jeopardize the long-term viability of agriculture.

Stretched to the limit using specialized equipment to produce single crops for special markets; heavily indebted; dependent on a narrow range of particular inputs, especially energy and money; and deeply invested in sophisticated technology geared only to do one thing, produce more of the same ... these farms are economically brittle. When things go wrong they go very wrong indeed.[5]

Moreover, once in debt, farming cannot sustain even short-term losses, much less long-term declines due to soil exhaustion and chemical saturation. The technology that is generating current high levels in agricultural productivity brings with it the prospect of long-term damage while the debt that finances this technology limits the options of farmers to ameliorate this damage.

Soil erosion, groundwater pollution and loss of habitats due to pesticide use have all entered the arena of environmental concern. That these environmental concerns should be integrated into trade issues has become apparent to most environmental advocates. However, claims that NAFTA is a green trade agreement overlook the interdependent nature of environmental issues. That environmental problems can be adequately addressed through ad hoc adjustment to a system that is fundamentally unsustainable is, at best, wishful thinking and may, in the long run, encourage a dangerously complacent attitude towards the future.

There are indications that policy-makers currently view environmental protection as inconsistent with competitiveness, an attitude which is at odds with the evidence that there is an essential interdependence between environmental and economic outcomes. Environmental and economic objectives may be complementary, even in the short run. Take, for example, the Canadian brewing industry, which currently enjoys barriers against interprovincial trade. This trade advantage is unlikely to survive continental trade under NAFTA where the US industry is highly concentrated. However, a disseminated brewing industry would be economically efficient, even under NAFTA, if a national reuse law were adopted. There is ample evidence that bottle return laws are effective in promoting conservation and reducing waste, both environmental objectives which must, eventually, be translated into reduced production costs.

Implication 4: Implicit in the decision to defer agriculture negotiations until 1996 is the hope that General Agreement on Tariffs and Trade (GATT) will resolve many of the conflicts that must arise in reaching an agriculture agreement under NAFTA. This belief, while convenient, ignores the reality that NAFTA is not, in fact, a trade liberalization scheme such as GATT but an alternative which may weaken the prospects for GATT advances. The emergence of regional interests leaves little scope for international agreements such as GATT.

Agriculture is the object of social and economic policy throughout the developed world and Canadian agriculture, as a major exporter, is already familiar with the grim consequences of global trade. In the agriculture sector, surplus production resulting from subsidy programmes is a problem only because commodities are being produced at prices that make sales on world markets impossible without an export subsidy. The inability of Canadian agriculture to compete on international markets may be more an indication of the relative insufficiency of export subsidies than of the relative inefficiency of Canadian farming. Increased efficiency through specialization can do little to help Canadian agriculture face enormous export subsidies on world markets. Moreover, apparent economies of scale may be a particularly misleading measure of efficiency when large scale agriculture is systematically subsidized. National treatment under NAFTA may limit Canada's ability to use direct programmes to protect domestic agriculture from the distortions of industrial agriculture without providing the expected efficiency benefits.

The Limits to Efficiency

The widespread and largely unexamined belief that market outcomes are necessarily efficient and therefore desirable rests on a foundation of perfect competition that has little practical relevance in assessing the impact of NAFTA. Agriculture, in particular, may suffer unexpected consequences under NAFTA. Moreover, a perilous willingness to adopt competitiveness as the gauge of social welfare ignores cultural, environmental and social effects that seem likely to be critical in evaluating the effects of the agreement. The existence of a continental market implies the acceptance of continent-wide social and environmental standards. The prospect of acquiescing to the introduction of the environmental degradation that is endemic to industrial agriculture reveals the inherent danger in blind pursuit of export efficiency.

The evidence that NAFTA can deliver economic prosperity and beneficial institutional change relies on assumptions about industry and market structure that are clearly insupportable for agriculture. That no agreement emerged from the original NAFTA negotiations is an indication of the difficulty of predicting the effects of trade liberalization. Expectations and, thus, outcomes in future agriculture negotiations may depend, critically, on perceptions of industry distortion. Superficial comparisons tend to suggest that Canada exhibits relatively high levels of agricultural support and these assumptions must be carefully examined if Canada is to avoid environmental degradation and economic dependence.

While the theoretical benefits of efficiency and gains from trade may be demonstrable, the practical prospects for achieving those ends under NAFTA are far from certain. Canadians have much to lose under NAFTA and only uncertain prospects of gain. Recognizing that institutional reform is imperative, Canadians should insist on explicit and active participation in a collaborative effort to formulate policies that protect social and cultural values while delivering needed economic reform.

Coda

When this chapter was presented, both GATT and NAFTA were being negotiated and the economic policy implications examined were substantially driven by cultural and political contexts. Since the adoption of both the Uruguay Round of GATT and NAFTA, changes in trade relations between Canada and the United States provide the opportunity for a critical evaluation of the policy implications of this chapter. Regrettably, there is a disquieting congruity between policy failures predicted in this paper and subsequent developments in trade relations among the trading partners. Significantly, cultural bias in the definition of subsidies is emerging as a crucial component in setting reform agendas and defining the direction of the framework for dispute resolution. Moreoever, agricultural policy looms as a particularly contentious issue in this context. Without some alteration in approach, Canada may find itself embracing agriculture reforms which are a detriment to both agriculture and the environment.

Trade disputes over agricultural commodities have accelerated since the Uruguay Round of GATT concluded. At the centre of these disputes is the largely semantic dichotomy in agricultural support policy. Grain farmers in the US Midwest have protested imports of Canadian wheat, citing the transportation subsidy received by Canadian farmers, disregarding the disguised transportation subsidy implicit in US energy policies. Under the current GATT, Canadian import quotas on diary products from the US become illegal and Canada is contemplating tariffs as high as 326 per cent[6] as a replacement which is unlikely to be sustainable in the face of wide-scale protest by US trade groups. Economists have long emphasized that public policy which distorts *free market* prices will be expensive and inefficient. Unfortunately, the distortions in US policy go largely unexamined and the efficiency of US agriculture is often implicit in comparisons made throughout the economic literature: "It costs Canadians $115,000 per job saved in agriculture in 1990 compared to $13,000-$20,000 in the United States."[7] However, a startling alteration to this icon of efficient agriculture emerges from a shift in perspective on the exact definition of agriculture subsidies. The Natural Resources Defence Council calculated the subsidies to irrigated agriculture in the Westlands Water District, one of the continent's richest agricultural producers, and found that the Westlands Water District paid about $10-$12 per acre-foot, an amount which is less than 10 per cent of the true cost of delivering water to the district. The resulting subsidy was estimated to be $217 per irrigated acre or $500,000 per year[8] for the average-sized farm. It would, indeed, be ironic if pressure on Western Canada to sell water, arising out of the enormous excess demand for water generated by this water subsidy, led to destruction of socially efficient segments of Canadian agriculture which cannot afford to compete with such subsidized production coming from the US.

Advocates of NAFTA identify domestic policy reform as a necessary implication and a vital social contribution of the agreement. Persistent inattention to the impact of disguised and indirect subsidies in United States agriculture may, indeed, emerge as the most serious threat to sustainable agriculture in Canada.

Endnotes

[1] Andrew Jackson, "NAFTA and the Myth of 'Win-Win,'" *Policy Options* 13(10) (1993), 24-28.

[2] Gene M. Grossman, *Imperfect Competition and International Trade* (Cambridge, MA: MIT Press, 1992).

[3] Herman E. Daly and John B. Cobb, Jr., *For the Common Good: Redirecting the Economy Toward Community, the Environment and a Sustainble Future* (Boston: Beacon Press, 1989), 271.

[4] P. Luciani, *Economic Myths-Making Sense of Canadian Policy Issues* (New York: Addison Wesley, 1993), 20-23.

[5] National Research Council, *Alternative Agriculture* (Washington, D.C.: National Academy Press, 1989), 10.

[6] "U.S. Goes Ahead With Wheat Probe," *The Globe and Mail*, January 19, 1994.

[7] OECD estimates as reported in *The Financial Post*, April 9, 1990.

[8] The estimates are taken from K. Frederick, "Water Resource Management and the Environment: The Role of Economic Incentives," in *Renewable Natural Resources: Economic Incentives for Improved Management* (Paris: OECD, 1989).

CHAPTER 8

THE ETHICS OF BEING A PIONEER: ENVIRONMENTAL ACCOUNTING RULES

David W. Conklin
T. Ross Archibald

David Conklin is an Adjunct Professor in the Faculty of Social Sciences, and a Research Fellow in the National Centre for Management Research and Development at The University of Western Ontario. He teaches in the Economics and Political Science departments, and he is currently participating in the development and teaching of a new environment of business course in the Western Business School. He received a B.A. from the University of Toronto and a Ph.D. from the Massachusetts Institute of Technology. He has worked in both the public and private sectors and has been the research director of several government task forces. The focus of his research is the relationship between business and government, and he serves as a consultant in the development of government legislation and regulations. His publications include a book written with Richard Hodgson and Eileen Watson entitled *Sustainable Development: A Manager's Handbook.*

T. Ross Archibald, Ph.D., F.C.A., is a Professor at the Western Business School of The University of Western Ontario. He has been actively teaching and researching topics in the financial reporting field such as pension, environmental and crisis accounting for over 25 years. He founded and directed the School's executive education course, Management for Accounting and Financial Executives, and has taught on the Western Executive Program since 1976. Archibald has provided consulting services to private and public sector organizations, taught specialized courses on four continents, given pension and problem solving advice, and acted as an expert witness.

Introduction

New international agreements are reducing trade barriers, with the expectation that residents of the signatory countries will, on average, be better off as a result. However, this process can expose certain corporations to unfair competition if they are compelled by law to perform cost-enhancing activities that their foreign competitors are able to avoid. The lack of international harmonization in environmental laws and their enforcement became a major issue of contention in the North American Free Trade Agreement (NAFTA) negotiations. Significant differences in environmental legislation and enforcement have developed between Canada and the United States, on the one hand, and Mexico on the other. This chapter examines a related subject. Of importance are not just the legal obligations for a corporation to incur the costs involved in compliance with new environmental laws. Also of importance are the decisions concerning financial reporting measurement and disclosure of these newly-recognized obligations. Governments have focused solely on the establishment and enforcement of new environmental laws and have not yet turned their attention to the question of whether corporations must provide information in their public records concerning the future costs that will have to be incurred. In view of the lack of international agreements in this regard, the establishment of new environmental accounting rules has raised many ethical issues.

At this point in time, the Canadian accounting profession has decided to be a pioneer in environmental accounting, establishing new and stringent requirements for Canadian corporations. Significant differences in reporting requirements among countries have now created an uneven playing field, placing certain corporations at a competitive disadvantage internationally. Since Canada is most closely linked to the United States with regard to trade and investment flows, this chapter focuses on differences within North America in regard to requirements for environmental accounting.

This situation raises a number of ethical questions that are important in their own right, and that also illustrate basic ethical issues that will likely arise elsewhere in the rapidly changing area of environmental regulation:

(1) Should corporations be compelled to reveal their future environmental obligations publicly in their financial statements and other corporate reports? Obviously, environmental costs incurred in the current year have to be recorded in the current year. Of concern here are obligations that will have to be fulfilled sometime in the future. Does the corporation bear responsibility for conveying this information to the public? Since future events cannot be predicted with certainty, how can the corporation quantify various estimates concerning future outcomes in ways that will best convey this information?

Involved in this set of questions is the degree to which current shareholders should be responsible for the financial burden of future environmental obligations. The complete reporting through comprehensive disclosure of these costs and liabilities will tend to reduce current stock prices, while a decision to delay reporting until costs are actually incurred could mask the economic reality and tend to shift the burden to future shareholders. The complete reporting of these may also lead the corporation to attempt to shift its environmental burden to customers through higher prices, to employees through lower wages, or to suppliers through lower prices for the corporation's purchases. The ability of a corporation to shift costs in this way will depend upon the structure of the market in which it operates. For Canadian exporters of primary products, there may be very little possibility for such cost shifting. At issue here then, is who should bear the burden for complying with new environmental legislation?

(2) If corporations should reveal their future environmental obligations in their financial statements, who should set the rules for quantifying these obligations and for determining appropriate presentation? In Canada, the accounting profession and certain corporate executives have chosen to be pioneers. Yet, these individuals will not personally bear the full cost of their decisions. Furthermore, these individuals do not fit readily into the traditional profile of responsible, democratic government. Should the accounting profession have the power to impose its decisions on corporations? Should Canada wait until the United States agrees to a common set of standards?

(3) Are there any basic principles that can serve as a guide for decision-makers? For example, should accounting rules be based upon conservative estimates of future costs in order to ensure that future shareholders will not be surprised by costs that exceed estimates? Alternatively, should corporations, their technical advisors, and their accountants seek to develop "best estimates" that represent their informed professional opinion concerning the most likely outcome of future events? Is it adequate to include future costs solely as a note appended to the financial statements, or should the future estimated costs be entered in the main body of the accounts, directly impacting current expenses, assets, and liabilities? Should governments require that corporations establish segregated funds in cash to cover these future financial obligations? Should governments declare a particular discount rate to be used in estimating the present discounted value of future obligations? Should governments develop enforcement mechanisms?

The Ethics of Accounting Standards-Setting

There is a legitimate question as to what group in society ought to be setting accounting standards, first for a country and secondly, but no less importantly, for the world. No doubt this is an age-old question that has been considered by philosophers in the past and more recently those individuals who are more directly concerned with the ethical problems that are facing society at the end of the twentieth century. The answer to this question would seem to be closely related to the reality that special privileges in society are granted to those who not only purport to have, but who in fact do have, special expertise.

There are a host of professions in our society which, because they have studied to attain special insights and proficiency in their areas of expertise, are, within constraints, given society's permission to exercise their professional judgement. This is perhaps clearest in the medical profession where some of the basic ethical principles date back to Hippocrates. The main point with professionals is that only they have enough training and skill to render aid and specialized services to other members of the society. Others are not sufficiently educated or trained to recognize their needs for the services, nor do they possess the skills that must be rendered to enhance their own self-interest. Perhaps this association can be compared to the principal-agent relationship where the agent is duty bound to use superior skills and information to act in the best interest of the principal.

This reasoning would appear to hold as we move to consider the setting of accounting standards. Accounting is a highly complex, some would argue arcane, art. A reasonable understanding of accounting requires a considerable amount of study, practice and experience. Thus, it can be argued that the accounting profession ought to be setting accounting standards. It is much more difficult to operationalize this general principle when appointing the appropriate accounting-specialized and non-accounting sophisticated individuals to set standards. It is also necessary to consider the total needs of society, perhaps best thought of in a more narrow focus as the needs of the users and the preparers of accounting information.

The positive argument for permitting standards to be set by professionals is often countered with the assertion that government can do it better and perhaps with a more even hand. Unfortunately, the government prescription does not appear to hold empirically. We have numerous examples in the twentieth century of situations where governments have exerted their control over accounting standards and poor economic outcomes have resulted. Recent occurrences with tragic financial consequences for many non-professionals, particularly depositors, were the bank failures in Western Canada in the mid-1980s.[1] At least in part because the government legislated the rules for accounting and financial reporting long ago and with different goals and criteria, certain required accounting methods were no longer appropriate in the evolving economic circumstances of the late 1970s and early 1980s. However, the legislated accounting methods were so deeply entrenched that the financial statements required by law bore very little relation to the underlying economic reality of the banks. The publication of financial statements which obscured the true state of affairs was at least partially responsible for the sudden bank collapse and the resulting financial disaster for depositors and other investors. Numerous examples of similar unfortunate economic outcomes could also be found.

Consequently, there appears to be considerable economic support for having accounting standards set, in large part, by the professionals who are appropriately trained to the task and who deal with the problems on a day-to-day basis.

Standard-Setting in Canada

The Canadian Institute of Chartered Accountants (CICA) has been legally empowered to set accounting standards in Canada by the various federal and provincial Companies Acts with the assent of such regulatory bodies as the Ontario Securities Commission (OSC), the Commission des Valeurs Mobilières du Québec (CVMQ), and other provincial securities commissions. On an extra-territorial basis, the Securities and Exchange Commission (SEC) of the United States recognizes the CICA as well. The accounting standards are issued in the form of the CICA *Handbook* and the general rule is that if an accounting standard appears in the *Handbook* it becomes the legally accepted standard for accounting in Canada. The most recent form of the body that sets standards came into being on October 1, 1991 as the Accounting Standards Board (ASB) of the CICA. The CICA is a national body of 55,000 chartered accountants, all of whom have been trained at one point in their lives as auditors or public accountants and receive their charter by writing and passing a uniform final examination which is designed to test their professional knowledge and preparedness to perform audits in all Canadian jurisdictions.

The Accounting Standards Board is a private sector organization composed of 15 individuals, 13 of whom are unpaid part-time volunteer members. The CICA appoints eight of these members and each of the following organizations is entitled to appoint one volunteer voting member:

- the Financial Executives Institute of Canada (FEIC), an association of 1,200 members comprised primarily of financial officers in large Canadian companies who, in that sense, represent the *preparers* of financial statements;

- the Society of Management Accountants of Canada (SMA), an alternative accounting body with 25,000 members concentrating on internal or management accounting;

- the Canadian Council of Financial Analysts (CCFA), comprised of 2,300 individuals who work primarily in financial analysis and are considered to represent the *users* of financial statements;

- the Certified General Accountants of Canada (CGA), a 22,000 member accounting body concerned with financial and management accounting with some members granted audit privileges in some provinces;

- the Canadian Academic Accounting Association (CAAA), a body of 650 individuals comprised primarily of academics and other education-oriented individuals who strongly represent accounting education and research concerns.

The additional two board members are senior CICA staff who serve as non-voting members. Accounting standards must be approved by at least 9 of the 13 voting members. All meeting and voting is conducted on a confidential basis and no published dissents are permitted.

The goal behind the composition of the ASB is to represent the constituent parties which include public accountants, preparers and users and also to respect linguistic (French and English) as well as regional differences in Canada. One stated goal of the organization of the ASB was to create a body for the purpose of approving matters of principle and policy. The ASB was also given the power and resources to delegate the development of new standards to volunteer task forces and/or professional staff.

Because the ASB members are volunteers, the CICA was careful to reflect on previous volunteer systems where the time demanded of members easily fell into the 300-500 hours a year range. In order to have an effective group, it was believed vital to reduce this time pressure and provide more research support. Thus, to facilitate this process, more individuals were hired as support staff for accounting studies and standards, and furthermore, other individuals with particular interest and expertise were sought out and asked to serve as volunteers on study groups that would conduct the necessary research and publish findings in research reports. For instance, the study group on the environmental audit was drawn from the business community, public accounting and academe. Similar patterns have been followed by other research study groups with an informed interest in a particular accounting issue.

Because certain accounting problems surface quickly, they cannot wait for the lengthy due process of the ASB. For instance, the formal process to create the new accounting standards for pensions, *Handbook* section 3460, took over five years to complete. The Emerging Issues Committee (EIC) was therefore created to provide timely guidance. The 14 members, representing users, preparers, public accounting, and regulators, meet every six weeks to respond to agenda items in a timely fashion.

General consulting on broader societal issues is provided to the ASB by the Accounting Advisory Board (AAB). The members, who meet two times a year, are drawn from the legal profession, the financial community and other socially responsible organizations. The support cost of the ASB is largely borne by the CICA and augmented by a modest contribution from the Financial Executives Institute of Canada. The CICA Board of Governors approves the ASB budget. Because the new system has been in place for less than two years, it is hardly appropriate to draw conclusions about the outcomes to date.

Standard-Setting in the United States

Since 1973, the Financial Accounting Standards Board (FASB) has operated in the United States as the designated organization for the establishment of standards in financial accounting and reporting. The FASB was empowered by the official recognition of the SEC, who gave them legal authority to establish accounting standards in the US. In this sense, the SEC has relied on the private sector in the form of the FASB to set accounting standards. The board is comprised of 7 full-time members who are appointed to serve five-year terms. Potentially, a member may be reappointed for an additional five-year term as well. As a private sector organization, the board is financed by voluntary contributions, largely from business organizations and the public accountancy profession. The board is an avowedly public organization that strictly follows due process and even goes to the length of holding all meetings in public. It is said that the board members are so concerned about maintaining the perception and reality of due process, characterized by the full and public disclosure of their deliberations, that they avoid three-person casual conversations over coffee lest the discussion be considered a board meeting. It follows that votes on accounting standards, which will pass on a four to three vote, are published and, in addition, dissenting opinions are permitted and published.

The Financial Accounting Foundation (FAF) oversees board operations, receiving contributions and passing the FASB budget. More than half of the funds contributed are from industry and the financial community. The Foundation is separate from all other organizations but its trustees are made up of nominees from sponsoring organizations whose members are believed to have special knowledge of financial reporting. These organizations are:

- American Accounting Association
- American Institute of Certified Public Accountants
- Financial Analysts Federation
- Financial Executives Institute
- Government Finance Officers Association
- Institute of Management Accountants
- National Association of State Auditors, Controllers and Treasurers
- Securities Industry Association

There are also three trustees at large, one of whom is selected from the banking industry.

The FASB is also consulted by the Financial Accounting Standards Advisory Council, a group of 27 members who are widely representative of the preparers, auditors, and the users of financial information.

Comparison Between Standard-Setting in Canada and the US

Exhibit A compares the ASB and the FASB on a number of dimensions. The most salient differences would seem to be the number of members, the public disclosure emphasis together with the full-time salaried membership of the FASB. The terms are shorter for the Canadian ASB, but it would appear that the membership constituencies are approximately equal. In terms of governance, the Canadians remain in the private sector and are largely responsible to the public accounting profession represented by the CICA. The FASB is also a private sector organization, but the governing board, the FAF, has a broad constituency base like the actual FASB membership. Both groups have created separate bodies to deal quickly with emerging issues and they also draw on a larger body as a consulting group containing a membership of 27 broadly-based individuals. There can be no question that both organizations are carefully monitored by their respective government regulatory authorities, but in typically Canadian fashion, the legislation authority is provincial; whereas, in the United States (and most other countries), it is federal.

Addressing the Ethics of Canadian and US Standard-Setting

It is difficult to argue that the standard setting in both Canada and the United States is not based on and developed by a broadly based constituency of informed individuals and that the structured groups have been empowered by legislatures elected by the general population. If this arrangement is not ethical, one could ask in what other way accounting standard-setting could possibly be organized to achieve the desired state of effectiveness.

The current situation in Ontario tests this question of standard-setting authority by way of a challenge by the CGAs of Ontario to be granted the power to perform statutory audits in the province. Currently in Ontario, one must be a chartered accountant (CA) to qualify for a public accounting license to perform audits and issue audit reports. A CGA who has not passed the qualifying examination which is set by the CAs is denied the right to participate in what is regarded as a highly profitable segment of the public accounting market. The ethics of this controversy have not been resolved and the decades-old battle continues. However, despite what some regard as a tactical challenge by the CGAs to the existing standard-

Exhibit A
COMPARISON OF FEATURES OF THE CANADIAN ACCOUNTING STANDARDS BOARD
AND THE US FINANCIAL ACCOUNTING STANDARDS BOARD

	Canadian Accounting Standards Board	US Financial Accounting Standards Board
Members	13	7
Votes to Pass Standard	9	4
Deliberations	Confidential	Public
Dissenting Opinions Published	No	Yes
Service	Part-Time	Full-Time
Compensation	Volunteer	Salary
Sector	Private	Private
Funding	CICA	Industry Financial community Public accounting
Term	Three years Two year additional appointment as chair permitted	Five years Five year reappointment pemitted
Constituencies Represented	Public Accounting Government Business (preparers) Financial (users) Academic	Public Accounting Government/regulatory Business (preparers) Financial (users) Academic
Overseeing Group	CICA Board of Governors	Financial Accounting Foundation
Emerging Issues	Emerging Issues Committee	Emerging Issues Task Force
Advisee Group	Standards Advisory Board	Financial Accounting Standards Advisory Council (27 members)
Other Parties	Provincial Security Comm. (OSC, VDMQ) SEC	SEC Congress
Securities Legislation	Provincial	Federal

setting process, the ethical arguments are seldom raised. There appears to be no chorus of voices in Canada condemning the ethical position of the ASB to be the sole Canadian standard setting authority.

Standard-Setting in Mexico

The Accounting Principles Commission (APC) of the Instituto Méxicano de Contadores Públicos (IMCP), is recognised as the primary authority for determining accounting standards in Mexico. The APC issues pronouncements on accounting and reporting standards and updates them whenever necessary. Although the Comisión Nacional de Valores (CNV) has legal authority to establish accounting and reporting standards for companies listed on the Mexican Stock Exchange, much as the case in the United States, it has deferred to the APC for the setting of accounting standards.

Members of the APC represent many different sectors of the economy and many different viewpoints on financial reporting and accounting matters. Voting members include representatives of the largest IMCP firms, representatives of the National Securities Commission, the National Bankers Association, the Mexican Stock Exchange, and the Association of Financial Executives, as well as the Mexican representative of the International Accounting Standards Committee.

Although standards set by the APC are mandatory for large and small companies, CNV has, on occasion, issued specific rules for companies listed in the Mexican Stock Exchange. In general, however, the standards used are quite similar to those set in Canada and the United States. Thus, standard setting in Mexico has also largely been delegated by law to the private sector and is heavily influenced by the public accounting profession.

International Accounting Standards

There are a number of organizations involved in international standard accounting setting activities. The major influencing bodies are:

- International Accounting Standards Committee (IASC)
- Commission of the European Community (EC)
- United Nations Intergovernmental Working Group of Experts on International Standards of Accounting and Reporting (ISAR)
- Organization for Economic Cooperation and Development Working Group on Accounting Standards (OECD Working Group)

The IASC, founded in 1973, is arguably the dominant organization and essentially functions as a private sector assembly. It actually represents private sector interests and organizations. The EC Commission, the OECD Working Group, and ISAR are political bodies created by international agreements and treaties.

In 1973, IASC was founded by agreement between professional accounting organizations in nine countries, including Canada, Mexico, and the United States. Currently, it is comprised of over 100 professional accounting organizations from more than 70 countries.

The main rational behind the IASC is to foster international harmony among nations on their accounting standards. Through 1991, the IASC issued as passed 31 standards and in 1989 issued E32, an exposure draft directly addressing *Comparability of Financial Statements*. Thus, the IASC continues to strive for a measure of international harmony of accounting standards.

Financial Reporting of Environmental Costs and Liabilities in Mexico and the United States–A Comparison

At this point, neither the FASB nor the Institute (IMCP) has a financial reporting or disclosure requirement for future removal and site restoration costs that matches the Canadian standards set out in *Handbook* section 3060.39. All three NAFTA countries have another accounting standard that could come into play and that is their accounting requirements on the reporting of contingencies. Even a corporation arguing that the site restoration 15 years in the future was not a current obligation (a specious argument at best) would nevertheless be obliged to disclose the contingency of this future cost and obligation. However, until these items are disclosed in the US and Mexico, it is highly unlikely that current or future shareholders or, for that matter, the securities markets, will properly adjust to the economic reality of environmental costs and liabilities.

An Illustration: CICA section 3060.39

The recent CICA *Handbook* section on Capital Assets requires, in section 3060.39, "... when reasonably determinable provision should be made for future removal and site restoration costs, net of expected recoveries, in a rational and systematic manner by charges to income." On the strength of this paragraph, willing or unwilling, Canadian standard setters are dragging Canadian financial statement preparers into the world of full disclosure of the economic consequences of activities that will influence the environment. The clear outcome is that a company undertaking a project, say a gold mine with an anticipated 15 year life, must, from year one, begin to account for the cost of the cleanup of that mine, and must, in each year's financial statements, disclose those costs and the attendant growing liabilities.

We will examine the consequences of this relatively innocuous appearing paragraph to consider its important ramifications for Canadian corporations. As the analysis proceeds, it will also be clearly seen that there are substantial ethical questions attached.

To begin with, most informed accountants would contend that the site restoration provisions and their disclosure represent the logical outcome of what is currently good accounting practice. An important accounting principle to bear in mind is that a specific point in time, the legal corporate fiscal year end, is generally referred to as the Balance Sheet date. The financial statements are attested to by the shareholders' auditor to be a fair presentation of economic reality under the existing accounting model and in the circumstances. There can be little question that corporations ought to be compelled to reveal their future environmental liabilities in their financial statements (of which the notes are an integral part) because those future liabilities, though difficult to measure, are real and most certainly will have an impact on current or future investors, primarily shareholders, but often the creditors of the corporation. The theoretical underpinnings of properly accounting for events currently committed and in progress, but occurring in the future, were clearly established in developing the accounting standards for pensions to be paid well into the future.

Who Should Bear the Cost of Environmental Liabilities?

Environmental liabilities are now arising regularly as the result of management decisions. They were in the past as well, but more often than not were ignored. They are clearly the responsibility of the corporation and through their ownership, the shareholders. It would be unethical to induce future shareholders to purchase equities without informing those individuals of the real obligations they are undertaking. Thus a reasonable ethical position would require that a clear and accurate statement of the accounting liability at any point in time be disclosed to financial report readers and in particular to potential investors.

There is a reasonable question as to who is going to bear the cost of a company's responsible management of the environment. In the case of a gold mine, the linkage is relatively simple. If you choose to dig gold bearing ore out of the ground and take the risk of selling it for a profit, you cannot avoid the fact that digging holes in the ground affects the environment. A common way of removing gold from the bearing ore is to use a cyanide process. Cyanide has the unfortunate characteristic of killing things. If you truly want gold from the ground, you have to be willing and able to return the property to, at the very least, a non-toxic state and possibly one that would hopefully look like you had not even been there. In the long run, the market price of gold will have to rise to cover the higher costs involved in this new responsibility for the environment. However, if only Canadian mines are so affected, then gold mining will be less prevalent and less profitable in Canada than in the past.

Commodities pose a special problem because they face severe global price competition. As a result of the new accounting standard in Canada (*Handbook* section 3060.39), those Canadian companies dealing in commodities are now forced to recognize, from the outset, the total full cost of producing the commodity. In the competition with other companies in other countries, conceivably with accounting standards and even environmental laws that do not reflect the economic reality of pollution costs, the competition's lower accounting costs may indicate a lower selling price for that particular commodity in the world market. In a sense, the Canadian method has done little more than measure and disclose the true costs of the operation. However, if the rest of the world either does not know the true costs or chooses not to disclose them, the lower non-inclusive cost may well be the reigning market price, and this would force the Canadian companies to suffer a loss or, at the very least, a lower profit than their activities would normally provide. Obviously, mine openings would shift from Canada to more profitable locations elsewhere.

One might argue that all this trouble has been caused by an overzealous Canadian standards setting authority. Nevertheless, we believe that a cogent ethical position with regards to the cost of insulting the environment is a part of the cost of doing business, and until other countries build such charges into their accounting standards, these countries are being derelict in their financial reporting duties. If Canada chooses to be a pioneer, then Canada has a responsibility to its corporations and their stakeholders to help negotiate uniform accounting standards internationally and, likewise, press for comparable environmental laws.

Accounting in the Context of Risk and Uncertainty

At the present time, considerable scientific uncertainty exists in regard to the linkages between various environmental issues and the state of human health. Scientific uncertainty exists over the regenerative capacity of the natural system and the degree to which a certain amount of pollution is acceptable within the sensible objectives of sustainable development. Scientific uncertainty also exists concerning the technologies that may be used to solve environmental problems. Management must deal with the question of how much corporate funds should be devoted to research and development that attempts to reduce these uncertainties. Accountants must deal with the question of how corporate financial statements can accurately reflect the corporation's position in regard to these risks and costs.

Risk assessment is a normal part of a day's work for accountants. Contrary to popular misconceptions, accounting is inextricably bound to the future. Even the depreciation rate estimated for a cast iron bridge involves a prediction of the future. Estimating the life of a telecommunications satellite is more complex, but the principle is the same: the accountant must undertake a forecast of future events.

The standard approach used by accountants over the decades of experience is based on intense interaction with the relevant professionals. Obviously, a quantity as mundane as the allowance for doubtful accounts is derived from a scientific investigation of probabilities generally developed jointly through the interaction of the credit manager and the accountant, with all judgements rooted in experience and the best current information available prior to determination. The estimates underlying pension provisions are determined for accounting purposes by interaction with pension plan actuaries, just as oil and mineral reserves are assessed through interactions with geologists and mining engineers.

A recent research study of approaches to dealing with risk and uncertainty was commissioned by the CICA and executed by Efrim Boritz with the aid of an eight person advisory group representing management, public accountants and academics.[2] The study addresses the broad spectrum of how to deal with uncertainty in an accounting context. Topics range from the nature of business operations through management's motives and intentions to the measurement and disclosure of relevant events utilizing the financial reporting system.

Accountants continue to develop techniques to deal with uncertainties, primarily by educating themselves in the details of the field, interacting with the relevant professionals, and gathering the relevant information up to the date of the evaluation. There is no reason to believe the same approach will not provide proper accounting and, therefore, vital management information for the vast array of current and future uncertainties.

The Future of Environmental Accounting

Traditional accounting practices based on the historical cost model do not report on the full economic costs of production because they were never designed to include many social costs imposed on the environment. As legislation begins to transform these social costs into real corporate obligations, accounting practices will have to develop new methods for placing financial values on assets and equities that have not been directly assigned monetary values by the market. Estimates of future financial obligations will be particularly difficult if new technology reduces corporate costs. Furthermore, risk and uncertainty play a major role and are difficult to quantify. For example, the future financial obligations connected with an oil spill may not be clear if the legal obligations underlying them are not clear. As suggested in a 1989 *CA Magazine* (Chartered Accountants) article:

> [O]ur accounting rules penalize, rather than encourage, the environmentally responsible corporation. The more a corporation spends on prevention and cleanup, the less its earnings per share. We lack a vehicle for recording "green assets" and monitoring their use, for distinguishing between the costs of renewable versus nonrenewable resources and for providing accounting incentives to improve environmental protection.[3]

> [There is a] need for a new resource-based statement of accounts, something beyond the rather short, bland and nonspecific annual report coverage of health and environmental issues. Investors and other stakeholders need more information on:

> • The actual quantities of resources consumed, rather than "borrowed."

> • A company's perceptions of the major risks to the environment and the risk-management plans developed to deal with them.

- Its level of investment in environmental protection.

- Its response capability, including the degree of reliance on an industry network.

- Potential financial liabilities exceeding insurance coverage.

- The full economic consequences of a major oil spill. And, in the absence of a major spill, a frank discussion of the social benefits realized.[4]

In the past, management and accountants have, in financial statements, provided for explicit contractual obligations that the corporation has incurred. Existing rules currently specify the disclosure of some types of contingent liabilities. Generally, these require that provisions be made in the financial statements when future costs are "likely" (Canada) or "probable" (United States), and when the amount can be reasonably estimated. However, the application of this concept is subject to the individual corporation's interpretation, subject to the review of the corporation's auditor. Generally, no financial statement provisions are required if future costs "cannot be reasonably estimated," but the existence of a contingency must be described in the notes. This, too, is subject to individual interpretation. It appears that new environmental accounting rules will follow this pattern of ambiguity, which will add to the difficulties encountered by the prospective shareholder or lending institution, in evaluating the net worth of the corporation. Anthony Hawkshaw has illustrated the current diversity of accounting practices in the statements of 26 Canadian companies.[5] The individual accountant does not receive much guidance concerning how the kinds of potential future costs that have been described above should be calculated for the purposes of financial statements.

Accountants are beginning to develop new guidelines to deal with these issues. The CICA, for example, has recently addressed some of the problems. Two exposure drafts were issued in 1993. The first, Contingent Gains and Losses, represents a revision of the existing Section 3290, Contingencies. The second deals with Measurement Uncertainty.[6] Both of these exposure drafts address accounting procedures and disclosures applicable to a complete range of crisis events from tax rulings to tornadoes. The CICA has also issued a new research study entitled, "Environmental Costs and Liabilities: Accounting and Financial Reporting Issues."[7] The planned outcome of the study will be a new *Handbook* section created to deal specifically with the recognition, measurement, and disclosure of environmental costs.

The Ethical Dilemma

The Canadian accounting profession has made the decision that Canada shall be the first country to implement new environmental accounting rules. Our objective has been to raise a series of ethical questions related to this decision. We hope that our discussion has enabled the reader to reach his or her own conclusion with regard to these. We hope also that this discussion illustrates issues that will arise in other policy areas related to new concerns about the environment. With each policy area, Canada has the opportunity to be a pioneer. Yet, there will likely be heavy costs imposed upon Canadian corporations, their employees, and their customers as a result of new policy directives. Within our tradition of responsible, democratic government, it is not clear who should be making these pioneering policy changes. Our discussion has indicated reasons for allowing a professional association to take the initiative. Yet here as well, the decision involves ethical issues whose resolution may be subject to different opinions.

Endnotes

1 For a detailed description see John Waterhouse and David Tims, "The GAAP in Bank Regulation," *Canadian Public Policy* xiv (2) (1988), 151-161.
2 J.E. Boritz, "Approaches to Dealing with Risk and Uncertainty," *Canadian Institute of Chartered Accountants*, (Toronto, 1990).
3 D.B. Rubenstein, "Black Oil Red Ink," *CA Magazine* 122 (11) (November 1989), 31.
4 Ibid., 35.
5 A. Hawkshaw, "Status Quo Vadis," *CA Magazine* 124(3) (March 1991), 26.
6 Canadian Institute of Chartered Accountants, "Exposure Draft, Contingent Gains and Losses," (Toronto, 1993a); and, Canadian Institute of Chartered Accountants, "Exposure Draft, Measurement and Uncertainty," (Toronto, 1993b).
7 Canadian Institute of Chartered Accountants, "Research Study, Environmental Costs and Liabilities: Accounting and Financial Reporting Issues," (Toronto, 1993).

PART III

TRADE, ENVIRONMENT

AND THE

WORLD ECONOMY

CRITICAL PERSPECTIVES

CHAPTER 9

SHOULD CANADA VOLUNTEER TO BE A NUCLEAR WASTE DUMP FOR THE WORLD?

David Conklin
Jeffrey Gandz

David Conklin is an Adjunct Professor in the Faculty of Social Sciences, and a Research Fellow in the National Centre for Management Research and Development at The University of Western Ontario. He teaches in the Economics and Political Science departments, and he is currently participating in the development and teaching of a new environment of business course in the Western Business School. He received a B.A. from the University of Toronto and a Ph.D. from the Massachusetts Institute of Technology. He has worked in both the public and private sectors and has been the research director of several government task forces. The focus of his research is the relationship between business and government, and he serves as a consultant in the development of government legislation and regulations. His publications include a book written with Richard Hodgson and Eileen Watson entitled *Sustainable Development: A Manager's Handbook.*

Jeffrey Gandz is Professor of Business Administration and M.B.A. Program Director at the Western Business School at The University of Western Ontario.. He holds a Ph.D. and an M.B.A. from York University, teaches organizational behaviour and human resource management and consults with many organizations including General Electric, The Royal Bank of Canada, Sears, and both provincial and federal government departments. He is the co-author, with Frederick Bird, of *Good Management: Business Ethics in Action*, a casebook and text for M.B.A. students.

The Nuclear Waste Problem

When nuclear power plants were first built, there was a general feeling of optimism that science would develop safe and cost-effective methods for dealing with nuclear waste, and decisions were taken to press on with nuclear projects in anticipation of scientific developments. For some, hope persists that future technology will be able to reduce the risk of contamination from nuclear waste. However, it is no longer clear that this is the case. A report issued by the Ontario Royal Commission on Electric Power Planning states that "it is apparent that after about fifty thousand years the waste is going to be more toxic than it is after about 5000 years because of certain internal changes that occur."[1] Furthermore, we are fast reaching a point where nuclear plants themselves have come to the end of their useful life, and will have to be safely decommissioned. Disasters at Three Mile Island (TMI) and Chernobyl have created special nuclear waste problems and anxiety exists that these experiences could be repeated. It is indicative that,

> at the same time as the government and the Canadian nuclear industry were at great pains to point out why there were no similarities between Russian nuclear technology and Canadian nuclear technology, and therefore we should all be assured .... we were in the ironic position of being told we couldn't have an inquiry until the investigation into a technology that was not comparable to our own, had been completed.[2]

Previous practices on the part of the nuclear industry suggest that the existence of uncertainty has been used to justify secrecy. However, a public backlash often occurs when there are accidents and when explanations are not easily understood. The aftermath of the Three Mile Island disaster demonstrates how the media and public activists can generate fear and hysteria when clear answers are not provided. While scientists may argue that the media distorts risks through exaggeration and misinformation, the position of the nuclear industry is virtually indefensible as long as the media are able to thrive on the element of secrecy. Many citizens are no longer content to remain excluded from the decision-making process or to remain recipients of filtered information.

The general public has rather suddenly become extremely worried about this situation, and are demanding an involvement as stakeholders in the disposal of nuclear waste. This popular concern is motivating politicians to play a more active role through tougher regulations. It is only recently that our legal system has begun to adjust to these realities, and we are entering a new era of litigation. Today, the ethics of nuclear waste has become a subject of pressing political and legal importance, as well as a subject of increasing concern in the minds of the general public.

As a society, we have reached a new stage in dealing with nuclear waste. Increasingly, it is becoming clear that both air and groundwater can convey nuclear waste far beyond the locality of a nuclear plant. Since nuclear wastes are expected to have a half-life of 10,000 years, the possibility of international transmission of nuclear waste will be with us indefinitely. Even if new technology is able to reduce the half-life to, say 100 years, nevertheless, the risk of contamination will still be present for a long time. In view of this, the nuclear waste problem has become international in scope.

> In a sense, Italian peasants, and French sheep farmers and Canadian city dwellers are paying for the choice made by Soviet nuclear engineers and Soviet society (or that part of it which makes those decisions).[3]

In particular, Canada's proximity to the United States makes us particularly vulnerable to their practices in regard to nuclear waste. Canadians can no longer sit by while the United States makes its own decisions in regard to appropriate government regulations.

The Experience of the United States

The United States must contend not only with spent fuel rods from nuclear reactors, but also with about 100 million gallons of liquid waste. The liquid waste may be more dangerous, because it is being stored below ground level in tanks that sometimes leak. A method called glassification has been put to use in France, Belgium and the United Kingdom, and is being developed as a means of hopefully disposing safely and permanently of high-level waste. Several glassification facilities are currently under construction, including a $920 million project at the Department of Energy's Savannah River Site, which will be the largest such facility in the world:

> Plutonium 239 and tritium have been produced there for use in atomic weapons since the 1950s, the height of the Cold War .... This deadly mush now has the consistency of peanut butter. A building in which to vitrify the material has been constructed, using 69,000 cubic yards of concrete and 13,000 tons of steel. The facility will be fully automated, for this truly will be a glass to see through not only darkly but at a distance .... Test runs of the equipment began in 1990 and are expected to continue into 1994, when the actual melting will start. To process the current inventory of high-level waste will require more than 15 years.[4]

Thirty-four million gallons of highly radioactive waste have been accumulating in storage tanks at Savannah River alone since 1954. One does not require scientific knowledge to appreciate the motivation behind research into the process of glassification. Propelled by the increasing accumulation of waste and subsequent pressure to slow down production, "the industry's sense of urgency has little to do with environmental or safety concerns."[5] Du Pont played a significant role in the project, considering several approaches to immobilizing the cesium and radioactive sludge. Borosilicate glass was selected because it is insoluble and leach resistant. Hundreds of specialized pieces of equipment, with strict construction tolerances, are required to withstand the highly corrosive materials. The success of glassification also ultimately depends on what occurs underground over the next few thousand years, a factor that our succeeding generations may not always be able to control.

In 1988, Yucca Mountain in Nevada was chosen by the Department of Energy as a permanent repository site for the disposal of high-level waste once it has been through the glassification process and is contained in steel canisters. Issues that could affect the site's integrity include future faulting, volcanism, and climatic changes. The site has been deemed suitable because it provides rock cover above the water table. This rock has chemical and mineralogical characteristics thought to be favourable to the retardation of waste migration should the waste become mobilized. However, "predicting the exit routes of chemical wastes is a site-specific task requiring data, most of which has not been collected."[6] The need to rely on models of rock-mass response influenced by construction and testing disturbance is of great concern as the existing models are viewed by many to be inadequate for repository prediction.

The accident caused by Unit 2 of the Three Mile Island nuclear power plant in Harrisburg, Pennsylvania, came very close to a meltdown and reveals the limitations of current methods used to evaluate risk. Cleanup costs included the damaged reactor (estimated value $1 billion) as well as the purchase of replacement power amounting to $800 million in the eight years following the accident.[7] While 99 per cent of the radioactive rubble and all of the water will be removed, some contamination will be left behind. Neighbours of the plant are seriously concerned about the prospect of a partially radioactive site. Three Mile Island has illustrated the cleanup difficulties associated with the nuclear waste problem. It has also shown experts how much there is to learn about what can happen during a nuclear accident. It is difficult to generalize the lessons that were learned during emergency procedures at TMI precisely because it is unclear whether or not the TMI crisis can be considered typical of potential disasters in the future. Nevertheless, one observation was that "the human factor was therefore as important in helping contain the accident as in making it happen in the first place."[8] The public response included support for participation by non-experts in order to maintain some degree of accountability:

a majority of people near TMI wanted nontechnicians to have at least as much influence in how the cleanup was conducted as the technicians. This could be interpreted as a desire to gain some control over technicians, in whom they had lost trust.[9]

Despite public opposition, the United States Supreme Court handed down its final decision on October 2, 1985 to reactivate Unit 1 on Three Mile Island. Sufficient risk to Unit 1 was not demonstrated by the accident at Unit 2 and therefore the incident did not warrant the permanent closure of Unit 1.

The United States government will use cost-plus contracting for a contemplated cleanup of the nation's contaminated nuclear weapons plants; the cost has been estimated as high as $200 billion. Martin Marietta and Westinghouse are likely to be chief players, and privately owned Bechtel, along with joint ventures among smaller operations, may also get involved. The cost-plus contracting scheme pays varying award fees to the contractors in addition to their costs for plans, equipment, and payroll. Westinghouse took over operation of the Savannah River plant in Aiken, South Carolina, which produces tritium, an essential component of bombs, on a cost-plus basis in April 1990, giving it an even stronger foothold on the cleanup contracts. It is interesting to note that the Savannah River plant has received spent fuel from the site at Chalk River in Ontario.[10] Meanwhile, firms like Martin Marietta have expressed interest in contracts for cleanup work at plants other than those they operate.

Both air and groundwater can convey US nuclear wastes to Canada. Consequently, for Canadians, these US developments are extremely important. Any failure could have impacts on Canadian citizens. The US developments also raise the question whether waste storage should be placed in the hands of private sector corporations, or kept under the direct responsibility of government agencies.

Canada as a World Nuclear Waste Dump?

Some scientists have noted that Canada has special geological formations which may be ideally suited for the safe storage of nuclear waste until the waste has gradually lost its contamination properties. The Precambrian Shield has rock formations that are exceptionally durable and have not been subject to geological movement for millions of years. Scientists working at Atomic Energy of Canada Limited are attempting to develop new technology that would facilitate such storage. In particular, the Atomic Energy of Canada Limited plant near Pinawa, Manitoba, is constructing an experimental shaft deep into the granite of the Canadian Shield. The purpose is to study the feasibility of long-term storage of nuclear waste. In this chapter, we raise the question whether, in view of these special geological formations and also in view of our extensive experience with nuclear safety precautions, Canada should volunteer to be a world nuclear waste storage dump.

While it is true that today's technology cannot accurately measure the risks involved in storing nuclear waste, nevertheless, countries around the world must somehow deal with this disposal problem. Gordon Edwards, founder of the Canadian Coalition for Nuclear Responsibility, states that "there is nothing we can do to render radioactive materials harmless. And, at the present level of technology we do not know how to destroy nuclear wastes without simultaneously creating more."[11] Atomic Energy of Canada has concluded from its "concept assessment" as well as its "site selection" investigation that any Canadian Shield rock area can be considered "a potential site for a nuclear waste repository."[12] As part of this research, new ways of constructing containers for nuclear wastes are also being developed. In particular, new ceramic industrial tools have proven to be resistant to friction, erosion, and high temperatures. The Whiteshell Nuclear Research Establishment at Pinawa has been investigating these possibilities.

Should Canada opt to become a nuclear dumping ground? Strong support for this position could rest upon the very undesirable aspects of the alternatives. For example, the alternative of leaving this responsibility to an array of other countries may pose greater risks because of unstable political climates, inadequate financial resources or lack of expertise. Recent revelations about Soviet nuclear wastes emphasize the risks to Canadians–and to all the world–of relying upon each nuclear country for disposal of its wastes. Along this line of reasoning, should any single country be allocated the responsibility? How can one be confident that Canada's political future hundreds or thousands of years from now is any more secure than a country that may be considered a high risk at the present time? Are issues like nuclear waste disposal of such significance that a world committee must be considered for decisions on site selection, monitoring and future research? These are only some of the questions that should be involved in decisions about becoming a nuclear waste dumping ground. The irreversibility of many of these decisions emphasizes the need to address these questions in a wide variety of forums.

Quite apart from the issues discussed above, there may be a strong economic rationale for an active solicitation by Canada with regard to serving as a world nuclear waste dump. This role would create many high-tech jobs, bringing considerable income to the Canadian economy, as well as skills development and personal financial benefit to employees in this new sector. Over time, the research and development conducted by this sector would be extensive, and it would likely result in stimulus to technological progress in other Canadian businesses.

For Canadian citizens, the possibility of becoming a world storage dump for nuclear waste is an ethical issue. Not only are there the risks of leakage, but also, the process of transporting nuclear wastes to such nuclear waste dumps could involve the risk of accidents. To a great extent, the general public has been left out of decisions concerning the geological research, concerning the processes by which construction and transportation to and from the nuclear waste disposal facility would take place, and concerning the procedure for risk assessment. Increasingly, Canadians are reacting to decisions directed by the nuclear industry, and they are demanding attention, as well as the right to participate in the decision-making process.

It is no longer a question of whether or not there will be any release of radioactivity into the environment. Research confirms that "even if 99.997 percent of this airborne material is filtered out, there still will be radioactive gases and particulates, including plutonium, released into the atmosphere before the waste is ever put into the repository."[13]

It is evident that the environment within which Canadians are demanding an increasing role is dominated by ambiguity and uncertainty. The process by which decisions about nuclear waste disposal are made must adjust to new information, to increasing complexity, to a greater number of stakeholders, and to the demand for accountability by Canadian citizens. Certainly, ethics will play an increasingly significant role in the discussion and evaluation of nuclear issues. However, if the requirement for an ethical decision is consensus, then the possibility of a decision that may qualify as an ethical one is unlikely. There is an evident challenge in allowing citizens with diverse interests to participate in the decision-making process. The uncertainty surrounding outcomes adds to the difficulties of ethical decision-making. A purpose of this chapter is to urge that the time has come to develop an ethical system or set of ethical criteria upon which decisions might be based, even if consensus in those decisions cannot ultimately be reached. We believe that the participation of interested citizens is a necessary component of the "ethical" process of reaching those decisions. Precisely for this reason, it is important to explore the roles of the various stakeholders who may be involved in the decisions about Canada's future as a world nuclear waste dump.

Many questions and possibilities arise from thinking about the different stakeholders, and many carry an ethical component that should be considered. For example, how should Canadians balance the information provided by specialists and scientists in the nuclear industry against the passionate pleas of less informed activists struggling to achieve a nuclear-free world? How can one anticipate and measure future technological developments concerning the nuclear burden that would be carried by future generations? What is the role of the political process in reaching decisions about the highly specialized nuclear industry–a subject unfamiliar to most Canadians–but also a subject that has global rather than simply national implications?

Determining an Ethical Decision-Making Process

For decision-makers, an important question concerns the process of decision-making and the mechanics through which various stakeholders should be represented in this process. A key issue is the obligation of corporate decision-makers to include the ethical judgements of others in their own ethical judgements. Here again, the passage of time has altered ethical considerations, and will likely continue to do so. In particular, the number of those who consider themselves stakeholders in these ethical judgements has expanded greatly, as has their knowledge of relevant scientific matters, their ability to command attention, and their legal right to intervene in regulatory public and legal proceedings. The process must be robust enough to cope with the positions of concerned critics who are legitimate stakeholders in the decisions because of their environmental concerns, and also those who are ideologically opposed to nuclear energy in any of its forms because of its association with the weapons industry.

Ethical issues require the involvement of many groups of employees within the corporation if the corporation is to develop a consistent position in regard to these various issues, and if the specific knowledge of these various employee groups is to be utilized in the decision-making of the corporation.

Corporate decisions concerning ethical issues will increasingly involve dialogue within the corporation, in order that employees at many levels and in many scientific specialties can contribute their factual knowledge and can understand the rationale for, and nature of, the official decisions. This is absolutely critical because of the regulatory and political processes which will expose executives in the nuclear industry, and its customers, to formal inquiries and media attention. Ethical issues also require the involvement of many groups outside of the corporation if the corporation's decision is to be publicly justifiable.

The successful negotiation of the legal, regulatory and political maze which now faces the nuclear industry depends on attaining and communicating with relevant stakeholders the hard scientific knowledge which is currently available, assessing and predicting the evolution of additional knowledge gained through developing experiences and scientific research, and engaging in processes of deliberation, argumentation, and justification which are perceived as being informed and candid. This public policy aspect of corporate decisions concerning ethical issues will create the need for new corporate practices, including:

- procedures for dialogue and decision-making within the corporation;
- procedures for dealing with those outside the corporation who consider themselves to be stakeholders in the decision-making procedures; and
- processes for compiling and integrating the ever-expanding complexity of ethical decisions due to the growing complexity of the relevant scientific knowledge.

A central focus will be the relationship between ethical judgements and the analysis of risk, including the probabilities of alternative outcomes. New quantitative indices, as well as qualitative measures, will have to be developed to assist decision-makers in arriving at ethical judgements. Hopefully, research may increase the precision of risk analyses and the calculation of probabilities among alternative outcomes.

Candid and continuing dialogue must be preferred over other strategies for dealing with stakeholders. Avoidance is not an option. The issue is politically front-and-centre and concerned groups have the ears of politicians and regulators. Nor is it feasible to coopt stakeholders at this late stage, or to engage in tokenism in relationships with them. The environmental movement as a whole, and the critics of the nuclear industry in particular, are too well-organized and sophisticated to allow themselves to be coopted.

To be effective in conducting this dialogue, the nuclear establishment must develop a multidisciplinary team who bring a variety of perspectives to bear on this issue but who have good working relationships with each other. This is logical for two reasons:

- The background and skills required to deal with senior business management, multiple and diverse stakeholder groups, and public policy-makers is unlikely to be found at high levels in one individual.
- The development of defensible positions on these highly contentious issues requires intense discussion within and between the groups who are developing the positions within the industry. This discussion must deal with the many positions which might be taken by different external stakeholder groups and critics and thereby anticipate and prepare for the ensuing debate.

It is important to note that certain other countries have placed a much higher reliance on nuclear energy than have Canada and the United States. To some degree this may reflect higher costs of alternative energy sources in such societies, but it may also reflect different social norms and values. Many societies will confront the ethical issues involved in nuclear waste, and in this process it is quite possible that different groups of people will come to different judgements. Canadians will be impacted not only by ethical judgements here and in the United States, but also by ethical judgements in other nations. This raises the question of the appropriate degree of international collaboration in regard to the ethics of nuclear waste.

Another important consideration is the role of the democratic process within nations and its affect on decisions concerning nuclear issues:

The social movements which occasionally emerge to challenge technological elites, however, may either be last grasps of representative democracy in an age of technocracy or novel symbols of an increasingly common political mechanism assuring some degree of popular sovereignty.[14]

While the democratic process emphasizes the opportunity for participation, there are several aspects that prevent the effective participation of concerned citizens. The reality of specialized experts determining the process of development dictates a certain degree of exclusion which has already been discussed. Another force which promotes the exclusion of public participation is the familiar free rider syndrome emphasized by Mancur Olson. While the world would benefit from environmentally healthy solutions, no particular individual or group is eager to bear the cost of coming to those solutions, or lobbying for their implementation. Philip Cantelon and Robert Williams warn against the control enjoyed by a single industry when there is a relatively disinterested population. With regard to the power of the nuclear industry, they state that "the most profound political power is the power of non-decision making, of deciding what never becomes a matter for decision–of setting up the system within which our choices are structured."[15] Allowing nuclear scientists to set political, research and financial agendas is a different situation from allowing them to provide specialized information. And yet, in such a complex area with so many uncertainties it is relatively easy to shift from performing the former function to controlling the second. The nuclear industry may be a symbol of an emerging technocracy that will come to replace the democratic process.

Of course there is a danger in the opposite scenario where the nuclear issues, and nuclear waste disposal issues in particular, become highly politicized. While this may be ethical from a democratic point of view, it is unclear whether or not it is ethical in terms of safety, and the general preservation of society. Is it really ethical to expose decisions about site selection and standards to the logic of political bargaining and pork barrel practices?

Sustainable Development

Sustainable development is concerned with trade-offs over time, in particular between the current generation and future generations. The concept of time plays a significant role in the whole issue of nuclear waste disposal, in that scientific research will continually add to human knowledge in regard to nuclear waste management. As time passes, human knowledge will become increasingly precise in regard to the relationships between nuclear waste on the one hand, and the environment and human health on the other hand. Consequently, wise ethical judgements will likely change over time with the accumulation of greater scientific knowledge. This means that decision-makers have to determine an appropriate time profile for the treatment of existing nuclear waste, allowing in this time profile for the future introduction of new technology for waste disposal when it becomes available. It is probable that new technology will permit a more precise differentiation of wastes, with various levels of risk and danger, as well as the ability to reduce the volume of certain wastes, particularly by turning liquids into solids. Even the scientific ability to predict earthquakes, volcanism, and climatic changes will likely improve over time. Scientific knowledge concerning the strength of materials used to contain nuclear wastes will also likely increase, together with the creation of new and more durable materials. From this perspective, there is a close relationship between ethical judgements and the current and anticipated state of scientific knowledge.

The concept of time is also significant in regard to the allocation of waste disposal costs between current and future generations. Both fuel disposal and the decommissioning of plants may impose substantial costs on future generations. It will be important to clarify the guidelines that decision-makers may use in determining the financial obligation of current energy users, and the time profile of probable future commitments. In practice, such ethical issues involve the question of providing an appropriate margin on cost predictions and the analysis of contingency factors that may affect cost outcomes.

Ethical issues also arise from the relationships between the nuclear industry on the one hand, and the customers, suppliers, and others with whom it has a contractual relationship. Of special concern, is the need to depend upon the ethical judgements of such third parties, when these parties are not under the direct control of the nuclear industry. The sale of nuclear energy and nuclear plants to other countries raises ethical issues in regard to their treatment of nuclear waste. In the United States, several non-government corporations are becoming actively involved in the disposal of nuclear waste, and possibly these firms could, in the future, participate in the disposal of waste from Canadian plants. Of course, the scientific relationships between nuclear power for peaceful energy and nuclear weapons has made the contractual relationships with third parties a prominent ethical issue.

The Increasing Importance of Ethics
and the Procedures for Incorporating Ethics in Decision-Making

Of central concern is the role of law, regulation, and politicians in clarifying societies' positions in regard to these ethical issues. "Technologies are bundles of social, psychological, cultural, and political characteristics as well as technical, economic and engineering characteristics."[16] The current and future role of the courts and regulatory processes should form a major focus of this subject. Recent US experience has demonstrated that important disagreements and conflicts can develop among geographical regions, as citizens seek to keep disposal sites away from their particular area of residence. "Citizen opposition to new hazardous waste facilities is formidable and is based on a convergence of real, potential, and imagined local impacts."[17] We have seen similar concerns around toxic waste in Ontario and PCBs in Quebec. Here as well, the scope of ethical issues and procedures for considering them have been rapidly changing.

Responsibilities of the nuclear industry arise from its special position in regard to scientific knowledge and they relate to the education of the public and to communications with other stakeholder groups. The processes for conveying information to various stakeholders will likely become increasingly important. Society will likely continue to demand a greater openness in regard to the corporate processes for considering ethical issues. Consequently, the public policy aspects of decisions in regard to these ethical issues will be a central concern.

Ethical issues will become an increasingly important subject in nuclear waste management. Both the scope and content of these issues will become increasingly complex, as will the appropriate procedures for addressing them. Consequently, the development of a specific solution embodied in specific regulations will not be adequate. Rather, corporate decision-makers will have to be continually involved in the examination of current procedures and the consideration of modifications, including procedures that take more fully into account the likely involvement of stakeholders outside the corporation. Henceforth, this process will be ongoing. It will involve experts in several disciplines, and it will involve stakeholder consultations from time to time indefinitely, into the future.

Endnotes

[1] Gordon Edwards, "Nuclear Waste in Canada," in Anne Wieser, ed., *Challenges to Nuclear Waste: Proceedings of the Nuclear Waste Issues Conference, September 12-14, 1986*, (Lac du Bonnet, MB: Concerned Citizens of Manitoba, Inc., 1987), 65.

[2] Bill Blaikie, "Nuclear Waste in Canada," in Ibid., 59.

[3] Arthur Schafer, in "Workshop on Ethical Issues," in Ibid., 102.

[4] "Glass: Capturing the Dance of Light," *National Geographic*, December, 1993, 61.

[5] Edwards, "Nuclear Waste in Canada," 71.

[6] Michael Greenburg and Richard Anderson, *Hazardous Waste Sites: The Credibility Gap* (New Brunswick, NJ: State University of New Jersey, 1984), 101.

[7] Peter Houts, Paul Cleary, and Teh-Wei Hu, *The Three Mile Island Crisis: Psychological, Social, and Economic Impacts on the Surrounding Population*, Pennsylvania State University Series, no. 49 (Pennsylvania: Pennsylvania State University Press, 1988), 96.

[8] Philip L. Cantelon and Robert Williams, *Crisis Contained: The Department of Energy at Three Mile Island* (Carbondale: Southern Illinois University Press, 1982), 121.

[9] Peter S. Houts, et al., *The Three Mile Island Crisis*, 100.

[10] Gordon Edwards, Fred Knelman, and Walter Patterson in "Workshop on Military Connections," in Wieser, ed., *Challenges to Nuclear Waste*, 127.

[11] Edwards, "Nuclear Waste in Canada," 63.

[12] Blaikie, "Nuclear Waste in Canada," 55.

[13] Edwards, "Nuclear Waste in Canada," 71.

[14] Edward J. Walsh, *Democracy in the Shadows: Citizen Mobilization in the Wake of the Accident at Three Mile Island* (New York: Greenwood Press, 1988), 182.

[15] Schafer, "Workshop on Ethical Issues," 107.

[16] John Sorenson, et al. *Impacts of Hazardous Technology: The Psycho-Social Effects of Restarting TMI-1* (Albany: State University of New York Press, 1987), 167.

[17] Greenburg and Anderson, *Hazardous Waste Sites*, 165.

CHAPTER 10

ISSUES IN ENVIRONMENTAL PROTECTION: A THIRD WORLD PERSPECTIVE

O.P. Dwivedi

O.P. Dwivedi, Ph.D., LL.D. (Hon), is a Professor in the Department of Political Studies at the University of Guelph. He has been a policy consultant to various departments of the Government of Canada, including Environment Canada. His international assignments include work for UNESCO, ESCAP (Bangkok), WHO Advisor to the Government of India, CIDA Advisor to the Government of Papua New Guinea, and the World Bank Advisor to the Government of Mauritius. He has published 17 books and over 60 articles in professional journals and scholarly books. From 1986-1989, he was a member of the Environmental Assessment Board of Ontario, a quasi-judicial tribunal. At present, he is Vice President of the International Association of Schools and Institutes of Administration in Brussels.

I   Introduction

Humanity's role in manipulating its surroundings is enormous and ranges from the obvious–damming of great rivers–to the subtle–the effects of DDT on the reproduction of wildlife. This concern over environmental impact generated a great deal of worry starting in the late 1960s. Many environmentalists therefore, began to propose a "right" to environmental quality. Their proposals included mostly decision-making tools, such as environmental impact assessment, duties and regulations imposed on private industries and corporations, and powers acquired by the state to monitor related activities both in the public and private sectors. However, environmental impact does not stop at measuring pesticide residues and the amount of mercury in fish. It involves the quality of life on earth, and indeed, the ability of man to interact with nature and survive in the long run. It also means that pollution, destruction of species and natural areas, and depletion of resources can not be placed second to man's materialism and his captivation for technological progress.

The continuing and accelerating deterioration of our planet's ecological base poses a major threat to the viability of our world. Nowhere is the evidence of global ecological deterioration better argued than in *Our Common Future*, a Report by the World Commission on Environment and Development

(Brundtland Commission). The real significance of this Report lies (1) in its thorough explanation of why we, the people inhabiting this planet, are collectively destroying the resources; (2) in its thesis that we cannot save the environment without development, *but* at the same time, we cannot keep on developing *unless* we save the environment; and (3) in its main recommendation that without restructuring existing institutional arrangements and legal mechanisms, fragmentation, overlapping jurisdictions, narrow mandates and closed decision-making processes will continue. As the Report states, "the real world of interlocked economy and ecological systems will not change, the policies and institutions concerned must."[1] The Commission suggested that nation-states should consider one of two approaches: (a) an "effect-oriented" approach which established environmental policy, laws and institutions that focus on environmental effects; and (b) a "sources and causes" approach which concentrates on the sources that are the causes of those effects.[2] Both approaches represent a distinct way of looking at solving environmental issues.

Most governments have adopted the first approach, *effect-oriented*, by establishing environmental protection programmes and agencies without much change in the existing institutional structure. Such agencies have mostly been given jurisdictions in those areas on which no other ministry or department could lay a concrete claim. However, as experience in some industrialized countries has demonstrated, this approach has resulted in focusing exclusively on reactive or remedial actions rather than on preventative measures. This has created some serious jurisdictional disputes concerning the environment, which is seen by many ministries as a shared responsibility. In some cases, the environmental protection ministry or agency has taken a sharp stand against economic development policies being pursued by other ministries. Thus, inter-ministerial jealousies have resulted in jurisdictional fights, policy fragmentation, and pursuit of narrow objectives. Instead there is a need to go into "sources and causes" of the environmental problems. This will require a change in people's role in treating nature and using it, as they have done so far in exploiting it.

The Brundtland Commission has already warned:

> The time has come to break out of past patterns. Attempts to maintain social and ecological stability through old approaches to development and environmental protection will increase instability. Security must be sought through change ... Without reorientation of attitudes and emphasis, little can be achieved.[3]

In order to break out of past patterns, people's attitudes must be changed, otherwise, the same old solutions, although presented in new bottles, would continue to crowd public perception as well as the public policy agenda. One of the approaches suggested relates to the concept of *environmentally sound and sustainable development*. This envisions a policy stand with the government's realization that long-term economic growth is only possible if a nation sustains its viable natural environment and adopts an integrated approach to sustainable development which recognizes the interconnectedness between scientific/technological, social, cultural and economic dimensions. The Third World has been told that the environmental policy of each nation ought to be based on environmentally sound and sustainable development. It is this policy stand which may engender the necessary interconnection and coordination between various policy sectors in that government, such as fulfilling basic needs and conserving the natural resources base. But this also requires a major change in the policy perspective of a government so that environmental considerations become an intrinsic part of national policy-making and not added afterwards. Among the steps to be undertaken on a priority basis is to act on local environmental health issues rather than worrying about the international resource and environmental problems.

For the developing nations, protecting the health of their people and conserving their natural assets is the most important policy action. Preventing adverse environmental impact is better and cheaper than fire fighting action after the disaster has taken place. That is why environmental values in decision-making should be recognized and interwoven into the policy framework by the governments of Third World nations. These range from biodiversity protection and conservation, sustainable resource use, and environmental protection, to fostering economic development of a kind that both harmonizes with the natural environment and augments the quality of life for all people, present and future. The realization, although emerging slowly, is now being acknowledged by Third World nations that their people have the right to live in ecological harmony.

II Environmental Values

As has been witnessed in many parts of the world, drastic alteration of the natural environment results in a breakdown of the natural balance of an area, with consequences such as accelerated soil erosion, aggravated flooding, loss of crop yield, declining air and water quality, and loss of wildlife and other species. "These factors are more than aesthetic irritants–they are early warning signs that social and economic problems lie ahead, and living standards are threatened."[4] These factors and their interrelationship are so complex and complicated that their implications are only beginning to be realized. In the name of economic expediency, coupled with humanity's blind faith in the superiority of technology, nations have taken steps without appreciating the full range of consequences on the total life-support system. Economic development and a better quality of life for everyone cannot be separated from environmental management. Therefore,

> in order to achieve a more rational management of resources and thus improve the environment, states should adopt an integrated and coordinated approach to their development planning so as to ensure that development is compatible with the need to protect and improve the environment for the benefit of their population.[5]

Nowhere is the need for such an integrated programme concerning population, resources, economic development, and environmental protection and conservation more important than in the developing nations. The environmental crisis in these countries is mainly the result of poverty and has led to the massive destruction of biological resources on which life depends–forests, grasslands, croplands, fisheries. This is *then* further aggravated by efforts to industrialize, which are in themselves attempts to alleviate poverty that pollute the air, land and water. The integrated approach encompasses an ethical dimension which relates to values, norms and behaviour of individuals as well as institutions (both in the public and private sectors). Individual and corporate behaviour must be responsible behaviour. That responsibility includes not only to avoid endangering the life-support system for the present generation but also that of future generations, because environmental problems, in one way or another, affect everyone, and hence each person has a responsibility to protect the environment. *The right to a healthy environment is an obligation as well as a responsibility.*

The right to a healthy environment is based on the premise that no one individual or entity (whether government or business) has the privilege to endanger the environment to the extent that it adversely affects the ecological sustainability of all natural resources including air, water and land resources. On the other hand, that right includes an *obligation to see that natural resources are held in trust for the use of present and future generations.*

This is the duty of all responsible and concerned citizens. However, not everyone in society is aware of this duty. So, an appropriate awareness has to be created. What institution is capable of doing that? It seems religions have such capability because religious teachings lead to the realization that there are limits to our control over the animate and inanimate world, and that our arrogance and manipulative power over nature can backfire. It is our religion and faith which says that a person's life cannot be measured by material possessions and that the ends of life go beyond material possessions and consumption. Thus, religious and cultural imperatives can be a powerful source for environmental conservation and protection.[6]

Do people of the Third World see these imperatives differently in comparison to the people of the North? Or, as some in the North would say: what do these people really want? Why are they not working as hard as we do so they can also enjoy the fruits of their labour? How long are we going to help them with food, machinery, material, knowledge, and expertise; and how much more should we sacrifice our quality of life so that their standards of living could become tolerable? These are the grumblings from ordinary folks in Canada and other Western nations who are bombarded every day with television images of barely alive human beings from Somalia, the famine stricken people of Ethiopia, the indiscriminate destruction of lives and property in the former Yugoslavia, and various civil disorders in other parts of the globe. People in the North are getting sick and tired of seeing a constant media barrage of human suffering so it is not surprising to see some of them saying: enough is enough–we have our own problems of economic recession, unemployment, riots, and ever-rising taxes–we cannot help those who constantly and regularly bother our conscience.

Perhaps, this is what the Third World wants–pricking the conscience of the people of the North so that they can appreciate the misery, despondency, and gloom which surrounds Third World people. For them, it is a classic fight between the rich and the poor. And further, they say that the one who has been giving us the medicine (for our development) is also the one responsible for our present state of crisis. If we are constantly suffering, it may be partly because of us, but surely it is mostly because of the policies and programmes of the West. The Third World was always kept at the periphery and was seen as the problem while the solution always rested with the centre (i.e. the North). This became evident during the Earth Summit when certain conventions were not agreed upon by the powerful and wealthy West.

III Developmental Frustrations

"Well in our country," said Alice, still panting a little, "you'd generally get
to somewhere else–if you run very fast for a long time, as we have been
doing."

"A slow sort of Country!" said the Queen. "Now here, you see, it takes all
the running *you* can do to keep in the same place. If you want to get
somewhere else, you must run at least twice as fast as that."

Lewis Carroll, *Alice Through the Looking Glass*

Third World nations have already discovered what the Queen told Alice in
the above quoted passage. The harder they work for development, the more
difficult it gets to reach the goal. It seems that perhaps this is what has
happened during the past four decades of developmental efforts. Their
relative position *vis-a-vis* the industrialized nations has deteriorated compared to what they had at the time of independence from their colonial
masters. A brief history of developmental efforts and the frustrations
generated over the years is given below.[7]

While some colonies received their independence immediately after World
War II, freedom came to most of the developing nations of Africa and Asia
in the 1960s. After a few years, however, the great enthusiasm which
greeted these nations lost its impetus. By the early 1970s, a spirit of
frustration and despair with the developmental process had set in. For one
thing, it appeared evident that externally induced modernisation had failed
to eradicate the basic problems of underdevelopment which it purported to
solve. While some significant increases of GNP took place, poverty, disease
and hunger had either worsened or remained unaltered. The same could be
said of the growing gap between the rich and poor nations, not to mention
that between different social strata within nations. In many regions of Asia,
Africa and Latin America, incremental reformism had failed to create a more
equitable socio-economic order and had proven to be an ineffective antidote
to radical change. In fact, frustrated reformism had fuelled a revolution of
rising frustrations. Large on the horizon loomed the Indo-China experience.
It demonstrated that over-administering was neither an efficient nor an
effective insurance against revolution.

Instead of affluence, growth and optimism, the developing nations faced
scarcity, stasis (or decline) and lowered expectations. Two basic trends are

related to this decline. First, at the level of praxis, a great deal of the international and domestic development efforts had proven less than impressive. Secondly, at a conceptual level, the failure of development and reformism in general resulted in an expanding analytical void. Increasingly, the objectives, methodologies, and even epistemologies and value assumptions of Western social science would undergo fundamental questioning.

It should be noted that by the late 1960s, the economic progress of the poor nations was taken for granted–it was just around the corner. All the West needed to do was create certain conditions to induce its becoming tangible. It was expected that with the help of foreign aid (mostly in the form of consultants, soft technologies, and purchase of specialized hardware– secured from the same source which provided the aid), developing countries would achieve economic progress. But by the mid-1970s, the very foundations of the development paradigm were severely in question. Not only was their usefulness in doubt in the Third World itself, but an intellectual crisis of purpose and confidence had also set in among the experts of the West. The gap between the centre and the periphery was widening rather than narrowing in both relative and absolute terms. Instead of development and nation-building, turmoil and fragmentation proliferated throughout Africa, Asia, the Middle East and Latin America. Urban crises, energy crises, cessation of growth, unemployment, and breakdowns of public institutions and public morality all had the effect of dampening the early optimism about the ability of the First World to solve problems everywhere. Even the "basic needs" strategy which emerged as a part of the New International Economic Order (NIEO) failed radically to redirect the very terms of reference of the development debate. Further, in the absence of a common strategy adopted by both the West and the Third World, the NIEO went the same way as the other concepts which had emerged earlier.[8]

It was not surprising that the very concept of development came under severe questioning. While it still meant economic growth for traditionalists, increasing numbers of analysts had begun to define it in terms of sustainable development and human values: quality of life, satisfaction of basic needs, protection and conservation of the environment, and so on. For many, development for what, to what and for whom were not merely rhetorical questions because they highlighted the real fact that development entailed prior normative considerations and value choices.

By the mid-1980s, there was a rude awakening among the developing nations when they found that, instead of being recipients of capital from the West, they were forced to make net transfers of their meagre resources to the West. In order to service their debts, several developing nations became virtually bankrupt. Restrictive trade practices prohibited the poor from exporting their products and even this problem was compounded when commodity prices fell to a level unknown during the previous 50 years while the prices of manufactured products kept rising. It is no wonder that starvation, destitution, inequality, and oppression have continued in most of the developing nations. The Golden Age of the 1950s turned into the Age of Pessimism and Rude Awakening by the end of the 1980s.[9] Nevertheless, there were some rays of hope which came from the worldwide awareness due to the Earth Summit in 1992 which impressed on all that no one group of nations could keep on "progressing" all the time while the majority remained hungry and poor. To some, this may sound very moralistic arguing for the duty of the North to help close the development gap in the South. Is there another way out however? Until now, the South has adopted a weak approach to negotiations with the North. This awakening means that new approaches are required in North-South relations.

IV Administrative Vision and External Pressures

Developmental efforts and the frustrations surrounding these are discussed above. However, when it comes to environmental protection policy and programmes implementation, these are equally fraught with many problems. Among these problems, two interrelated issues which influence the management and administration of such programmes in the Third World nations are discussed below.

(A) Environmental Crisis and Administrative Vision

Although environmental concern has achieved considerable global acceptance and popularity, the perception of crisis is not being shared by all in various ministries and the administrative sphere. Those who articulate this sense of urgency are sometimes considered as emotional and irrational power-grabbers and empire-builders. But the magnitude of environmental crisis demanded a more measured, systematic and holistic response. Specifically, it demanded institutional coordination, policy adjustments and structural adaptations. And when this demand had to be met, the existing governmental structure had no capacity to face a challenge so pervasive and complex as potentially disturbing the administrative edifice of a nation. It is not surprising, therefore, to see individual ministries trying not only to protect their turf but also to expand their power base by claiming more administrative capability and vision relating to environmental protection.

In such an atmosphere, the task of coordination becomes extremely difficult as the agency which has been entrusted with this task is seen by others as an undesirable intruder and obstructionist of their normal functions. One result is futile gestures or withdrawal symptoms at worst, or unenthusiastic support at best. Often, the resisting administrative agency employs such techniques as prevention, curtailment or circumvention of anticipatory policy pronouncements. Finally, even when a new ministry or a department of environment has been established, it does not do better than be accorded a marginal position in the administrative hierarchy. Compounding the situation is the perception among many administrators that environmental policy and management is still a discrete function, something added on elsewhere to an administrative structure whose basic mandate has not been altered.

(B) External Inducements for Building Institutional Capability

During the 1980s, many international aid agencies (such as the World Bank, United Nations Environment Program, and Northern nations aid agencies) started showing great interest in a nation's capacity to manage its own environment. These external inducements helped to expedite the process of institutional acceptance and administrative accommodation relating to capacity building for environmental protection. In some places, the initial hesitation about the role of this "new kid on the block" is still continuing. This was clearly evident in India when the Department of Environment was formally established in 1980, or in Mauritius when the new Ministry of Environment and Quality of Life was constituted in 1991. It was not surprising to note that some officers of other ministries harboured concern about the new role of such an agency. Of course, this is nothing new because it has happened in other countries when a new multidisciplinary environmental protection agency was created. Institutional strengthening takes a back seat when doubts (possibly to the point of outright resistance) persist among the key ministries about the new organization. In such a situation, direction from the office of the Prime Minister or President becomes crucial for ordering coaptation, integration, and coordination.

As environmental problems cut across ministerial responsibilities and jurisdictions, there is a need for more forceful articulation of environmental concerns in national planning and policy-making, as well as for improved coordination, institutional structures and legal instruments in the implementation of policies involving environment and development. For example, the World Bank noted in its report entitled *Economic Development with Environmental Management Strategies for Mauritius*:

> Diluted authority and diffused legislation have implications for rational, efficient and sustainable natural resource management. To be successful, a concerted effort to tackle environmental problems will require a systematic review of institutional, legal and regulatory arrangements, and the establishment of a comprehensive national policy for environmental protection and management.[10]

A similar situation exists in many Third World countries.

A note of caution: externally induced changes, while easily instituted, must be given time to achieve acceptance by the body politic and the existing administrative and legal mechanisms. Placing too much faith in instantaneous changes and expecting a "magic wand remedy" for bringing requisite organizational effectiveness and motivational changes in the administrative apparatus has sometimes resulted in disappointment. And when expected results do not follow, the recipient country turns against those organization(s) which induced such recommended changes. That is why great care should be taken before rushing towards instituting externally suggested changes. Like a human body, governmental institutions also require time to accept foreign organs. At the same time, one should be ready for rejection from the body. It will be beneficial to all the Third World nations to undertake an assessment of the "induced change" in the administrative, institutional and legal mechanisms pertaining to environmental protection.

V   The First and Third World Environmental Issues

Interaction between the rich North and poor South will have to be based on certain accommodations. From the perspective of Third World nations, the following items appear to be a part of their global demands that they would like industrialized nations to consider for the protection of the planetary environment:

(1) *Internationalization of the Polluter Pays Concept:* There is a need to internationalize the "Polluter Pays Principle." At present, the concept is being used by some industrialized nations, but restricting it to their domestic borders. However, they (or their multinational corporations) are not recognizing that they are the main polluters of our world, and they ought to "pay" for it. Because pollution has been caused in the past and is being caused now mostly by industrialized nations, either directly or through their commercial concerns in the Third World, it is only appropriate that these nations should apply the principle upon themselves. Industrialized nations should establish, based on their past and present contribution to the world pollution aggregate, a permanent fund for the cleaning up of their collective and individual actions. Further, environmental technology transfer should be freely available to all nations, free from any restrictions such as copyright, patent, and trademark.

(2) *Green Imperialism:* Several developing nations have a basic distrust of the promises and policies of the North. They think that the current emphasis on pollution control by the industrialized nations is merely a continuation of their economic domination and trade barriers. Suggested constraints on development, barriers on their exports, and requirements of the Structural Adjustments Programmes have led the poor nations to strenuously oppose any environmental conditionality.[11] Further, industrialized nations should take the lead in reducing per capita energy consumption because overconsumption causes fast depletion of non-renewable energy resources and, at the same time, affects the global environment. The North should also control auto emissions at home and also require their multinational corporations (which produce and sell automobiles to the Third World) to introduce catalytic converters and the use of lead-free gasoline.[12]

(3) *Consumption and Materialism, not Population, are the Culprits:* The South believes that consumption patterns and the continuous emphasis on a materialistic way of life in the North are the basic culprits of global environmental problems, as opposed to rising population among the poor nations. For example, the United States emits 1000 billion tons of carbon gases while India's share is only 230 billion tons, even though the

US has only one-quarter as many people. Consider other indicators. In 1990, 251 million Americans used more energy for cooling their homes than 1.1 billion Chinese used for all purposes. The North accounts for 73 per cent of total industrial carbon dioxide emissions in the world. Production of CFCs should be halted. Alternative technology, for refrigeration and air-conditioning, must be found and must be made available to Third World nations. From a resource-use viewpoint, a rise in population among poor nations is not much of a problem compared to even a very slight population growth in the North.

(4) *Differing Perceptions About Global Environmental Problems*: The North and South differ about the priority to be given on various environmental issues. From the South's viewpoint, poverty alleviation is the most crucial task of the day, not ozone depletion, the release of hydrocarbons, or the like. As Prime Minister Indira Gandhi stated during the 1972 United Nations Conference on Human Environment in Stockholm:

> On the one hand the rich look askance at our continuing poverty–on the other, they warn us against their own methods. We do not wish to impoverish the environment any further and yet we cannot for a moment forget the grim poverty of large numbers of people. Are not poverty and need the greatest polluters?[13]

It is obvious that not much has changed during the past twenty years since Gandhi made that statement. Developing nations are still struggling with poverty, hunger, and providing basic health care to their people. To most of them, environmental concerns are the affliction of "over development."

(5) *Need for an International Environmental Monitoring and Enforcement Agency*: At the United Nations level, an organization should be set up to monitor the state of the environment of our planet and to prepare an annual environmental audit report relating to the enforcement of environmental international treaties and conventions and to infractions caused by individual nations as well as by multinational corporations. Such cases should be brought before the International Court of Justice for prosecution. No country would have veto power over this organization.

Third World countries cannot afford the costly react-and-cure approach to dealing with environmental problems that are becoming more complex and pervasive and more difficult and expensive to clean up. Further, these nations can no longer afford to ignore environmental considerations in properly assessing our economic performance. Environmental degradation and mismanagement of their environmental resources impose social and economic costs.

At the same time, one thing should also be made clear. People of the Third World are going to face some difficult choices and are likely to see the costs of environmental protection reflected in higher prices. But these costs will be offset by improvements in the quality of air and water, and ultimately, in human health. Moreover, new economic opportunities will be provided by a growing environmental industry sector–opportunities that governments and businesses must explore, given the challenges of an increasingly integrated and more competitive world economy. In the final analysis, the economy should experience net gains as a result of integrating environmental consideration into decision-making.

VI Concluding Observations

Every generation receives a natural and cultural legacy in trust from its ancestors and is supposed to hold it in trust for its coming generations. This trust imposes upon each generation the obligation not only to conserve and protect the environment and that natural legacy but also to enhance it so that the future generations can enjoy the fruits of such trust in a most appreciable manner. Of course, trustees are permitted to use the resources of that trust for the purposes either set down in writing or enunciated through cultural and religious systems for each society. However, trustees are not given free will to exploit the legacy so that only a dwindling amount is left for the future generation of trustees. It is from this perspective that we have to see how our actions (present as well as past) impose serious environmental burdens on future generations.

These burdens can be divided into four groups: depletion of natural resources; degradation of environmental quality of specific areas; protection and enhancement of the natural legacy; and reparation for the exploitation and over use of environmental resources by previous generations.

Renewable natural resources like forests, fish, and sand get depleted faster when we consume them much more rapidly than their rate of regeneration. Already, we have problems due to deforestation and overfishing in our seas.

These stocks should be replenished (or time and effort invested towards this process). Our legacy to the future generations will be hollow otherwise. Similarly, non-renewable natural resources, such as minerals, ought to be used wisely because once these are exhausted, future generations will be unable to reap the same benefits which our present generation has been getting.

Concerning the degradation of environmental quality, it should be noted that the way we dispose of our wastes in the water and in the air affects not only us but also our children and their children. Our system of waste disposal may be such that it could be life-threatening not only to human beings but also to the rest of the animate and non-animate world. That is why it is crucial that human activities which degrade the environment be minimized, if not altogether terminated. Towards this, each nation-state should formulate an Environmental Investment Program to improve the air and water quality within its boundaries.

Third, it is our moral duty to leave a healthy legacy for future generations not only by protecting the environment from the harmful ways of our activities, but also by attempting to restore the status quo of two generations ago. This is not going to be an easy task, nevertheless, attempts will have to be made. This requires an attitudinal change on the part of all of us, but undoubtedly, the industrialized countries among us who are consuming the natural resources too fast too soon have the heaviest burden to carry.

Finally, it is a duty for us all to see that the future generations receive appropriate reparation for the damage which our and the immediately preceding generation have visited upon us by their careless and exploitative tendencies.

As a final summary, the following two observations are presented.

(A) Transfer of Pollution-Free Technology[14]

Although developing nations would gladly accept technology, they are worried that they may be given technologies by the North which were being used two or three decades ago and which brought us to the brink of the environmental disaster that the entire planet faces today. Developing nations require technology to be transferred for four major purposes: (a) cleaner and more efficient production; (b) minimization of energy requirements, industrial waste, and pollution; (c) prevention of air and water pollution; and (d) to fulfil the agreements in certain international conventions, such as the Montreal Protocol, which mitigate the adverse impacts of environmental damage caused, in the first place, by the industrialized world. Another consideration which worries the South is the issue of intellectual property rights and commercial profits by the multinational corporations. In this respect, a new global partnership is required to create mechanisms which ensure the availability of financial resources at moderate and reasonable rates, and to transfer environmentally sound technology on non-commercial terms so that the developing nations could make a swift technological transition. The international community must appreciate that the current culture of the West, which is based on mass production, mass consumption, and mass waste generation and disposal, would also have to change. A commitment from the North would have to come on two fronts: a need to change its lifestyle, and to provide assistance to the developing nations for environmental conservation and protection, not in the form of bilateral aid or multilateral loans, but as a partnership-grant between nations. This means a grant or aid among partners; the emphasis here is on partnership rather than a relationship in which one is a giver and another is a receiving destitute.

(B) Environmental Common Interests and Common Good

People living in all parts of the world can be held together in this common enterprise of protecting our common heritage by the values and ideals that each community subscribes to, as well as by self-interest in the best sense. By combining their concerns, talents, energies and resources, people can build a common future on earth to be able to share their fortune (meagre or in abundance) so as to equalize opportunities among all neighbours, among all regions, and to sustain the right of all to fulfil their ends of life. That is why the globalization of environmental issues is important.

In addition, there is an urgent need to encourage cooperation among people of the world. This can probably best be done by fostering the convergence of the shared fundamental value: protection and enhancement of the environment. Of course, there are differences concerning lifestyles across the globe. Further, people do not want identical lives, cultures, and beliefs. Nevertheless, there are several mutually reinforcing values rather than incompatible cultural ones which provide us with a remarkable degree of agreement towards this issue. Given an opportunity to act locally on these global issues, communities can respond to regional and global challenges. For this to occur, some institutional changes will have to be undertaken. Reforms would be needed in the international laws and treaties and attitudes of people would have to go through some fundamental changes with respect to their lifestyle. Flexibility, adaptiveness, and the ability to reconcile the needs of different communities and local interests, would have to be carefully nurtured. The reality of our world, the central fact that we must take into account in the design of global environmental policy and programmes is not independence but interdependence. The complexity and scale of environmental problems no longer permit a "water tight" division of environmental issues. The challenge before us is in the reform and renewal of the existing world system, and in securing a firm place for the rights of future generations. It is to this end, the ethics of caring for our planet, that much of our efforts must now turn during these last years of the century if this planet of ours is not to get further damaged. This challenge is not limited to the Third World alone. We are all in it together.

Endnotes

[1] World Commission on Environment and Development, *Our Common Future* (New York: Oxford University Press, 1987), 310.
[2] Ibid., 310.
[3] Ibid., 309.
[4] International Union for Conservation of Nature and Natural Resources, *Why Conservation?* (Gland, Switzerland: IUCN, Commission on Ecology, 1985), 3.
[5] For further reference see, UN, Conference on the Human Environment, *Declaration on the Human Environment* (New York: UNO, December 1972).
[6] For further elaboration of this author's views on environmental ethics, see the following two articles: "Man and Nature: A Holistic Approach to a Theory of Ecology," *The Environmental Professional* 10(1) (1988), 8-15; and "An Ethical Approach to Environmental Protection: A Code of Conduct and Guiding Principles," *Canadian Public Administration* 35(3) (Autumn 1992), 363-380.
[7] For an overall review of developmental efforts between 1940s and the 1980s, see O.P. Dwivedi, *Development Administration: From Underdevelopment to Sustainable Development* (London: Macmillan, 1994).
[8] For further details see, O.P. Dwivedi and J. Nef, "Crises and Continuities in Development Theory and Administration: First and Third World Perspectives," *Public Administration and Development* 2 (1982), 59-68.
[9] For further elaboration, see O.P. Dwivedi, "Development Administration: Its Heritage, Culture and Challenges," *Canadian Public Administration* 33(1) (Spring 1991), 91-98.

[10] The World Bank, *Economic Development with Environmental Management Strategies for Mauritius*, Report No. 7264-MAS (Washington, D.C.: The World Bank, November 1988), 2.

[11] For this point, the author is grateful to Dhirendra K. Vajpeyi, of the University of Northern Iowa, Cedar Falls, USA.

[12] This reminds me of my frustration in 1990 trying to import a car into Mauritius which required the use of lead-free gasoline. I discussed the matter with relevant government officials in Port Louis. They were very helpful and arranged a meeting between me and the regional representative of Shell International Company. Using my case in point, I suggested that the time had come to introduce lead-free gasoline in Mauritius. I was advised instead that developing nations do not need a costly product like catalytic converters and lead-free gasolilne. When I pointed out that the National Environmental Policy of the Mauritius Government contains a provision for introducing lead-free gasoline, I was informed that irrespective of the policy pronouncement, there was no legal requirement for the petroleum companies to sell it. Eventually, I was able to secure lead-free gasoline as a special privilege through the kind intervention of the General Manager of the State Trading Corporation of Mauritius. The reluctance of some multinational corporations to introduce technological changes which are now taken for granted in the industrialized nations is amazing.

[13] Quoted in O.P. Dwivedi, "India: Pollution Control Policy and Programmes," *International Review of Administrative Sciences* 43(2) (1977), 123.

[14] See for further elaboration, O.P. Dwivedi, ed. *Perspectives on Technology & Development* (New Delhi: Gitanjali Publishing House, 1987).

CHAPTER 11

RECONCILING THE IRRECONCILABLE: THE GLOBAL ECONOMY AND THE ENVIRONMENT

Deborah C. Poff

Deborah Poff is Dean of Arts and Science and a professor of Philosophy at the University of Northern British Columbia . She is the editor of an international, interdisciplinary journal, the *Journal of Business Ethics*, and co-editor of *Business Ethics in Canada*. Poff is the author of numerous articles on ethics of violence, sexuality, feminism, global economic development and justice issues. She has been the recipient of some 20 research grants, with a total value in excess of $1,000,000.

For the past decade, we have been listening to a number of inconsistent and irreconcilable recommendations for solving the serious economic and environmental problems in both domestic and international economies. Our current language with respect to the significant sea changes we have witnessed in the global economy are filled with, to use that most appropriate euphemism of the 1980s, disinformation.

This chapter will focus on how the relationship among structural adjustment policies and practices, the business activities of transnational corporations and what Robert Reich has called "the coming irrelevance of corporate nationality" makes environmental sustainability impossible. To begin, a brief discussion of the global economy and its relation to the diminishing significance of national boundaries will be undertaken.

The Global Economy and the Erosion of Statehood

In their 1989 book, *For the Common Good*, Herman Daly and John Cobb argued that if Adam Smith were alive today, he would probably not be preaching free trade. Their argument is based on what they believe to have been a necessary commitment of the eighteenth century capitalist to a sense of community and to an identification with his own nationhood. On this point, Smith is perhaps most universally known. He states:

By preferring the support of domestic to that of foreign industry, he [i.e. the capitalist] intends only his own security; and by directing that industry in such a manner as its produce may be of the greatest value, he intends only his own gain, and he is in this, as in many other cases, led by an invisible hand to promote an end which was no part of his intention.[1]

Daly and Cobb argue that the cornerstone of the free trade argument, capital immobility, that factored so strongly into Smith's belief that the capitalist was committed to investing in his or her own domestic economy has been eroded by:

a world of cosmopolitan money managers and transnational corporations which, in addition to having limited liability and immortality conferred on them by national governments, have now transcended those very governments and no longer see the national community as their residence. They may speak grandly of the 'world community' as their residence, but in fact, since no world community exists, they have escaped from community into the gap between communities where individualism has a free reign.[2]

These capitalists have no disinclination to move their capital abroad for the slightest favourable preferential rate of return. The concern which Daly and Cobb articulate here is frequently posed as a question or series of questions. For example, "with the globalization of the economy, are we living in a world system in which national economies are merely vestigial remnants of modernity or the earlier industrial period?" or, "are nations as political and social regulatory systems necessary agents for global economic negotiation and cooperation?" What we have had as answers to these questions is essentially political positioning in two oppositional camps. As Arthur MacEwan and William Tabb summarize:

The extreme globalist position often carries the implication that no change is possible except on the international level, and since there is no political mechanism for such change–aside from that of formal relations among governments–oppositional political activity is easily seen as useless. On the other extreme, those who view the national economic system as a viable unit are led to formulate programs that ignore the importance of economic forces which transcend national boundaries. Such an outlook can lead to both unrealistic programs which fail because of capital's international flexibility and implicit alliances with reactionary nationalist groups to advocate, for example, increased 'competitiveness'.[3]

Although I will later argue that both of these alternatives are inadequate, I would first like to spend some time discussing how we have gotten into our current economic crisis. That means a brief sojourn into the world of structural adjustment, the world we have essentially been living in for much of the past decade.

Structural Adjustment

The only aspect of structural adjustment that will be addressed here is consequences of the debt crisis and the stagnation and economic insecurity of the 1980s. Those familiar with the literature on the current economic crisis know that a complete picture starts with the Bretton Woods conference of 1944 which set guidelines for the International Monetary Fund and the International Bank for Reconstruction and Development (the World Bank, as it is now known). Bretton Woods also guaranteed the dominance of the United States in the world economy. As Jamie Swift notes, "the U.S. dollar, linked to gold, would be the world's most important reserve currency and the United States effectively became banker to the Western world, with the right to print and spend the principal currency."[4] What ensued in the next 40-plus years is too complex to examine here. It is sufficient to note that during that time, Japan and Germany rebuilt; the United States, faced with a growing trade deficit and budget deficits, abandoned the gold standard; and an unprecedented exchange of world currency as commodities emerged. This was followed by extensive loans to Third World countries. With those loans went conditionality, the conditional being structural adjustment.

Structural adjustment as the salvation from national and international economic insecurity was a natural by-product of the Reagan-Thatcher-Mulroney era, posited as it was on an idealized nineteenth century laissez-faire. It comes from, as J.B. Foster notes, a "renewed faith in the rationalizing effect of market forces in the face of economic stagnation."[5] Structural adjustment involves, in fact, a number of complementary actions, all mutually targeted to producing a so-called level playing field on a global scale. These actions include privatization, deregulation and liberalization of national economies. Much of this is familiar to Canadians for this is precisely what the Canadian government has been pursuing with the Canada-US Free Trade Agreement and with the North American Free Trade Agreement. The impact of structural adjustment, it is assumed, will remove supposedly artificial obstacles and allow for the rational correction of the current crisis by removing the obstructions to natural market forces.

Part of adjusting to create a level playing field, however, means "a weakened, restructured labour force with lowered expectations."[6] Thus, part of restructuring for global competitiveness has meant deregulating or decertifying unions in the United Kingdom, New Zealand and elsewhere in the developed world. In the developing world, it has meant devalued domestic currencies, high unemployment, increased poverty and starvation, inflation of the cost of living and, as a strategy for global competitiveness, the establishment of free trade zones within a number of these countries.

Furthermore, within the developing nations, all of these factors have led to disproportionately increased poverty among women. This appears somewhat ironic, since much of this increase in poverty happened during the second half of the United Nations Decade for Women. However, since women are the poorest and most politically and economically vulnerable members of the global community, they also represent the largest so-called surplus labour force. Hence, we have the incongruity that while both nationally and internationally, more equity legislation was introduced into charters and constitutions and international agreements than ever before in recorded history, at the same time, the transnational corporations of advanced economies were utilizing the world's poor women as an avenue out of the stagnation of their own domestic economies by moving some of their operations to free trade zones. As Lourdes Benería states:

> The existence of a large pool of female labour at a world scale is being used to deal with the pressures of international competition, profitability crises, and economic restructuring that characterize the current reorganization of production. The availability of cheap female labour has also been an instrumental factor in the export-led policies of their world countries shifting from previous import-substitution strategies.[7]

The 1989 United Nations World Survey on Women concludes that :

> [T]he bottom line shows that ... economic progress for women has virtually stopped, social progress has slowed, social well-being in many cases has deteriorated and, because of the importance of women's social and economic role, the aspirations for them in current development strategies will not be met.[8]

Environmental Sustainability

Having briefly outlined the parameters of structural adjustment, one can now ask, "what does this mean for environmental sustainability?" It is evident that any attempt to repay debts and remain competitive in such a global market under such conditions is almost impossible for a Third World country and increasingly difficult for developed nations like Canada. To look first at the seemingly more favourable conditions in Canada, consider that environmental protection in developed nations like our own is only a relatively recent phenomenon. Laureen Snider argues that even within the boundaries of a nation-state, where a conflict arises between business interests and environmental protection, business wins. Thus, both in Canada and the United States "environmental protection varies from poor to nonexistent, basically ... because of the power of business."[9] When we add to this the power of transnational corporations which take on supernumerary roles, traversing the globe and engaging in negotiations that change the quality of life and laws in various domestic economies, we begin to realize the resistance which any attempt to protect the environment meets. To quote Snider again with respect to the situation in Canada:

> As with occupational health and protection laws, provinces and countries fear they will be at a competitive disadvantage if they strengthen environmental regulations unilaterally. Industries have always tried to minimize the costs of operation by moving to the cheapest locations they can find. Free trade between Canada and the United States has often resulted in industries from Canada and northern U.S. states relocating to the less regulated south ... With an extension of the free trade agreement to Mexico, many can be expected to join the already extensive migration ... ,taking advantage of cheap labour and lax environmental regulations there.[10]

In developing countries, the situation is exacerbated by the very nature of their so-called competitive edge outlined by Snider (i.e., cheap labour, lax environmental regulations). The combination of a heavy debt load, structural adjustment, and a radical change in the basis of domestic economies in Third World nations guarantees that such nations cannot put the environment before economic survival. As Swift summarizes the problem:

> It is simply not possible to push the idea of sustainable development while insisting also on debt repayment, favourable access to minerals and agricultural resources for transnational corporations, and cuts in the public

sector and lower levels of social spending by Third World governments. Such an economic model is bound to focus not on environmental safeguards but on achieving a better trade and payments balance–the kind of policy package known as 'structural adjustment'. The notion that the same ideologies of industrial growth that created the environmental crisis can bring about 'sustainable growth' is, in the end, not only puzzling but also dangerous.[11]

Food aid distribution over the past decade has involved countries where, predictably, famine follows deforestation and desertification and developed nations' do-gooders attempt to teach modern farming methods to previously agrarian peoples who destroyed their environment cash-cropping for markets in the developed world. The perversity of this pattern is sufficiently mind-boggling to make us search for alternative, more coherent explanations of the problem.

Essentially, we have here three cycles of activity. The first is the externally imposed requirement within a Third World country to move from traditionally agrarian subsistence farming to large scale cash crop farming. This results in a cycle of famine. This, in turn, results in foreign food-aid and the attempt by non-profit organizations from industrialized countries to bring modern agricultural farming methods to the famine-stricken area, along with the food-aid, as a means of eliminating starvation. The latter cycle may initially be done in relative ignorance by well-intentioned individuals who are unaware that the cycle of famine was predictably engineered by previous development strategies. Rather, it is sometimes assumed that there is an inability among poor nations to deal with what are believed to be naturally caused disasters such as famine in Ethiopia or flooding in Bangladesh. These disasters, however, are not caused by whims of nature. Nor are they caused by the ignorance of peoples who merely need instruction in ecological conservation. Rather, "Third World countries are caught up in a desperate and vicious process of destroying their natural resources simply to service debt and allow short-term survival."[12] They are also doing so because they have lost control of their domestic economies and of national self-governance.

The environmental damage seems reminiscent and evocative. It brings to mind images of the pollution and environmental degradation which was endemic to the Industrial Revolution. The difference here is that the negotiations and damages incurred by development have been transnational in nature and have seemingly gone beyond the capacity of nation-states to control effectively . This is not just a difference in scale but a difference in kind. As J. P. Berlan summarizes:

> Transnational companies are involved in all manner of hazardous ventures in Third World countries. They are building nuclear power plants, constructing massive dam projects, undertaking large mining and mineral-processing ventures, and investing in manufacturing that uses dangerous chemicals and produces hazardous wastes. In most Third World countries health and safety regulations inside plants are either non-existent or weak. Environmental standards to govern industry are just starting to be taken seriously. Most Third World governments are so desperate to attract investment that companies are in a good position to reduce their costs by saving on expensive pollution controls and health and safety equipment for workers.[13]

Such radical shifts in power from national economies to transnational corporations and supranational monetary funds has lead some intellectuals to embrace a new political cynicism and existential ennui captured by the general heading, post-modernism. David Harvey summarizes this state as a loss of faith in progress, science and technology and a total agnosticism with respect to any political or collective solutions. At least psychologically, if not epistemologically, this is similar to the political inertia noted at the beginning of this chapter, the position of the extreme globalist, and

> carries the implication that no change is possible except on the international level, and since there is no political mechanism for such change–aside from that of formal relations among governments–oppositional political activity is easily seen as useless.[14]

The Remnant State?

This brings us to these final questions: "Do we have both conceptually and factually or descriptively an erosion of nationhood or statehood?" And, if so, "What does this mean for such global problems as environmental sustainability?"

Robert Reich has argued that it is no longer meaningful to speak of nations in terms of national economies because the emerging global economy has rendered those economies irrelevant. He states:

As almost every factor of production–money, technology, factories, and equipment–moves effortlessly across borders, the very idea of an American economy is becoming meaningless, as are the notions of an American corporation, American capital, American products, and American technology. A similar transformation is affecting every other nation, some faster and more profoundly than others.[15]

This perspective is echoed in the discussion of national governance in the 1991 UN World Investment Report which notes:

One of the trends highlighted in the present volume is the growing regionalization of the world economy. National economies are becoming increasingly linked in regional groupings, whether through initiatives at the political level, as in the case of the integration of the European Community, or through activities at the private-sector level ... As described in this report, regionalization is one of the important factors behind the recent growth of foreign direct investment and its growing role in the world economies.[16]

For those concerned with Canada's involvement in free trade agreements, the question of Canadian sovereignty is central. As Manfred Bienefeld notes with respect to financial deregulation.

[T]he political content of financial regulation is usually entirely neglected when the multilateral agencies stress the importance of international regulation while advocating national deregulation even though this means giving up a large degree of autonomy in domestic... policy.[17]

To this, Easter adds:

In Canada, our true sovereignty as a nation is being lost as we replace political debate and decision-making for community goals, with the absolute rule of the market ... Almost all ... [good policies] ... are now being lost or rendered useless under the guise of "competitiveness" and "open borders".[18]

But there is something to remain cognizant of when we look at the literature on the loss of national economic autonomy and sovereignty. It is nations that are the key agents in negotiating deregulation, privatization and free trade deals. In the worst literature on the globalization of the economy it is as if Adam Smith's invisible hand had been replaced by the invisible man, for all we hear about are global economic forces that require structual adjustments.

In liberal democracies, we view nation-states as protectors of basic rights, both positive and negative, and basic civil liberties. Today, they are, in fact, involved in global negotiations that may erode the very principles on which they are based. This affects not only rights meant to ensure the quality of life, including the fight to live in a clean and sustainable environment, within given nations but also diminishes the possibility for the growth of democracy and democratic rights on a global scale. As Foster points out:

> [A]s each state makes its economy leaner and meaner to enlarge its own internally generated profits and export the crisis to others, the stress on the world economy intensifies, and international cooperation–always a dim possibility–becomes more remote.[19]

Interestingly, as regional deprivation within developed economies increasingly mirrors the economies in developing nations, we witness what we previously only saw in countries like India, where at Bhopal, the prime minister of the country was willing to put jobs at any cost before anything else. As we add the nations of the former Soviet Union to this mix, we observe with seeming fatalism the bottom-rung position which both environmental protection and quality of life issues take in the turmoil of establishing political and economic security.

Not only, however, do forward-looking principles of rights and benefits get undermined, as nation after nation positions for a competitive advantage that results in levelling to the lowest common denominator. Global negotiation, coupled with financial deregulation and the development of information technology, has resulted in unbridled corruption and crime. As a chief financial officer of the Bank of Montreal noted:

> I can hide money in the twinkling of an eye from all of the bloodhounds that could be put on the case, and I would be so far ahead of them that there would never be a hope of unravelling the trail ... Technology today means that that sort of thing can be done through electronic means.[20]

In a related argument, Clive Thomas claims that:

> [T]he contradictory development of bureaucracy in the face of ideological assaults on the state ... includes a burgeoning growth of corruption, which has reached such staggering proportions that some social scientists see it as an "independent productive factor".[21]

With respect to the environment, this level of corruption, coupled with desperation, has been evidenced in the Third World as nations vie for position to accept toxic waste from developed countries in contravention of international law.

So, does all of this mean that the notion of statehood has shifted, diminished or been eroded? I would say unequivocally not. What has been eroded is not statehood but democracy and the ability of citizens within democratic states to exercise democratic rights. Democracy has been undermined or subverted and people have been disempowered, but states have not. This is not only true with respect to developed countries which have some type of democratic governance, but also bodes ill for the establishment of new democracies. Canada is less democratic to the extent that deregulation, privatization and economic liberalization have been accomplished. To the extent that nations are willing to use such factors as economic bargaining chips, the possibility for democracy in other nations is weakened. With deregulation, privatization and economic liberalization, environmental sustainability becomes one more barrier to competitiveness, as do social programmes and other quality of life indicators.

Assuming as I do that democracy is a good thing, what should be done about this? At the beginning of this chapter, I pointed out what I thought were false alternatives: on the one hand, extreme globalism that accepts the world defeat of nationhood and, on the other, naive nationalism which we encounter frequently in Canada these days as Canadians try to claw back Canada's social democracy from its recent demise. So, what is my solution? Well, it is not a new idea. Essentially, all nations need to negotiate internationally from a position where they can set their own national priorities with respect to the social, political and economic needs of their citizens. This is something that increasingly has been given up even in nations like Canada where there is still the possibility of exercising collective political will. All nations have to negotiate from a position of national self-sufficiency. Transnational corporations have a political and undemocratic message that citizens in all nations have to be more competitive and that is to be accomplished by dismantling national institutions, social programmes and environmental protections. The fact that competitiveness without the protection of our natural resources, our infrastructure and social programmes amount to mass suicide is rarely considered. What I conclude here may sound reminiscent of the cultural imperialism of a former era, but it behooves those of us with the privilege to still resist global degradation and the erosion of basic rights and freedoms to do so and not allow our nations to bargain away the world. As John Maynard Keynes noted in 1933:

> The divorce between ownership and the real responsibility of management is serious within a country when, as a result of joint-stock enterprise, ownership is broken up between innumerable individuals who buy their interest today and sell it tomorrow and lack altogether both knowledge and responsibility towards what they monetarily own. But when this same principle is applied internationally, it is, in times of stress, intolerable–I am irresponsible toward what I own and those who operate what I own are irresponsible towards me.[22]

The solution to the problem of divorce here is reconciliation rather than resignation and resistance to the false and alarming rhetoric of global greed that has benumbed our better sensibilities.

Endnotes

[1] Adam Smith, *Wealth of Nations*, Erwin Cannan, ed. (New York: Random House, 1977), 423.

[2] H.E. Daly and J.B. Cobb, *For the Common Good: Redirecting the Economy Toward Community, the Environment and a Sustainable Future* (Boston: Beacon Press, 1989), 215.

[3] A. MacEwan and W. K. Tabb, eds., *Instability and Change in the World Economy* (New York: Monthly Review Press, 1989), 24.

[4] Jamie Swift and the Ecumenical Coalition for Economic Justice, "The Debt Crisis: A Case of Global Usury," in J. Swift and B. Tomlinson, eds., *Conflicts of Interest: Canada and the Third World* (Toronto: Between the Lines, 1991), 82.

[5] J.B. Foster, "The Age of Restructuring," in MacEwan and Tabb, eds., *Instability and Change in the World Economy*, 281.

[6] Ibid.

[7] L. Benería, "Gender and the Global Economy," in MacEwan and Tabb, eds., *Instability and Change in the World Economy*, 250.

[8] United Nations, *1989 World Survey on the Role of Women in Development* (New York: United Nations, 1989), xiv.

[9] L. Snider, *Bad Business: Corporate Crime in Canada* (Toronto: Nelson, 1993), 194.

[10] Ibid.

[11] L. Swift, "The Environmental Challenge: Towards a Survival Economy," in J. Swift and B. Tomlinson, eds., *Conflicts of Interest: Canada and the Third World*, 215-216.

[12] J. P. Berlan, "Capital Accumulation, Transformation of Agriculture, and the Agriculture Crisis: A Long-Term Perspective," in MacEwan and Tabb, eds., *Instability and Change in the World Economy*, 222.

[13] Ibid., 221-222.

[14] D. Harvey, *The Condition of Postmodernity* (Oxford: Blackwell, 1990).

[15] R. Reich, *The Work of Nations: Preparing Ourselves for 21st Century Capitalism* (New York: Alfred Knopf, 1991), 8.

[16] United Nations, *World Investment Report: The Triad in Foreign Direct Investment* (New York: United Nations, 1991), 40.

[17] M. Bienefeld, "Financial Deregulation: Disarming the Nation States," *Studies in Political Economy* 37 (1992), 31-58.

[18] W. Easter, "How Much Lower is Low Enough?" in J. Sinclair, ed., *Crossing the Line* (Vancouver: New Star Books, 1992), 93.

[19] Foster, "The Age of Restructuring," in MacEwan and Tabb, eds., *Instability and Change in the World Economy*, 294.

[20] R. Naylor, *Hot Money and the Politics of Debt* (Toronto: McClelland and Stewart, 1987), 12.

[21] C. Thomas, "Restructuring the World Economy and its Political Implications for the Third World," in MacEwan and Tabb, eds., *Instability and Change in the World Economy*, 337.

[22] J.M. Keynes, "National Self-Sufficiency," in D. Moggeridge, ed., *The Collected Writings of John Maynard Keynes*, Vol. 21 (London: Cambridge University Press, 1933).

CHAPTER 12

BIOREGIONALISM VS. GLOBALIZATION

John Cartwright

John Cartwright teaches courses in Third World and environmental politics at The University of Western Ontario where he is a Professor in the Department of Political Science. His major current research interest is the politics of maintaining biodiversity, and in particular, the problems of maintaining tropical and temperate zone forest ecosystems. He has done work for the International Union for the Conservation of Nature and is currently president of the Federation of Ontario Naturalists.

Many governments today are pursuing sharply divergent agendas in the spheres of environmental and economic management. Their environmental agenda almost always professes to focus on the ecological concepts of "bioregionalism" and the "ecosystem approach," emphasizing the interdependent network of interactions among all life forms within a bounded area, although the practice does tend to lag behind the professions. However, the same governments' economic management is guided by the economic concept of "globalization," which in essence means the integration of all areas of the world into a single market economy. It is my contention that *globalization is the direct antithesis of the bioregional or ecosystem approach,* and furthermore poses far and away the most serious threat to the long-term viability of individual ecosystems and bioregions.

An ecosystem is essentially all of the interactions among living organisms, and between these organisms and their physical surroundings, within a more or less bounded area. A "bioregion" is the next step up in the scale of biologically interdependent units, and thus for the purposes of this chapter, I shall use the two terms interchangeably. What is significant here is that concern for an ecosystem or a bioregion implies that we will try to work within the *limits* of that bioregion, that we will not log the trees or till the soil beyond their capacity to regenerate and sustain the elements of the bioregion. Two further implications are that the people who live in one bioregion should not assume that they can make up any overuse of the resources in their area by drawing on the resources of another bioregion, and that because we do not fully understand the role of most specific organisms in maintaining an ecosystem, we should try to maintain the maximum biodiversity of genes and species within each ecosystem.

Globalization, by contrast, refers to the capacity of international private businesses to shift their capital and technology freely, anywhere in the world, as the need for resources and markets drives them. This ability to move freely throughout the world's markets allows the possessors of capital to use up the resources of any given bioregion and then move on to seek more of those resources wherever else they may exist. In saying this, I am not suggesting there is anything immoral or wicked about these businesses. What they are doing is following the law of the market (and the requirement of their shareholders) that they maximize their profits. Whatever the individuals who manage a particular business may feel personally about their responsibility for a particular bioregion, if they refrain from exhausting the resources of a bioregion and then moving on, while other businesses do ditch that region and move along, then those managers are likely to be looking for another job. In short, we should not expect private businesses to practise voluntary self-restraint, since this is essentially asking them to commit suicide.

The job of imposing restraints upon businesses' exploitation of particular bioregions rests squarely with a quite different type of organization, namely the governments of the world's states. Unfortunately, since the end of World War II, there has been a concerted effort by the United States, generally supported by other industrialized capitalist states, to limit the ability of *any* jurisdiction to provide effective protection against the destruction of any or all ecosystems within its boundaries. This has been done through a series of worldwide and regional treaties whose ostensible purpose is to liberalize international trade by establishing a framework of international rules which facilitates the free movement of international business and, at the same time, handicaps any state which tries to pull out of the world market system. These treaties lock rich and poor countries alike into a system whose main beneficiaries are multinational private corporations which are free to roam wherever they wish on the planet in search of the resources they need to conduct their business.

Why it is Important to Use an "Ecosystem Approach"

From a broad environmental perspective, there are compelling reasons to consider the long-term health of every ecosystem, every bioregion. Each one represents a unique web of interdependence among organisms, each of which has adapted itself in order to exist in a relationship with others, and it is a rather arrogant assumption of God-like powers for us to take upon ourselves the right to decide which shall continue to exist, and which shall disappear. Even from a more narrowly anthropocentric viewpoint, it seems somewhat arrogant to assume that the rich industrialized nations can use up the resources of a particular bioregion when those who depend upon that bioregion for their whole existence have no place else to go. If logging companies clear-cut the Northern Ontario forests, destroying the game and the fish of the area in the process, the aboriginal people can hardly take up farming or move to Toronto.

There are also more positive reasons for ensuring the continued viability of all bioregions. First, we scarcely know what potential benefits, in the form of natural resources and also of knowledge, await our discovery in even the best known temperate zone ecosystems, let alone the more complex tropical ones. For example, it is only in recent years that we have learned about the mouse-fungus-conifer relationship so essential to the growth of our highly valued commercial trees,[1] or the anti-cancer drug taxol, which is found in the bark of a previously despised "weed tree," the Pacific yew. Second, we do know from experience some of the losses that can be incurred from destroying ecosystems: for example, the silting up of hydro dams and other water supply systems when the forests in their watersheds are logged.[2] Third, we also know that the ramifications of the destruction of one ecosystem extend beyond its boundaries: for example, the recent declines in neo-tropical bird migrants to Canada seem at least partially attributable to tropical deforestation.[3] If we are going to maintain healthy ecosystems, it is important that we take an overall perspective of the ways in which they function and the requisites for their survival. We cannot afford to allow single-purpose agencies, be they forestry officers, dam-builders, or mining companies, to pursue their goals regardless of the side effects on other concerns.

The Drive for Global Free Trade

Yet it is precisely at this juncture, after our expansion of economies and of population has driven us into almost all the bioregions of the world, and when we are just beginning to become aware of the potential costs of disrupting all of these bioregions, that there are unprecedented thrusts to intensify long-standing patterns inherent in the world capitalist system to over-exploit individual ecosystems and then move on. We are heading toward a crisis because at the same time as we have reached the frontiers of the planet's ecosystems, we have increased our capabilities to move rapidly from one bioregion to another.

One element in this increased capability is simply our technological progress. One man operating a feller-buncher can cut and place at the roadside 12 cords of wood in the time the most expert lumberjack with a chainsaw can cut and stack one[4]–and the feller-buncher can work 24 hours a day. However, in the past two decades, the most important steps in stripping away the defences of individual bioregions around the world have been an interlocked series of *political* developments, whose thrust have been to strip away the ability of nominally sovereign states to protect themselves against invasions by outside capital.

The key political developments are, first, the intensification of efforts to "free" international trade in areas that essentially benefit the countries whose economies are most "developed" (intellectual property, patenting of genes in agriculture, and trade in services, as well as reducing protection for local industries); and second, the neo-conservative campaign to denigrate the ability of states to use their powers for the good of their citizens, which has resulted in a diminution of the ability of states to control economic activities within their borders for societal ends. The effect of this propaganda campaign has been shown most dramatically in the rush of the Eastern European states to embrace the "market economy," jettisoning all the social safeguards their previous regimes had developed. It has been equally effective, however, in persuading Western states chanting the mantra of "free markets" to lock themselves out of the right to act in key areas through provisions in trade treaties, such as the Canada-US Free Trade Agreement (FTA), the North American Free Trade Agreement (NAFTA), the European Community treaties, and the General Agreement on Tariffs and Trade (GATT). The result of these two thrusts of "trade liberalization" and the curbing of the power of individual states has been a power vacuum which has allowed multinational businesses to assert increasing power in the name of "free markets" and a kind of pseudo-competition in which the people of the world are free to choose which multinational corporation's products they will buy and consume, but not whether they will buy and consume the products of multinationals.

GATT is the major mechanism for regulating international trade. Its basic purpose is simple–to reduce the impediments to the free flow of trade among nations, to ensure that such restrictions as a country applies to the movement of trade goods are applied equally to goods produced inside and outside its borders, and to change any non-tariff barriers to trade into tariffs, which can then be gradually reduced. From its inception in 1947, this approach was applied to the movement of physical goods. In the Uruguay Round, which began in 1986, the United States and other industrial states have sought to widen its application to other "property," notably services and "intellectual property." Defenders of GATT argue that it does include in Article XX the means whereby a country can control imports or exports for environmental purposes, but the wording seems rather restrictive:

> [Provided] such measures are not… a disguised restriction on international trade, nothing in this Agreement shall … prevent the adoption … of measures… necessary to protect human, animal or plant life or health.

As Shrybman points out, "there is no reported precedent under GATT that invokes this provision to justify environmental protection measures,"[5] though there certainly are precedents for countries being told they *cannot* claim any environmental justification for measures. For example, the United States used the GATT to challenge a Canadian law requiring salmon and herring caught in our West Coast waters to be landed in Canada for inspection–and won, despite the Canadian claim that this measure was necessary in order to control the numbers of fish caught.[6] Similarly, Ontario's attempt to impose an "environmental tax" on beer cans, while letting returnable bottles stay untaxed, seems likely to be successfully challenged under GATT.

It is true that in many cases, allegedly "environmental" regulations are really intended as disguised protection of domestic businesses–the salmon landing rules probably, and Ontario's environmental tax on beer cans almost certainly (because it does not apply to soft drink cans), are cases in point. However, there still is an element of environmental protection in each of these measures which surely needs to be weighed against the benefits of freer trade in commodities. The fundamental problem here is that "freeing trade" is elevated to an absolute good, while "environmental protection" is treated as only one of a number of competing claims.

The general prohibition under GATT against import and export controls has a number of serious anti-environmental effects. One effect is that countries cannot insist upon processing raw materials within their borders, an approach which could help Third World countries obtain more value from such commodities as timber and thus reduce the amounts of forest they need to cut in order to pay their debts. Ironically, the proposed provisions against controls on exports may even be used against the United States, where the states of Washington and Oregon have tried to restrict whole log exports to Japan.[7] Another effect is that countries or lesser jurisdictions which have imposed high standards on pesticide, growth hormone, and other residues in agricultural products, or imposed environmental restrictions on how products may be obtained, can find these rules overridden by GATT's terms. Again, the United States and the European Community, which have each put strict (although different) rules in place about these residues, can expect that as a result of "harmonization" of different GATT members' rules, their standards will be lowered to those that can be accepted worldwide.[8] To some extent, this is a fight between two branches of the United States government. The US Congress has imposed rather strict limits on the allowable residual amounts of pesticides such as DDT, while the Bush administration sought to have the limits set according to "scientific evidence" to be provided primarily by the international Codex Alimentarius, whose standards tend to be a good deal weaker than those of most Western industrialized countries.

The most serious effect of GATT's export rules, however, will be upon those Third World countries which have a significant agricultural export sector and a large number of rural dwellers who simply do not have the cash income to buy their food supplies in a market. These people, who comprise much of the population of Latin America, South and Southeast Asia, and most of Africa, can manage satisfactorily as long as they can grow their own staple foods, but they must have access to land to survive outside the market economy. Under the present GATT, Article XI, 2 (a) only allows export restrictions to be *"temporarily* [my emphasis] applied to prevent or relieve critical shortages of foodstuffs ...," and the US has sought to abolish even this minimal protection for local food self-sufficiency.[9] Because landowners and other elites in most of these countries benefit from export sales, and also because the governments are being pressured by the West to pay their debts, it is not surprising to find that increasing amounts of land are being pre-empted for export crops, and that the small farmers who need to grow their own food are being pushed into ecologically unsuitable areas, such as hillsides in Mexico or the rainforests of Brazil, Peru, or Kalimantan. Thus, in order to provide exports to the rich Western countries, whole tropical ecosystems are being destroyed, and this process is being maintained on pain of sanctions under the GATT.

Regional trade arrangements work equally strongly against environmental measures. The European Community's Court of Justice ruled in 1988 that despite the Community's mandate to protect the quality of the environment, Denmark's attempt to require all beverages to be sold in returnable bottles tipped the balance too far against free trade and toward environmental protection. This ruling made clear that, within the European Community, there is no absolute right for a country to protect its environment. The Canada-United States Free Trade Agreement is replete with examples of an anti-environment bias. For example, there is no protection against charges of "trade-distorting subsidization" for a province that pays the cost of replanting its forests, as British Columbia learned to its cost. However, Section 906 provides explicit protection for subsidies in aid of oil exploration, although such exploration in areas such as the Beaufort Sea and the coasts of Newfoundland risks a major environmental disaster, and more broadly, our continuing reliance on fossil fuels engenders myriad environmental problems.

One particularly insidious proposal is the attempt to introduce patent protection for "intellectual property" into the Uruguay Round agreement. Now if this were simply an attempt to control the pirating of books and records, one could feel some sympathy for the people whose goods were being taken. However, this proposal includes international protection for the patenting of life forms–in other words, for the seeds that farmers plant and the domestic animals that they raise. The country which provided the basis for this patentable material may not only get nothing from it, but may even have to pay for the privilege of getting its genetic material back. A classic case is the chance acquisition of a genetic source which enabled American tomato growers to add some US$8 million a year to the value of their tomato crops, thanks to a botanist who spotted a small weedy plant by a Peruvian roadside and sent its seeds back to a US plant breeding programme.[10] So far as I know, none of that money ever went back to Peru, and under the proposed new rules, if Peruvian farmers want to obtain the improved tomato seeds, they will have to pay handsomely for the privilege.

One ironic twist in the attempt to protect commercial biotechnology through the "intellectual property" rules is the proposal to allow "cross-retaliation." This means that rather than retaliating in the same area (say, agriculture), the country imposing retaliatory sanctions could act in the area of, say, textile imports. The FTA, which provides simply for retaliation by taking away "equivalent benefits" in any area the griever chooses, may be the pattern of the future. If the right of "cross-retaliation" is imbedded in the GATT rules concerning intellectual property, it will mark a sharp departure from the principle (as *The Economist* put it), that "a country cannot restrict trade on one product (say, Japanese computers) to enforce unrelated environmental policies (say, on whales)."[11] The interests within a country wanting cross-retaliation on intellectual property are, needless to say, quite different from those who want it to be applied for environmental purposes.

A key question in examining the process of regulation under GATT or the regional agreements such as the FTA and NAFTA is, "Who are the arbiters who make the determinations? and to whom are these arbiters accountable?" Essentially, the arbiters are individuals selected through a closed executive process, with no public investigation of their biasses or values.[12] In the GATT, their findings have to be accepted by the governing council, which is comprised of representatives chosen by the executive bodies of the member states, and thus are at one remove from any electoral accountability. Although one probably does not want electoral accountability for persons who are in effect acting as judges, it seems equally undesirable for the final decision to be in the hands of persons who are acting for "reasons of state." The two most dangerous aspects of this process, however, are:

(1) that because the process by which determinations are made is essentially an executive one, there is almost no public examination of the reasons behind determinations, nor even of the individuals who make them; and

(2) because the whole process involves the application of global rules, there is no room for consideration of the needs of the particular bioregion or ecosystem that will be affected by the ruling.

My general conclusion, then, is that the GATT and the regional agreements involving major industrialized states have served to tie the hands of any state which may seek to impose regulations to protect the bioregions within its boundaries against exploitation through international trade, which means by and large through transnational corporations. Ironically, but perhaps not surprisingly, these restraints are being imposed at a time when the citizens in the industrialized states are becoming more vocal than ever before in demanding that their governments provide effective protection for their environments. To accommodate these citizens' demands, governments *want to be seen to be* setting out elaborate rules and procedures for environmental assessments of projects, stringent limits for the use of toxic chemicals, and so on. While all this public activity is going on, however, an almost diametrically opposite agenda is being pursued by these governments behind the scenes, in that they are tying their own and future governments' hands against the possibility of tightening regulations on the untrammelled exploitation of natural resources, the use of chemicals in agriculture, the dumping of toxic wastes, and a wide range of other issues that have caused concern.

The secretive way in which governments' ability to protect their citizens against harmful environmental effects is being weakened gives rise to justifiable suspicions that this is a deliberate attempt to circumvent the growing efforts by citizens to prevent environmental damage. It is specious to argue, as do the more devout believers in the efficacy of markets, that as long as consumers have information on the environmental effects of their purchases, their individual decisions will produce all the environmental benefits that are necessary.[13] Even if full information could be winnowed out from the torrent of advertising campaigns for the "greenness" of particular commercial products, it is hard to imagine any consumer having the time to absorb it even for all the products he or she uses daily. The problems of determining what impact production processes have on the environment at all stages in transforming raw materials into a finished product, including calculations for those effects which are imperfectly known, would pose considerable difficulty for any private individual or group. It seems pretty clear that only governments have the resources to undertake full environmental assessments on behalf of all their citizens.

What, then, might we do to reconcile international trade with environmental needs? I have two proposals which could improve the situation, though neither is a panacea. First, we need to change the GATT, and also the regional agreements such as the FTA, to incorporate explicit safeguards for any country wishing to impose rules that will protect its environment. These would include the right to levy a countervailing duty on goods entering from any country whose environmental standards were lower than its own, sufficient to cover the savings in costs of production for the offending country. Such a rule would encourage a "leveling up" of environmental standards rather than the present "leveling down." They would also have to include the right to stop the export or import of any product which was producing harmful environmental effects. There would, to be sure, be very substantial problems in determining when an environmental ban was in fact being imposed simply to protect a domestic industry, but here an international tribunal could surely still be used. The key point is to strengthen the requirement that the environmental costs of activities be considered in relation to the other considerations that are currently examined. Second, the process by which determinations of violations of international agreements are made needs to become more "transparent," to be carried out by individuals who operate in a more public fashion, so that their reasoning and the positions they have taken could be publicly discussed. Something akin to an open trial in the International Court of Justice might be appropriate. Neither of these changes would guarantee sounder decisions, but they would at least provide a system which would be pushed to pay more heed to public concerns as opposed to the more secretive self-interest of major corporations.

Endnotes

[1] Chris Maser, *The Redesigned Forest* (Toronto: Stoddart, 1990), 22-35.

[2] To give but two examples: By the mid 1970s, silting of the Panama Canal caused by deforestation had forced large ships to divert around Cape Horn; in Tegucigalpa, the capital of Honduras, a study showed that the cost of treating water from the protected La Tigra forest reserve was 1/23 the cost of treating water from an unforested reservoir. *IUCN Bulletin* 18 (1988), 10, 4.

[3] See David Hussell, "Declines in Migrant Birds at Long Point," *LPBO Newsletter* 24 (1) (Spring 1992), 12-14; John Terborgh, "Why Songbirds are Vanished," *Scientific American* (May 1992), 98-104.

[4] Jamie Swift, *Cut and Run: The Assault on Canada's Forests* (Toronto: Between the Lines, 1983), 140.

[5] Steven Shrybman, "Free Trade v. the Environment: The Implications of GATT," *The Ecologist* 20(1) (January/February 1990), 33.

[6] See Canada-United States Trade Commission, "Chapter 18 Panel Report: In the matter of Canada's landing requirement for Pacific coast salmon and herring. Final Report of the Panel," (October 16, 1989).

[7] Mark Ritchie, "GATT, Agriculture and the Environment: The U.S. Double Zero Plan," *The Ecologist* 20(6) (November/December 1990), 215.

[8] Ibid., 216.

[9] Shrybman, "Free Trade v. the Environment," 31.

[10] The discovery of the tomatoes and their genetic effect is told by their discoverer, Hugh Iltis. See his "Serendipity in the Exploration of Biodiversity: What Good are Weedy Tomatoes?" in E.O. Wilson, ed., *Biodiversity* (Washington, D.C.: National Academy Press, 1988), 98-105.

[11] "The Greening of Protectionism," *The Economist*, February 27, 1993, 25.

[12] Articles 22 and 23 of the GATT lay down the following procedure if the parties involved cannot agree: 1) the complainant requests a panel; 2) the Council (GATT's member states) approves the request; 3) the parties try to find three persons of appropriate background from countries not party to the dispute; 4) if the parties cannot agree, the Director General appoints panel members; 5) the panel takes its recommendation to Council for ratification.

[13] For an example of the pro-market argument, see "The Greening of Protectionism," 25-28.

CHAPTER 13

BIOREGIONALISM VS. FREE TRADE: AN EXPLORATION OF THE ISSUES

Susan Holtz

Susan Holtz is a private consultant who specializes in energy, environment, and sustainable development policy. She also works in public participation as a programme analyst and facilitator. Holtz has served on numerous advisory bodies and boards, including the C.E.D.A.R. Balanced Fund, the Canadian Environmental Advisory Council, the Canadian Environmental Assessment Research Council, and the Nova Scotia Round Table on Environment and Economy. She is currently Vice Chair of the National Round Table on the Environment and Economy. As an adjunct professor, Holtz teaches several courses in the Environmental Planning Department of the Nova Scotia College of Art and Design.

Introduction: Talking Past Each Other

To say that I have been distressed by the quality of public debate in this country for the last few years is a polite understatement. "Driven crazy by it" gives a better sense of my private reaction, if not my public demeanour. If I were to characterize recent discussion of such issues as the Goods and Services Tax, constitutional reform, or the North American Free Trade Agreement (NAFTA), "closed-minded," "under informed," and "smugly self-righteous" are just the beginning of a string of phrases that come to mind and I am referring here to statements by all sides.

Although I do not admire the tone of the debate, what I mainly object to is not that there is emotional heat, but rather that the heat that is generated sheds so little light. The reasons for this situation are built into the way public discourse is structured, particularly by the media, political parties, and advocacy groups. In dealing with trade-environment issues, my intent is to look first at what is making this discussion so acrimonious and unenlightening.

To start with, much media commentary on any issue is based on winning and losing. This is appropriate enough if there are only two possible outcomes of the debate, such as a guilty or innocent verdict. However, the real task of public policy is the framing of problems and the generation and refinement of solutions. Obviously, this supposes a multitude of possibilities, but it is in the interests of journalists to simplify and polarize the discussion into opposing positions. Such a presentation reduces the need to master facts and nuances, and also turns the dry complexities of policy into drama, with all the colour of personality, confrontation, and competition.

In addition to this simplification of policy debate into pros and cons, the fact that policy is so closely tied to a heavily enforced system of partisan politics turns every proposition into a test of political loyalty. Even when narrow party loyalty is not an issue, the rise of advocacy groups, coupled with widespread public disaffection with government, tends to make every issue into a credal affirmation of political alignment with opposition or support for the status quo. This ensures that debate will focus on attack and defense, rather than an open-minded search for truth and good judgement.

Such, it seems to me, are the socio-political circumstances of debate surrounding trade and environment. But it is the *analytical* consequences of this polarization that are most distressing. People are not discussing real disagreements, they are simply talking past one another. It reminds me of the intellectual stand-off on the topic of energy and the environment in the mid-1970s, after the first OPEC oil embargo, but before Amory Lovins' ground-breaking article, "The Road Not Taken," in *Foreign Affairs* in 1976. That debate, and this one too, are characterized by four things:

- lack of clarity about the assumptions, facts, and even interests on which each side's positions are based;
- lack of acknowledgment of the legitimacy of any interests and concerns of the opposing side;
- unwillingness by the opposing sides to acknowledge any shared assumptions and facts; and
- unwillingness to explore exactly where and why any shared understandings begin to diverge.

Trying to sort out the entire debate about trade and the environment along these lines is a huge job, well beyond the scope of this chapter. Nevertheless, it is an essential task. A more widely shared understanding of the links between trade and environment is central to making progress on sustainable development. Its actualization, I am convinced, will depend on finding ways to ensure that trade's role consistently reinforces both ecological sustainability and development. Of course, sustainable development requires other significant changes in direction for policy and institutions as well, but my point is that few other dimensions of sustainable development are so complex, so muddled, and so controversial. The topic is perhaps the most important conceptual impasse on sustainable development today.

As a small contribution, then, I will examine one of the great divides in the trade-environment debate: bioregionalism vs. free trade (or trade liberalization). My main purpose is not to come down on one side or the other, but to clarify the underlying interests and assumptions as a first step to laying the basis for a more pointed discussion. I will also briefly examine these positions relative to the broad concept of sustainable development. The values of sustainable development involve both human well-being and the well-being of Earth's biosphere. Neither aspect can be subordinated to the other. Thus, both a misanthropic and a narrowly anthropocentric ethical focus are ruled out by a sustainable development perspective.

Describing the History of the Debate

Perhaps the first task in trying to clarify the viewpoints underlying the environment-trade discussion is to provide an overview of the issue's history. One's own vantage point, however, obviously determines how one sees the field. As someone complaining about the quality of debate, let me therefore try to practice what I preach about the need for transparency and set out my own not-very-expert perspective.

I have been an environmental consultant for ten years, but for nearly ten years before that, I worked with or for citizens' groups in the environmental movement. I still consider myself an environmentalist. Although I have worked on many issues and projects, some of my most in-depth policy work has been in energy planning. I think it is fair to say that environmentally oriented energy analysts like myself–those who worked on the so-called soft energy path–were among the first environmentalists to recognize the profound interrelationship of environment and economy, and to be comfortable with all the dimensions of that relationship.

Nonetheless, and despite this orientation, international trade was not an area that we soft path energy analysts dealt with in any great depth. This is not to say that the subject was ignored. Rather, our treatment of it was rather superficial and inconsistent. On the one hand, the accepted approach we used was based on the desirability of internalizing all real environmental (and other) costs, using whatever mechanisms were most useful–regulations, taxes, fees, or whatever. That done, and, of course, it will be a long process to get that done thoroughly and accurately and as fairly as possible, then the allocative mechanism of the market was quite acceptable, in fact desirable, for making decisions about consumption, including decisions involving local, national, and international trade. Considering the many environmental consequences of energy use in the transportation sector, I think environmentalists of my background assumed that including all the environmental costs in energy prices would tend to increase transportation costs so much that these higher transport costs would become a barrier to trade for some commodities. However, it was not particularly important to try to foresee which products might be affected. The market would sort that out as time went on and technology changed.

At the same time as we were routinely using this unremarkable neoclassical approach to macroeconomics, certain aspects of the energy policy debates of the 1970s and 1980s pushed environmental policy in other directions with respect to trade.

In particular, the OPEC oil embargoes of the 1970s brought up concerns about security of supply, especially for commodities and resources essential to the functioning of society and to physical life-support. Water shortages in the American Southwest and reduced world grain reserves added to this awareness. With this new realization of how extended the physical and human networks are which provide many countries with basic human needs came fears of system breakdowns and of political and military intervention by stronger nations in order to maintain this status quo. Environmentalists, whose primary orientation was toward biophysical reality, tended to see security in terms of reducing the size of these extended networks and of constraining resource demands to local supplies. Managers in the business community, however, saw increased security in terms of enhancing management of the human networks through greater coordination.

With regard to oil, it is perhaps interesting to note that increased cooperation among countries and oil companies and also significantly reduced demand were both important, as it turned out, in managing the so-called oil crisis. It is also ironic, in retrospect, that the environmentalists' vision, which has always, in its rhetoric, stressed the necessity for cooperation, mainly put its faith in reducing the need for cooperative management. More on this topic later, however.

It is also important to recognize, in this history of the positions on trade-environment issues, that a further concern about relying on an extended network for life-support is that the environmental damage from resource extraction is felt locally and directly only by the people in the exporting country. In theory, if all the environmental costs are internalized, the price of environmental damage will be passed on to the buyer of the resource. If that price is very high, the buyer may find substitutes, or look for supplies elsewhere.

In practice, however, an urgent need for the resource, combined with its lack of availability in specific geographic areas (as in the case of oil, water, or hydroelectric potential), may well limit alternatives so greatly that even a high price will be met. As well, in cases where the main environmental concern is physical restructuring, such as in developing a new oil field in a wilderness area or building a dam, with the attendant loss of habitat and landscape value, pricing which accurately reflects this environmental change is notoriously difficult to devise.

New development means permanent physical restructuring of land. There-fore, from the perspective of trying to include all environmental costs, we are talking about incorporating the opportunity cost of losing that land-scape. Being able to justify a high enough opportunity cost to stop development in such a case is quite unusual. Assigning such a value is more a political than a narrowly economic act. The cost of environmental controls that limit pollution or even regulate some physical changes, like road construction practices, can be internalized through strict regulation and enforcement, but incorporating the costs of an irretrievable loss of a land-scape is difficult in theory and almost never happens in practice.

To get back to the inconsistent way we environmental energy analysts treated trade-related issues: along with full-cost pricing and, implicitly, the acceptance of a liberalized trade regime, we also advocated certain prag-matic constraints on trade in energy. These constraints included the prohibition of some large scale developments, such as hydroelectric dams proposed for sensitive wilderness areas and the exploitation of offshore Arctic oil, the energy production of which was dedicated to export. (Later, other analysts applied similar thinking to inter-basin water transfers.) The distinction between projects for export and projects for domestic use turned primarily on the political ability to influence demand. If reducing demand as much as possible within one's own jurisdiction still resulted in some permanent physical landscape change, then perhaps that simply was the environmental price to be paid. But outside the domestic political jurisdiction, the most effective tools for limiting demand, such as taxation policies, education and incentive programmes, or even rationing, could not be used.

As a result, another country's profligate use of an essential resource might well provide a market for new resource development in Canada that would not otherwise take place. And if such developments could not really be costed adequately because of the difficulty of internalizing opportunity costs, another, directly trade-limiting approach to certain developments might be used.

Framing the Trade and Environment Debate Today

The values filter of sustainable development, brought to the fore by the Brundtland Report in 1987 and various follow up actions, has broadened the focus of social, economic, and environmental policies. Environmental constraints on human activities are now widely accepted in theory, and at least to some degree, in practice. However, the sustainable development values shift has not resolved all issues, and the desirability of expanding economic activity remains contentious for some environmentalists. Nevertheless, the dominant frame for today's trade-environment debate remains the theoretical model of free or liberalized trade.

International trade experts believe that, through comparative advantage, expanded trade increases the size of the economic pie that everyone shares. Therefore, barriers to trade limit overall prosperity by distorting production and other costs. They also prevent the most efficient allocation of resources.[1] Since inefficiency necessarily incurs higher environmental costs, the trade experts argue, eliminating trade barriers to the greatest extent possible supports both economic development and environmental quality goals, both of which are vital for sustainable development.

However, the powerful neatness of this argument is flawed, at least as the universally accepted frame for the debate, in two ways. First, and most obviously, if you do not accept that expanded economic activity is a critical goal, the important role trade plays in advancing economic growth has little power. Indeed, if you reject the desirability of economic growth, then trade as an economic amplifier has negative value. Perhaps I should state here that I, at least, do accept Brundtland's argument that expanded economic activity is essential if the world is to address the needs of its poorest people, and that redistribution of wealth by itself is neither feasible nor sufficient to address the problem of poverty. I also accept that it is imperative to decouple physical throughput from economic growth.[2] Indeed, the degree to which this can be done will determine the size of a sustainable global economy, an economy which is, of course, ultimately limited by ecological constraints. In other words, population, technology, and ecological factors all interact to limit the size of the world economy, but technology and population can be influenced to some degree by human choices. If you believe both of those assumptions, and also do not want to predict just how much progress can be made through technological change or the degree to which population growth can be slowed, then the economic growth vs. no-growth debate fades as the critical question. But many environmentalists either do not understand or do not accept these views, and so for them, and for the broad policy discussion, the economic growth debate remains pivotal.

The second flaw in this framing of the debate is, I think, more serious. Although inefficiency does carry environmental costs, there is no single unit to measure environmental damage. Human activities *all* cause chemical, physical, and biological changes in the environment, but the magnitude and severity of change varies widely. The ecological significance of change depends on exactly what the change is, how extensive it is, how long it goes on, and what the affected environment is like. It is quite possible that the location and type of environmental change from an inefficient allocation of human economic activities would have less significant environmental consequences than those from more economically efficient actions. If, for example, economic efficiency dictated much human activity in a zone of particularly sensitive habitat, damage could be much greater than ineffi-cient activities in a resilient locale. It is an empirical matter which must be investigated in detail in each particular instance. I think no general conclu-sions can be drawn.

A third objection to this pro-trade paradigm is also brought forward by some critics, especially those involved with international development. They point out that in practice, existing economic arrangements and the disparity in political power between rich and poor nations, and between rich and poor within the developing world, will prevent any trade-related increase in economic activity from improving the lot of the poor. Moreover, these critics say, the South lacks the infrastructure and money to regulate environmental problems, and so the likely impacts of increased trade will simply be an increase in the horrible conditions that prevail in, for example, the industrial zones near the US border in Mexico.

This argument, however, does not really attack the *validity* of the trade liberalization paradigm. Rather, it asserts that the distributional effects of increased trade are more important than trade's wealth-generating potential. In other words, for these critics, the focus of the discussion is on the wrong issue: it should be on income distribution rather than on wealth generation. In its most extreme form, this argument claims that the impacts of increased trade are regressive for income distribution and negative for environmental quality as well, and therefore, trade liberalization should be opposed.

It is not my purpose to assess every strand of argument in this debate, but to try to clarify underlying assumptions. For this distributional argument, I would make two points. First, the relation between increased wealth and its distribution is a complex one, and whether trade as an engine of growth has any built-in bias toward regressive or progressive income distribution cannot be treated as a purely theoretical question. Its resolution must involve substantial empirical research, and I suspect that, like the question of whether there are any environmental benefits to economic efficiency, the answer varies with the particular circumstances, and the only general response is, "It depends."

My second point, however, does go to the philosophical thrust, rather than the facts of the debate. I doubt that ethically-minded supporters of freer trade would be indifferent to any regressive distributional impacts of trade if they thought that those effects actually occurred and were also part of an increasingly entrenched pattern that was clearly related to trade *per se*. (I would suggest that such a scenario would be morally offensive to anyone.) However, I also suggest that trade advocates do not believe that to be an accurate picture of reality. In the absence of definitive economic research, however, participants in the debate must take refuge in models of reality. This is where disputants really do see the world differently.

The difference is, I think, in what constitutes the engine for change. The critics' point of view is fundamentally static: the world as it is will be the pattern for the future. It is now an inequitable pattern, and so it will remain–at least until explicit, politically determined redistributive mechanisms are put in place.

By contrast, I would guess that most advocates for trade believe that a growing economy is a political as well as an economic prerequisite for greater economic equality. In their view, change toward less economic disparity can only happen if the economy is growing. As well, it is only in a growing economy that more resources will be able to be put toward environmental regulation and enforcement. Trade thus becomes a key factor in a model that is, above all, focused on the dynamic–on the levers of change–and these are fundamentally tied to economic conditions. Politically directed redistributive policies will ultimately fail, in this view, without economic growth. From this perspective, liberalized trade is a necessary, if not sufficient, condition for greater equity.

What shall we make of this debate? Obviously, it is a chicken-and-egg discussion about whether progressive political policies or economic development are the more important factor in reducing economic disparity. My point here is not to evaluate the argument–I do not have the knowledge, in any case–but to point out that almost no one is explicitly presenting their viewpoint, or for that matter, responding to their critics in these terms.

As I asserted earlier, the free trade paradigm has provided the implicit framework for much debate about trade, environment, and sustainable development. Even with the flaws which prevent it from being an unchallengeable way of structuring discussion, it still has much utility as the framework model. Many of the most contentious specific issues, such as whether to raise, lower, or harmonize environmental and labour regulations, can be quite productively discussed by environmentalists, as well as other interests, under the heading of trying to achieve "full-cost pricing," an objective that is almost universally endorsed by environmentalists. There is little need, in such a discussion, even to address the fact that internalizing environmental and social regulatory costs as an approach to environmental concerns is also consistent with a framework that highly values trade liberalization in principle.

What is rarely acknowledged by the trade community, however, is that there is another and far more challenging framework for trade-environment issues put forward by many environmentalists. This framework, which I will summarize by the term bioregionalism, essentially harks back to the early concerns I discussed that were not adequately addressed by the full-cost pricing approach used to integrate the environment and the economy. What I think is actually happening in the trade and environment debate is that some environmentalists are switching back and forth between the bioregional and the free trade paradigms, while the trade community, who neither fully grasp nor accept the bioregional framework, remain within the free trade model. This does not make for a very productive discussion.

The Bioregional Model

Bioregionalism has various degrees, but in what I call its strong form, its principal tenets involve restructuring both economies and political jurisdictions to make them coincide with the boundaries of ecological regions. (How, exactly, these natural boundaries would be determined has not had much rigorous debate. I suspect that, should such a quite unlikely political reorganization take place, there would be huge divisions within the ranks of bioregional supporters. I think it is noteworthy that, in the political upheavals of recent years, I have not yet heard of a serious proposal to redraw boundaries along biophysical rather than cultural lines.) Less radical proponents (the weak version of bioregionalism) merely emphasize that economic priorities should include maximizing regional self-reliance, particularly in those resources used for basic life-support, such as food, energy, and water. Trade in non-necessities is permitted, but tariffs should be used to create trade barriers for all essential commodities. Radical reduction of consumption levels is generally part of the programme, and cooperative or non-profit organizations are often put forward as preferable to profit-making enterprises.

The concerns behind such a vision are obviously related to a perceived urgent need to reduce consumption, and to provide security against the failure of extended trade networks. From this perspective, the collapse of human civilization is imminent, caused (though the exact mechanism is not necessarily identified) by ecological degradation. In this context, almost all trade is essentially seen as a security threat.

It is not my intent here to critique in detail this paradigm, although I do think that it fails to address the need to generate sufficient wealth not only to address global poverty, but also to finance massive environmental remediation and the technological innovation needed for ecological sustainability. Probably its greatest uncertainty is political – whether, in fact, it is a desirable scenario for most people. If overall economic prospects are stable or declining, are people more likely to support limiting their consumption through political programmes that constrain income and/or increase their taxes for income redistribution, or will they try to protect their own immediate interests instead? Generous-spirited egalitarianism does not seem to me to be the obvious outcome. However, my main point is that this bioregional model provides the background paradigm for most environmentalists, probably even for those who do not consider themselves in the ideological camp of bioregionalism.

There are at least two problems with this paradigm in the context of the trade-environment discussion. First, bioregional thinking carries a strong anti-trade bias on grounds of enhancing security. Nevertheless, this is rarely made explicit, let alone debated on its merits, when the framework for the debate is assumed by the trade community, and sometimes, even the environmentalists, to be the free trade model. But the persistence of environmental resistance to reducing trade barriers, I am convinced, goes back to bioregionalist thinking. Second, the problem with the bioregional paradigm in the trade debate is that it is so invisible or marginal to the trade community that its merits and flaws are not even examined.

I am convinced that some aspects of bioregionalism have value. In particular, the weak version of bioregionalism, which emphasizes regional economic self-reliance for basic resources used for life-support, has some intuitive appeal. Although such a policy focus clearly cannot guarantee security, it can arguably enhance resilience to unforeseen disruption.[3] It can also add to the number of cultural solutions humans create to solve the problem of how societies provide for basic needs. Moreover, an increased and increasingly self-aware reliance on meeting the special problem of the continuously generated requirements for food, energy, and water from local sources has value in grounding an appreciation of ecological limits. Arguably, a place is not truly "home" for human beings when too much of our life-support is external to the locale. Although humans are capable of maintaining life in space, in the deep ocean, and in Antarctica, these places are not home to our species. An awareness of local human carrying capacity for continuously required life-support is useful information in understanding sustainable levels of population for human settlements in a region, even if it does not by itself determine planning.

In short, although I think that bioregionalism does not by itself provide an appropriate framework for the trade and environment discussion, it can add useful dimensions to some of the issues addressed.

Conclusion

My own conclusions about an appropriate frame for the issue of trade and the environment, it turns out, are not so very different from the original way of thinking I described. They involve a requirement to internalize all real costs, combined with a willingness to let the market then work, in other words, to liberalize trade. Pragmatic exceptions can also be made where costs are difficult to internalize.

But notice that the essential first step is the internalization of costs. In practical terms, a necessary mechanism for doing this is regulation. This is the classic solution to the tragedy of the commons. As well, even if the mechanism through which regulation occurs is community tradition, as is the case with some aboriginal fishing and hunting management regimes, the principle is the same: mutual coercion, mutually agreed-upon. It is equally a matter of regulation if market mechanisms, such as tradeable emission permits, are the means by which control is exerted.

Thus, a key issue even using a trade liberalization perspective harks back to the locus of control over the internalization of costs. Who, in other words, gets to control regulation? It is here, I suggest, that democratic political communities, typically at the nation-state level, *must* be the ultimate arbiters of environmental quality goals and the regulatory mechanisms used to achieve them. (I think this principle applies to social goals as well, but I will not explore that here.) The concept of a "clean" or "healthy" environment is evocative, but is next to meaningless as an operational target. We are talking here about politically determined choices, not scientific absolutes. (The rules of the General Agreement on Tariffs and Trade do allow trade barriers on environmental grounds, although my sense is that there is a reluctance in the trade community to really accept this.) Who, then, gets to make these choices?

It is here, perhaps, that the community-based perspective of bioregionalism has the most insight. The underlying concern of bioregionalism is control, and, although I think the dismantling of existing political boundaries in favour of biome-based regions is frankly silly, the insistence on the primacy of a democratic local, regional, or even national community is, I think, correct.   The legitimacy, transparency, and accountability of decision-makers and the processes they use are matters of great significance, both in governance generally and, more specifically, in environment-related rule-making for trade.   The political accountability of decision-making about trade rules must be grounded in, and tied to, a felt level of community. Accountability to that political community must be the touchstone for the rule-makers' legitimacy. Although a fence against trade is, I believe, wrong-headed, the power of communities (including national states) to have the ultimate say in trade-offs and judgements concerning environmental quality must not be handed to anyone less accountable, or to any decision-making process that is less transparent and accessible than that of the affected political community.

Endnotes

[1] Although this assumption of rationalizing economic activity through trade liberalization is widely accepted in economic theory, it has been challenged recently by Daly and Cobb on the grounds of the modern mobility of capital, which has the effect of changing one of the "given" factors of production that result in greater economic efficiency and a larger economic "pie"; Herman E. Daly and John B. Cobb, Jr., *For the Common Good: Redirecting the Economy Toward Community, the Environment, and a Sustainable Future* (Boston: Beacon Press, 1989), chapter 11.

[2] This is also the distinction that Daly and Cobb made between growth and development.

[3] This was the essence of the argument that Lovins and Lovins make, directed to the more limited topic of energy security. Amory B. Lovins and L. Hunter Lovins, *Brittle Power: Energy Strategy for National Security* (Andover, Massachusetts: Brick House, 1982).